The ♥ of Resilience

Nurturing Your **Inner Strength** for a **Joyful Life**

Chuck Fisher, PhD
Meri McCoy-Thompson, MA

To maintain the anonymity of the individuals involved, we have changed most people's names.

Copyright @ 2024 Chuck Fisher and Meri McCoy-Thompson
All rights reserved.

ISBN: 979-8-9850475-4-7 Hardback
ISBN: 979-8-9850475-5-4 Paperback
ISBN: 979-8-9850475-6-1 Paperback (full color edition)
ISBN: 979-8-9850475-7-8 Ebook

Printed in the USA. First edition August 2024

By Chuck Fisher and Meri McCoy-Thompson
Edited by Michelle Higgs
Cover art by Teddi Black
Layout by Megan McCullough
With design elements by Marsha Gilbert and Illustrations by Megan Marschall
Mindset photos by Ricardo Gomez Angel, Javier Allegue Barros, and Rustam Mussabekov

Published by Dovetail Learning
6312 Tristania Court
Forestville, CA 95436

Other We Are Resilient™ resources are available:
www.dovetaillearning.org

Contents

Introduction

1. The Heart of Resilience 3
2. What is Resilience? 13
3. The Story of We Are Resilient™ 27

Protective Patterns

4. What are Protective Patterns? 31
5. Distrusting 45
6. Hypervigilance 57
7. Hyper-Caretaking 67
8. Avoiding 81
9. Defending 93
10. Attacking 103
11. Our Evolving Protective Patterns 113

Cultural Patterns

12 What are Cultural Patterns?.. 121

13 The Power of Exploring our Cultural Patterns 141

14 Creating the World we Want 161

Resilient Mindsets

15 Resilient Mindsets 173

16 Curiosity 181

17 Choice 199

18 Courage 217

Centering Skills

19 Centering Skills 233

20 Noticing Myself 243

21 Breathing Mindfully 263

22 Letting Go 277

23 Finding Gratitude 295

24 Positive Reframing 309

25 Nurturing Myself 325

Living in the Heart of Resilience

26 Living in the Heart of Resilience 341

Acknowledgements

We are incredibly grateful to the many people who contributed to this book. First, to our colleagues at Dovetail Learning. The We Are Resilient™ approach is the result of a generative and creative effort by our team: Ashley VanBezooyen, Bryan Clement, Cheryl Parker, Kristie Cannady, Lydia Jensen, and Sonoma Bates, with contributions from our board chair, Di Cullen.

We appreciate tremendously the many people who bravely and vulnerably shared their stories with us. Your courage deepened our understanding of the concepts in this book. Some prefer to remain anonymous. Those we can thank publicly include: Subha Aahlad, Jodi Allen-Maslowski, Xan Augerot, Sonoma Bates, Lori Bauer, Tamia Cardenas, Bryan Clement, Matt Coblentz, Renée Cooper, Veronica Cruz, Di Cullen, Jim Cullen, Vanda Davis, Jennifer Dovichi, Mark Duncanson, Jamison Evans, Yasuko Fukuda, Karla Galvez, Janet Gates, Nanfuka Haawa, Patty Haykin, Veronica Heredia, Erin Jackman, Gina Johnson, Ina Jubert, Radhika Kakarala, Maggie Lee, Selena Liu-Raphael, Erin Lund, Christine Lundblad, Sona Manzo, Grace Martin, Kim Martin, Alejandra Mata, Teresa Mayes, Mark McCoy, Matthias McCoy-Thompson, Soniya Mehra, Cathy Messenger, Annie Millar, Amy Moellering, Elissa Moriarty, Alexander Morris, Laura Moyles-LaBarge, Sharon Mulgrew, Karen Murillo Santillan, Sandra O'Sullivan, Cheryl Parker, Joanna Quintanilla, Ralph Rajs, Leisa Rattray, Zurisadai

Rivera, Amy Robinson, BIll Rutledge, Nicole Salvi, Carol Sarshik, Nancy Schlachte, Teresa Shannon, Dave Stiehr, Ebonie Thomas, Lisa Thomas, Garrett Toschi, Robyn Toschi, Clint Tripodi, Maria Tripodi, Kiyo Tukman, Alex Volpe, Celeste Walley, Rosario Williams, Bryan Umeki, Diane Velasquez, Rhonda Young, and Christopher Zorn. These individuals and many more are the heart of this book.

We are also thankful to those who have generously and consistently supported Dovetail Learning as we tested and evolved the We Are Resilient approach, particularly Debbie Fleischaker, Derek Jernstadt, and Jim and Joy Phoenix. Their faith in what's possible gave us courage.

Our board of directors played a pivotal role in the development of this book. They were our first readers and greatest cheerleaders, instilling in us the confidence that this book would make a valuable contribution to others. Our heartfelt thanks go to Di Cullen, Gina Johnson, Bill Rutledge, and Clint Tripodi for their unwavering support.

Finally, we are grateful to our families for their patience as we wrote this book and for their love and support as we strived to be our best selves. A special thank you to our life partners, Sandy Fisher and Steve McCoy-Thompson, for being willing to share their personal stories in this book and, for the great joy and resilience they have brought to our lives!

Chuck & Meri

Chapter 1

The Heart of Resilience

"Our connection with others can only be as deep as our connection with ourselves."

~ Brené Brown, *Atlas of the Heart*

Cultivating Inner Strength for a Joyful Life

Franklin was unhappy. "I loved my wife, Silvia, but she was depressed a lot, and we often got into big, angry fights. I felt badly about myself, like I was failing my marriage." As a teacher, he enjoyed working with his students and spent more time with them and his colleagues than at home. Silvia felt neglected and complained about it. Franklin felt criticized and reacted by withdrawing and spending even more time with his colleagues.

After a big blowup, his wife suggested couples counseling, where Franklin came face to face with how he prioritized work over his relationship with Silvia. "I thought my duty was to put bread on the table. I justified my long hours of work and grading papers as necessary to provide for my family. Now I realize that I was just trying to prove my self-worth. Much of it was about me, and I had to change. My attitude and behavior pushed my wife away." Their couples therapist helped them see how their *Protective Patterns* ran the show. Franklin was *Avoiding* difficult conversations, and Silvia was *Attacking* to try to hang on. Over time, they both learned how to improve their relationship by using their *Protective Patterns* less and their *Resilience Skills* more.

Franklin is not the only one who developed hurtful reactive patterns with loved ones. Zainab, a young adult, had a difficult relationship with her mother. Her mom, Batool, often confronted her in ways that felt intrusive. Her mom would say things like, "What's wrong with you? You are always so distant." Zainab felt like saying, "Mom, stop bothering me! You have no idea what I am going through." Instead, she reacted by *Avoiding* her mother even more.

However, this time, Zainab tried a new approach. She paused and *Breathed Mindfully* before responding. In that pause, she courageously said, "I am sorry, Mom. I need time and space for myself."

After saying this, Zainab was afraid of what her mom would think. She thought her mother wouldn't hear her if she expressed her needs. Instead, Batool was so moved by Zainab's authenticity that she asked permission to hug her daughter. Feeling stronger, Zainab continued. "I would appreciate it if you could stop blaming me when I need space." Her mother listened, and Zainab and Batool finally had an honest heart-to-heart conversation.

Zainab still has an imperfect relationship with her mom. But she took an essential step of being vulnerable, strengthening her resilience, and improving their relationship.

The relationships between Franklin and his wife, and Zainab and her mom, exemplify those that so many of us have with our loved ones (or friends, neighbors, colleagues). We have harmful patterns that push us apart—we make assumptions about each other, blame each other when we bump heads and hearts, struggle to say the right things, and hurt each other. Too often, we don't get it right. Then, we feel disconnected from those we care about and feel terrible that we were unkind.

We don't treat ourselves with kindness either. We judge ourselves harshly, and our self-talk becomes critical. We often don't know how to set boundaries to protect against others' intrusive behavior. We also may have unrealistic expectations and fail to give ourselves the nurturing we need to thrive.

For many of us, we had no idea that relationship patterns could be improved. Some of us were lucky enough to have family, teachers, coaches, or other adults who modeled healthy resilience skills. Others muddled through without the benefit of skills or mindsets to strengthen our resilience. We learn to protect ourselves by shutting others out or getting aggressive around our needs. Without adults who embody and model resilience, children have difficulty integrating healthy emotional development into their lifelong behavior.

We can do better. By understanding ourselves more clearly and developing resilience skills that help us thrive in our relationships, we can take our life beyond "good enough." We can better navigate our *Protective* and *Cultural Patterns* and learn to use mindsets and intentional practices to build a deeply fulfilling life that meets our most profound needs for authenticity and connection.

We Are Resilient™ is a simple yet powerful path toward authenticity. We can cultivate an inner strength within ourselves and our relationships for a more joyful life.

Learning how to build a thriving life is the story of this book. The We Are Resilient™ approach can help us make small, intentional changes that lead to big results. We can make breakthroughs in longstanding behavior that improve the trajectories of our relationships. This approach helps us to see more possibilities, open our hearts, and create more optimism, confidence, and connection. How we think, feel, and act directly impacts our relationships with others and how we experience the world.

This book is for those of us who want to:

- Develop greater empathy and compassion for ourselves and others
- Bring ourselves back to center when we get thrown off
- Become better equipped to cope with change and challenging situations
- Develop skills to help ourselves and others flourish
- Experience joy in the midst of the difficulties of daily life

We all can use these tools to navigate challenges. Jerome is a 60-year-old former CEO who lost his job and has to reinvent his career. Jacinda, a 16-year-old gay Latina, struggles with toxic relationships at school and how to fit in with her extended family. Ariana, a retired tech executive, wants to communicate better with her husband. Eve is an 80-year-old author whose primary challenge is caring for her very ill husband while retaining her role as his wife and best friend. Hampton, a Black man who struggles with many health issues, is trying to ensure his son learns to cook healthy foods and doesn't develop diabetes. Celeste is a recent college graduate and former foster child who grapples with boundaries with her extended family. For all of them, how they feel, think, and act impacts on how well they can handle their difficulties.

Whether we have similar issues or not, most of us have struggles that keep us up at night. It may be how to handle our teenagers or deal with a disagreement with our business partner. It may be how to manage a workplace that feels stifling or find a better-paying job. Many of us have challenges with our health, partners, children, parents, employees, or colleagues.

A hidden secret is that for each of us, like all the people whose stories are included in this book, stronger resilience is the ticket to dealing well with what keeps us up at night so we can flourish in life. Stronger resilience can set us up for more authentic relationships, positive and rewarding work, and an optimistic worldview.

When we know how to center ourselves in challenging situations, we can have more empathy and compassion with others. We can also more effectively collaborate to solve the critical problems we face in our families, schools, clinics, businesses, and communities. We face issues in ourselves and others every day. Understanding how we get thrown off-center and how to get ourselves back into balance is what strengthening resilience is all about.

This book is a guide to a deeper level of personal and relational wellbeing, what we call "the heart of resilience." While we are hardwired for connection, it is difficult to put down our armor and expose our vulnerability in a way that creates the most fulfilling connection and a more joyful life.

We, Chuck and Meri, illustrate how this is possible through our personal stories and more than one hundred other stories from people who shared intimate parts of their lives with us that are woven throughout the book. (We have used pseudonyms to protect confidentiality.) How we have learned to navigate the circumstances of our lives has directly led to our deep exploration of resilience. Each chapter ends with concrete practices and questions to reflect on our challenges and how we might approach them more successfully.

We identify some key concepts that support resilience, and those phrases are capitalized and italicized throughout the text—for example, *Protective Patterns*. Each concept will be defined and explored fully in subsequent chapters.

Our Paths Toward Understanding Resilience

Chuck's Story

Chuck—Even though I had spent my entire career helping others—as an Outward Bound instructor, school counselor, director of a substance recovery program, a founding director of Dovetail Learning, and developer of a social and emotional learning program for children—I still struggled to accept myself.

My childhood was rough. My dad was an alcoholic, and my mother enabled him. Because of my dad's job, we moved every two years—to the Philippines and Peru, and up and down the East Coast from Washington, DC, to Miami, to Boston. By the time I started tenth grade, I'd been in ten different schools. I was a terrible student because I didn't have adult support to gain the skills to deal with my life. I rarely did my homework and lied so I wouldn't get in trouble. I failed sixth grade and was ashamed of having to repeat it. Most days, I stuffed my feelings and pretended everything was fine. I acted like I didn't care, but I cared so much it hurt. I was filled with self-doubt and self-loathing. I didn't think I was loveable or a good enough person.

> **"Resilience is knowing that you are the only one that has the power and the responsibility to pick yourself up."**
> ~ Mary Holloway, resilience coach

Along the way, I discovered flashes of resilience. One day in Peru, in third grade, I got so upset from repeatedly being sent to the principal's office for bad behavior that I hid under the school stairs. Then, I ran away from school and stayed in a vacant lot until the end of the day. Looking back, this was a powerful act of resilience. I protected myself by removing myself from humiliation.

Another time, I stood up to a group of Peruvian kids who bullied me on my walk home from school. On this day, they shoved me to the ground and pulled off my best friend's watch that I had borrowed.

I was so set on protecting my friend's watch that I refused to let them take it. I was scared and angry but held my ground. I centered myself and talked them into giving it back. From that day on, they never bothered me again. I discovered that by being centered and courageous, I was powerful.

However, I still had so very much to learn. Physical, emotional, and sexual abuse damaged my belief in myself. As a teen, I got lost in drugs and alcohol. I smoked pot before classes to numb myself from nagging self-criticism. I thought of myself as slow and called myself stupid under my breath. I struggled to graduate from high school and dropped out of college.

Along the way, I discovered rock climbing, where I had to be focused and centered. It opened a path to self-knowledge for me. My desire to help others gradually brought me back to school, and I eventually earned a Master's in Counseling and became a school counselor. I started trusting my inner knowing but still felt a gap in my self-concept. I earned my Ph.D. in Transpersonal Psychology and wrote my dissertation on self-acceptance because I wanted to have it myself. Finally, two major health crises pushed me even further to recognize that I HAD to learn how to accept the beauty of who I am. I needed to be authentic to stay alive, to do this work I care about, and to be the person I wanted to be for my wife, daughters, and grandchildren.

My life's work has revolved around an essential life question: **How do we live into the beauty of who we are—the joy of accepting ourselves and others as whole human beings?**

Meri's Story

Meri—My need to strengthen resilience comes from the stuff of my life. We all have trauma in one form or another. It's not just the blatant trauma like a natural disaster, a violent crime, or physical, emotional, or sexual abuse. It's the everyday trauma we don't discuss, like a relationship breakup, the death of a pet, losing a job, getting bullied, or being rejected by a friend group. Most of us have experienced being excluded or shamed in our family or in front of our friends. Most of us lose someone whom we care about. These "everyday traumas" can affect us profoundly, and the more resilience skills we have to deal with them, the better.

I was a shy, awkward girl who had trouble making friends. I spent most of my time reading books. In middle school, I finally made some friends, leaving me vulnerable to rejection by several friend groups. One group of girls said they didn't want to walk to school with me anymore. Another group "disinvited" me to a party we had jointly planned. Life at home was also difficult. My father moved out when I was in seventh grade, and my mother was left to manage our minimal finances, finish her teaching credential for special education, and work full-time. My mother was depressed and spent much of her time at home crying in her bedroom. My two older brothers, my younger sister, and I had to figure out most things on our own. Fortunately, I became better at making friends and created a friend group that mostly stayed together through high school. I was good at school and won some awards, and that success also boosted my confidence.

"I am not what happened to me, I am what I choose to become."

~ C.G. Jung

Navigating the ups and downs in my life, plus the modeling I received from my mother as she made it through her challenges, taught me about Resilience. Though I didn't have the words to describe it, I was able to keep my *Protective Patterns* sufficiently in check that they didn't sabotage me as I worked toward achieving my life goals. I learned that choosing friends I could depend upon and investing a lot in those relationships is one of the most important gifts I could give myself. I still maintain some childhood friendships to this day. When I went to Boston for graduate school, I knew very few people on the East Coast. I made it my highest priority to find and invest in friendships, even above academics. I knew poor grades wouldn't hurt my resilience as much as a lack of connection with others.

Fast forward several decades. I had married, raised two children, and had a fulfilling career in nonprofits around the world. I worked with girls' education in Afghanistan; AIDS in India; preventive healthcare for kids in the U.S.; social entrepreneurship in Beijing; water, sanitation, health, and tech training in Nairobi; agricultural training in West Africa; and family engagement in the U.S. In all these roles, it was clear that while basic needs are essential, providing for those did not ensure people thrived. And even some destitute people could figure out how to work the system and get what they needed to transform their lives and the lives of their families. They were models of resilience.

This led me to my essential life question: **What does it take to make significant change, to transform the systems that create inequality and exclude so many?**

While Chuck was committed to helping people on their internal journey of living more authentically, and Meri was committed to changing external systems to help people experiencing life on the margins, their essential life questions led to the same place:

A desire to develop inner strength in ourselves and inspire it in others so we all can live more joyfully and make a positive difference in the world.

Chapter 2

What is Resilience?

> "Resilience is an Ordinary Superpower.
> It does not come from rare and special qualities
> but from the everyday magic of being human."
>
> ~ Ann Masten, *Ordinary Magic: Resilience in Development*

Noemi, a marketing coordinator, realized she was finding it harder and harder to get out of bed in the mornings. When she noticed her gloomy feeling, she became curious about it and thought about why she might be feeling that way. She realized she was absorbing negativity from some of her coworkers who were anxious about losing their jobs. After several years of rapid growth, the company was struggling, and layoffs were looming. Noemi knew that catastrophizing about her future would not help, so she chose to *Avoid* those coworkers to protect her own mental health.

Hampton had just finished his part of a high-stakes presentation to the city council when he felt his stress building and heart rate speeding up. He had to focus because he controlled the next slides for his colleague's presentation and wanted to be ready for the questions afterward. Hampton started *Breathing Mindfully*. Regulating his breathing allowed

13

him to release his tension, calm his thoughts, and quiet his heart. He felt centered when the council began their onslaught of questions.

Like many older women, when Eun-jung fell, she broke several ribs. She was in a lot of pain and could not care for herself or her husband like she wanted to. Rather than be depressed over her limited mobility, she looked for the bright spots. When her daughter installed a bedrail to make it easier to turn in bed, Eun-jung *Found Gratitude* that the bedrail gave her a place to store her cell phone so she wouldn't misplace it and could call her family at any time.

Like Noemi, Hampton, and Eun-jung, all of us already have resilience inside us, and we use it every day. Resilience helps us handle and recover from difficulties and discover positivity in our lives. Our resilience changes over time and will be higher or lower in different situations. Eun-jung felt like she was handling her aging body well until, suddenly, she had to deal with the consequences of a fall. Noemi felt discouraged but then realized that distancing herself from negative coworkers could create a more optimistic perspective. Hampton thought his presentation was going well, and then his anxiety and heart rate shot up. They all called upon resilience skills to shift their perspectives and improve their situations.

Defining Resilience

The standard definition of resilience is how we bounce back from a difficult situation, which is the start of our definition. We also emphasize that resilience can be learned and strengthened. Most importantly, we see resilience as a prerequisite to our capacity to become a better person and create a better world.

1. Resilience is the ability to adapt and respond to meet challenges effectively. At its best, it can help us thrive in uncertainty.

2. Our resilience will be higher or lower in different situations. We can strengthen our resilience by practicing our skills.

3. Resilience includes the awareness, mindsets, and skills to become the best possible version of ourselves and to contribute to our family, school/workplace, community, and world.

Finding our Superpower

> "Do not judge me by my success, judge me by how many times I fell down and got back up again."
> ~ Nelson Mandela

Most of us don't know how to tap into the superpower of our resilience very well. We ride the rollercoaster of life and take the hard knocks, hoping to get through intact. The good news is when life becomes challenging—as it did for Noemi, Hampton, and Eun-jung—there are ways we can smooth out the bumps and set ourselves on a more positive trajectory. Stronger resilience means we can flow more easily through difficulties while maintaining our cool, and when we do get knocked off-balance, we have the skills to recover more quickly.

The true importance of resilience is often hidden.

Our resilience superpower influences all aspects of our wellbeing and our experience of life itself. When we feel vulnerable, it helps us find a way to safety. Intentionally applying our resilience skills helps us be in charge of our wellbeing, rather than the victims of circumstances or other people. When we intentionally apply resilient mindsets, notice our thought patterns and behaviors, and strengthen our resilience skills, we can create more of the life we want. Even though we don't have control over many things that impact our lives (our environment, upbringing, and life's difficulties), we thrive when we intentionally tap into our inner capacity for resilience. Stronger resilience brings us home to ourselves, so we have the courage and skills to change the things that matter.

Just as important, resilience helps us attend to the challenges beyond ourselves—in our families, communities, and world. We can learn how to make inner changes that transform our relationships. We can think more clearly and be more intentional in our choices and interactions. Being resilient helps us be effective so we can contribute to creating a world of kind, connected human beings.

Our level of resilience affects us and everyone around us tremendously. When we act in less resilient ways, we cause harm to our loved ones, friends, neighbors, clients, patients, associates, employers, employees, and ourselves. When we act more resiliently, we support not only the wellbeing of ourselves but also our family, neighborhood, workplace, and, ultimately, the wellbeing and safety of our community (local to global).

At its core, resilience strengthens us, it makes us better people, and helps us to serve others and our communities.

The We Are Resilient™ Approach

To unlock the incredible power of resilience and better understand how it helps us become better people, the We Are Resilient™ approach distinguishes two sets of patterns, three resilient mindsets, and three kinds of skills (see Figure 1).

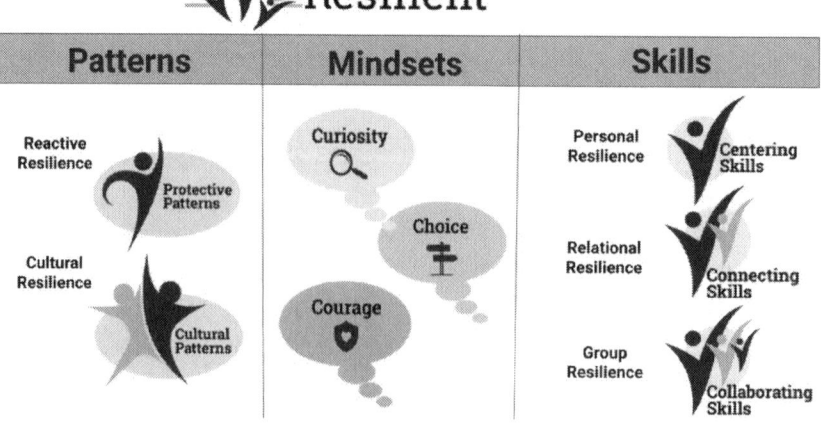

Figure 1

The Five Types of Resilience

Part of what makes resilience a superpower is its multifaceted and interactive nature. Let's look at five different scenarios and see how they map to the five types of resilience in the chart below.

- Julia's cranky mother-in-law verbally attacked her whenever they were together, so Julia avoided spending time with her. Julia used her *Reactive Resilience*.

- Olive and her sister had very different politics and tended to disagree about how to see the world. However, Olive appreciated other things about her sister and enjoyed discussing their shared interests at family gatherings. Olive used her *Cultural Resilience*.

- Omar loved to care for his family. He spent time taking good care of himself—exercising and eating healthy—so he had the energy to better care for them. Omar used his *Personal Resilience*.

- Donna's daughters were sad when their stepfather died. Donna spent time listening to each of them and just trying to hold space for them as they figured out how to heal. Donna used her *Relational Resilience*.

- Liam and his siblings spent much time on the complex care their elderly mother required. When each person reported completing a task in a family text, they sent thank yous to each other. Liam and his siblings used their *Group Resilience*.

Julia, Olive, Omar, Donna, Liam, and his siblings all displayed resilience, though in different ways. Exploring these five types of resilience helps us tap into this superpower. The following charts introduce the five types of resilience and the patterns or skills that contribute to each type.

Type of Resilience	How we use it	How it Impacts us	Patterns that Contribute
Reactive Resilience (see page 31)	How we REACT to the world.	We instinctively respond without thinking. Julia used the Protective Pattern of Avoiding to shield herself from her mother-in-law's attacks.	**Protective Patterns** come from our Reactive Resilience.
Cultural Resilience (see page 121)	How we VIEW the world.	We absorb ideas, beliefs, and stories from our family, community, and culture. Olive recognized and appreciated her sister's different Cultural Patterns.	**Cultural Patterns** shape our Cultural Resilience.
Personal Resilience (see page 233)	How we CREATE our INNER world.	We find the strength inside ourselves to feel calm and centered, enabling us to handle problems. Omar used the Centering Skill of Nurturing Myself to keep himself physically strong.	**Centering Skills** build Personal Resilience.

Type of Resilience	How we use it	How it Impacts us	Patterns that Contribute
Relational Resilience*	How we CREATE CONNECTIONS in the world.	We trust another person and feel safe to work things out when we have conflicts. Donna used the Connecting Skill of Heartfelt Listening with her daughters to support their healing.	**Connecting Skills** build Relational Resilience.
Group Resilience*	How we CREATE BELONGING in the world.	We feel safe within a group, are kind to each other, and work well together. Liam and his siblings used the Collaborating Skill of Appreciating Others to show how they valued each person's contribution.	**Collaborating Skills** build Group Resilience.

*Note: We will explore Relational Resilience and Group Resilience in our next book. For more information, see our Open Educational Resources on our website: www.dovetaillearning.org. These resources can be downloaded for free, adapted, and shared as outlined in our Creative Commons Attribution-ShareAlike 4.0 International License.

Each of the five types of resilience influences each other. When we strengthen one, it impacts the others. When we improve at using all of them, we become our best selves, improve our relationships, and strengthen our groups and communities.

This is our first book on the We Are Resilient approach. It focuses on how to develop inner strength for a more joyful life. Its goal is to help us intentionally strengthen *Personal Resilience*. We start this journey by showing what gets in our way, which are most often our *Protective Patterns*. We then place resilience in the context of *Cultural Patterns* so we can see ourselves more clearly. Our *Reactive* and *Cultural Resilience* are intimately connected to our ability to have strong *Personal Resilience*. We also explore how our *Mindsets* can guide us with our patterns and skills and how our *Centering Skills* can improve our wellbeing.

We developed We Are Resilient from a trauma-informed perspective. We explore some painful issues and want to acknowledge that some of the stories may activate you, especially if you have experienced trauma. Take a break or reach out to others to care for yourself if needed. For example, *Cultural Resilience* can be a particularly sensitive topic, so exploring it after strengthening our *Centering Skills* is best for some of us. We respect your needs, so skip any sections that don't feel relevant and perhaps return to them later.

Resilient Mindsets (see Chapters 15-18)

When we want powerful keys to unlock the heart of resilience, we can use our *Resilient Mindsets*. These Mindsets help us learn about our patterns and strengthen our skills.

Hugh, a strategic advisor, was slowly easing into his morning by drinking his coffee when suddenly he found himself in the middle of a big argument with his wife and daughter. What a difficult way to start the day! After leaving the room, Hugh became *curious* about what was happening with him. Why was he so bothered by their comments? He realized he felt upset about work, which made him cross with his family. Hugh recognized he needed to take some time to center himself before continuing with his day.

As a sophomore in high school, Sage was not taking school very seriously. Then, President Obama was elected. Seeing someone who looked like her become president inspired Sage to change her behavior. She realized she had a *choice* to change her study habits and become the excellent student she knew she could be. Sage made that choice, and it changed the trajectory of her life.

Two years ago, Nettie chose to walk away from a job that drained all her mental and physical energy. It was a scary time because, as a single mom, she needed to support her young son. Although going through that period of unemployment was difficult, she used her *courage* to take a step that allowed her to find a much more rewarding job.

As Hugh, Sage, and Nettie discovered, our attitudes determine how we experience life. Our *Resilient Mindsets* help us succeed. These positive attitudes are powerful forces to help us improve our relationships and our approach to life.

- **Curiosity**—Hugh's curiosity helped him discover that his grumpy attitude toward his family was really about him and not them.
- **Choice**—Sage chose to become a different type of student.
- **Courage**—Nettie used her courage to align her life with her values and leave a job that hurt her and her family.

Resilient Mindsets can connect us deeply to the heart of resilience because they guide us in effectively using patterns and skills. When we are curious about ourselves and others, understand that we can make choices that make a difference, and have the courage to align our actions with our values, we open up tremendous possibilities for ourselves.

When Resilience Feels Like a Dirty Word

"I don't have a good feeling about the word resilience. It feels like a negative word that requires us to 'get through anything,'" said Marlee in one of our training sessions. She echoed what others were feeling. Ruth added that sometimes we show up as TOO resilient, so it's hard to see or understand the personal cost. Sometimes, others expect us to show up and be resilient when we really need a break. We feel obligated to carry a heavy load and still bounce back. We may be told to "batten down the hatches" and weather the storm when a better approach would be to leave the situation and avoid the storm altogether.

Izzy, a lifelong athlete, has played and coached at the college level. Because of how the word resilience is used in athletics, she has a love/hate relationship with it. While it can help with peak performance, sometimes it means we are supposed to continue to take what is handed to us, even when it is not good for us.

Zainab addressed a deeper issue. "Sometimes it seems 'resilient' is what other people tell us to be, instead of changing the system causing our difficulties." Zainab was speaking for all who are struggling or marginalized, whether they face discrimination and racism or are simply working too hard to put food on the table.

Marlee, Ruth, Izzy, Zainab, and the others are right. When people apply the word resilience TO us, it can feel like an additional burden we are expected to bear. "Resilience" can mean "continue to show up and take whatever the situation is, at whatever the cost." Like other concepts, it can be used as a word to oppress others. It can mean a refusal to acknowledge the systems that are creating unequal burdens and insurmountable barriers to success. In those situations, we must examine how this call for resilience impacts us. Are we expected to do or be too much?

Like all expectations, it is helpful to examine where it comes from. Is it from ourselves? Our workplace? Our family? Our culture? We need to separate others' expectations of us from our own needs. Being resilient does not mean unquestionably accepting what feels wrong.

The We Are Resilient approach is not about letting anyone else define us. It is about owning our power to define ourselves. It is recognizing our situation—seeing and acknowledging deep pain and suffering where they exist—AND it is about giving ourselves the tools to create our best possible life given our situation. It is about working together to make the changes in the systems (economic, political, environmental, education, healthcare, etc.) that support wellbeing.

Relying on resilience shouldn't prevent us from advocating for the tough systemic changes that need to be made. That even requires extra resilience. For all of us, particularly those in marginalized communities, We Are Resilient can help us embrace our history while moving from victimhood to healing and new beginnings. Ultimately, our resilience can help us work toward removing the conditions and changing the systems that require so much resilience in the first place.

The approach is also not about defining others. It is never our job to tell people they need to build resilience. We each may react to the same situation differently. We all will be at different stages and have our own timelines for this process. This approach invites us to make space for everyone to be on their own journey.

Ever-Evolving Resilience

Chuck—I woke up early, and by 5:30 a.m. I was on my daily walking meditation on our back country road. The sun was just starting to burn through the fog. I felt fantastic, and it was a good day to have a great day. Out of nowhere, a truck whipped by me in the fog, almost side-swiping me. It scared me terribly, and my anger flared. "Who the *^#k does that guy think he is!" I was thrown off-balance, literally and emotionally. A little further down my walk, I found myself still ruminating on it. "Calm down," I told myself. "*Breathe Mindfully.*" I then used the *Resilient Mindset of Curiosity*. What must be true for that driver, and what was his experience? I started to see what he must have seen and began feeling *Empathy*. Though I was still unhappy about my close call, I also *Found Gratitude* for my safety, the sun coming through the fog, and being on my walk. Using my *Centering Skills,* I found my balance pretty quickly.

Our resilience is constantly evolving. We may cycle back and forth between feeling centered and off-center several times a day, or within a few moments, in response to an evolving situation. Both the external situation and our ability to use our *Resilient Mindsets* and *Skills* influence us tremendously. When we intentionally use our ordinary superpower, we can more easily create the life we want.

> **"Always walk through life as if you have something new to learn and you will."**
> ~ Vernon Howard, American philosopher

Two Insights

First, when we have challenges in our relationships, often our initial instinct is about how we want the other person to change.

This book is not about fixing other people. Of course, we don't have control over others. More importantly, we have learned that small shifts within us can create significant shifts within our relationships. We have tremendous capacity—in this resilient superpower—that can change how we feel about ourselves, how we operate in the world, and how we engage in relationships. When we intentionally strengthen our ordinary superpower, amazing things can happen.

Secondly, we also know that self-awareness and developing inner strength takes work and mental energy. We aren't going to get it right all the time. We are going to fail. That is okay. It is part of the process. Every small step we take moves us in the direction we want to go. Being aware of the energy required for self-awareness gives us more compassion for those who have difficulty finding it.

Change can be scary, but not changing causes stagnation. We need growth and change to get where we want to be. Intentionally leaning into our "growth edges" can produce rewarding results.

This book is for all of us, so we can build a world that inspires us. We need practical social and emotional skills to create a world where everyone thrives. The journey of resilience is a courageous undertaking. It includes uncovering patterns of thought and behavior that have been years in the making—and it may take a lifetime to fully unlearn those habits and relearn behaviors that serve us better. The good news is—like all journeys—it starts by taking the first step.

We invite you to join us on this journey.

~ Meri and Chuck

Chapter 3

The Story of We Are Resilient™

> "Enthusiasm is common. Endurance is rare."
> ~ Angela Duckworth, *Grit: The Power of Passion and Perseverance*

For over ten years, Dovetail Learning developed and trained educators in a social and emotional learning program that transformed schools in over 38 states across the U.S. and a few foreign countries. This program benefited hundreds of thousands of children, teachers, and parents.

However, Ayesha, a parent who liked our social and emotional learning program, was frustrated with its implementation at her child's school. Teachers would yell, "Calm down! Stop screaming!" without recognizing they behaved the same way as the kids. Ayesha felt her children were missing the program's power because the teachers did not have the skills to model how to handle life with vulnerability, grace, and confidence. We knew Ayesha's story was not unique.

Research from UC Berkeley, Harvard University, and many others revealed that the best way to help children gain resilience is to ensure that the adults who serve them have strong social, emotional, and resilience skills. With stronger skills, adults—especially parents, caregivers, educators, and pediatric providers—can buffer children from life's stressors and pass along effective skills through modeling.

By tapping into the expertise of our whole team, we created a strengths-based approach that helps us all understand how to navigate our challenges and develop inner strength. We integrated evidence-based research demonstrating how resilience skills can be transformative. We Are Resilient™ is built on universal human capacities for personal growth, healing, healthy relationships, and community resilience.

We also drew upon our own lived experience of surviving adversity and trauma and learning to thrive. One member of our team, Bryan, experienced his parents' divorce at age ten. He and his younger brother shuttled between them. He went through some tough times, including being shot at on the streets late one night. He was also mentored by some great coaches who helped him succeed in sports and finally in school. His dad worked in schools as a janitor and coach, inspiring him to become an educator and principal to advocate for other struggling children.

Like Bryan, all of our team struggled with resilience in our personal lives, our organizations, the people we encounter, and the world around us. Though a small team of eight, we considered ourselves a typical cross-section of society, collectively having experienced (primarily in childhood) the following:

- Family living with mental health conditions
- Emotional and/or physical abuse by parent/caregiver
- Sexual harassment or abuse
- Physical violence
- Loss of a family member to suicide, violence, incarceration, alcohol and substance use
- Financial insecurity
- Parental divorce
- Spousal abuse

Despite these challenges, we knew we were not victims of our lives but co-creators of our growth and development. In designing this approach, we realized we had to address what gets in the way of resilience. We understood the impact of trauma and adverse childhood experiences and that the work needed to follow the principles of trauma-informed care. We explored the thought patterns and behaviors that limited us and uncovered how *Protective* and *Cultural Patterns* both help us and harm us. Noticing when these patterns get in our way is essential to getting to the heart of resilience and leading a joyful life. Our efforts also revealed how *Resilient Mindsets* and *Resilience Skills* are vital to thriving.

Through a collaborative partnership with UCSF-Benioff Children's Hospital Oakland (BCHO) and a grant from the office of the California Surgeon General, we began training for pediatric clinics across California. We quickly realized that the We Are Resilient approach was much bigger than a method for adults to help children. Many types of people started benefiting from our training. Educators, primary care providers, behavioral health teams, first responders, parents, business executives, and others joined our training, ongoing coaching, and support groups.

Myles worked on the front lines as a paramedic in San Francisco. "I was in the worst parts of San Francisco dealing with homeless people on the streets, drug overdoses, and violent crime—very traumatic work. I spent over a year in a We Are Resilient group, and it changed my life. I was extremely prejudiced and judgmental about people in the worst of conditions. Now, I'm changed. I see through and beyond each person to understand why they are the way they are. I have deep empathy and compassion for them, in facing their difficult lives. And, for myself, when I'm witnessing and interacting with others' trauma. It's been a lifesaver for me."

Those who learned the We Are Resilient approach reported feeling calmer, less stressed, and more able to handle whatever life throws at them, creating a hopeful future. They discovered how their *Protective* and *Cultural Patterns* were hampering them, so they made minor shifts in their habits. Their relationships with their spouses, parents, and children improved. They speak in more empowering ways to their supervisors, colleagues, and employees. They had greater ability to manage their daily challenges with confidence and optimism. In short, they were more resilient.

Our team has created a framework and approach that is helping transform the lives of thousands of people. We will always be grateful to Bryan, Cheryl, Di, Kristie, Lydia, and Sonoma for their heartfelt and meaningful contributions to this work.

Meri—The people we have trained echo my own experience with the We Are Resilient approach. Understanding these concepts and practicing Resilience Skills is steadily improving my relationships and my life. I am a better wife, mother, sister, daughter, and friend because I can remain calm and be more empathetic in the face of conflict and adversity. Moreover, many of our clients work with low-income or marginalized people, and over the course of a training or coaching session, I have seen how the work is transforming them and making them more effective advocates for change. I can see how the systems change I have dreamed about can come, with each person learning to be a better version of themselves and more able to envision and create the positive solutions we all need.

Chuck—Building and applying the We Are Resilient approach has broken me open in the best way possible. Every day, it helps me to see, understand, and be more skillful at accepting myself and the world around me. Teaching this to others has given me immense compassion for those who hurt me. I understand how their trauma—and their *Cultural* and *Protective Patterns*—influenced who they became. When I see how dramatically this work impacts the wellbeing of so many others, I am awed by how the beauty of who we are—accepting ourselves and others as whole human beings—supports our shared humanity.

We are inspired by all who use this work for personal development and systems change. Having the inner strength of resilience is a game-changer. We hope you, too, find more resilience within yourself and your family, your community, and our world.

> "Life doesn't get easier or more forgiving,
> we get stronger and more resilient."
> ~ Steve Maraboli, motivational speaker

Chapter 4

What are Protective Patterns?

"Life is 10% what happens to me and 90% how I react to it."
~ John C. Maxwell, author

When we talked to Hilde, she shared how she liked being a social worker, but her Protective Pattern of **Distrusting** is often activated. She works hard to protect children but is critical of the child welfare system. Hilde feels that too frequently, she and her fellow social workers have been given false hope, weren't told the truth, or essential things were missed. Her Protective Pattern of *Distrusting* has led her to disappointment, heartache, and burnout. On the other hand, *Distrusting* also helps her see what needs fixing and has energized her to remain a part of a system that needs people who care.

Meri—My husband Steve's chronic illness recently activated my Protective Pattern of **Hypervigilance**. Steve has a lung condition that makes him vulnerable to pneumonia and TB-like infections. He can be perfectly healthy for many months and then suddenly fall ill. When he starts coughing, my ears perk up, and I move to high alert. I wonder—Is this a normal cough, like everyone gets, or one that signals the need for medical attention? When he is sick, my body practically vibrates with Hypervigilance. I feel like my "resting state" is not really resting because I am ready to jump at a moment's notice.

Chuck—I just wanted to help. My wife, Sandy, felt terrible about being upset with our granddaughter during a game. Our granddaughter made a rude comment that pushed Sandy's buttons, and Sandy felt hurt. Rather than letting Sandy handle it and sort out her feelings, I jumped into my Protective Pattern of **Hyper-Caretaking** when I saw that she was upset. I tried to save her. I said, "Oh, that wasn't about you at all. She was taking it out on you because of what had just happened with her sister." To relieve my own discomfort, I tried to fix her feelings rather than truly listening.

Meri—My financial advisor tried to make an appointment with us for several weeks, and I kept avoiding the call. I thought he might have some bad news about our family's financial situation, and I didn't have the time or energy to deal with it. I used the Protective Pattern of **Avoiding** to pretend there was no problem.

Chuck—It seemed like the simplest thing. Sandy asked me if I'd taken out the trash, and I said, "Of course I did." But I said it with attitude. My internal dialogue was something like, "I'm not a slacker! She knows I take the trash out every Thursday night, so why did she question me?" I slid into my Protective Pattern of **Defending** to prove I was dependable. My defensive reaction made things worse. Sandy just wanted to ensure the trash was out because our barrel was full, and we were going on vacation the next day.

Meri—After an hour on hold with customer service, I could feel my **Attacking** Protective Pattern creep into my body. My stomach felt tense, my breathing was speeding up, and I felt angry. I really wanted to let the customer service representative have it! I wanted her to know how disrespected I felt.

All of these stories illustrate how Protective Patterns can show up in daily life.

Protective Patterns

- **Everyone** has them.
- They are **automatic reactions** that arise by **default as an ingrained habit.**
- We might feel vulnerable or unsafe **emotionally, socially, physically, or mentally.**
- They emerge **when we believe we are unsafe**. In reality, we may be just fine.
- They give us an essential type of resilience: **Reactive Resilience.**

***Reactive Resilience** is an instinctual capacity for meeting challenges. Reactive Resilience appears as Protective Patterns.*

The We Are Resilient approach describes six types of Protective Patterns that we use when we feel vulnerable or unsafe: Distrusting, Hypervigilance, Hyper-Caretaking, Avoiding, Defending, and Attacking. (See Figure 2.) These Protective Patterns sometimes help us but often get in our way.

Protective Patterns

For Reactive Resilience

- Distrusting
- Hypervigilance
- Hyper-Caretaking
- Avoiding
- Defending
- Attacking

Figure 2

Chuck—My wife is always concerned about my health because of my history of heart disease. She wants me to eat well, exercise enough, and be free of stress so that we can share a long, healthy life together. However, sometimes, her concern moves into her Protective Pattern of *Hyper-Caretaking*. Then I feel like she is trying to control me, and I resent it. My *Defending* Protective Pattern emerges. This morning, she asked if I'd been out of my office chair today, and I responded with, "What do you mean? I got up at 6 a.m. and took a run!" Ouch! My Reactive Resilience initiated a serious argument. I wanted to prove I was right, while she just wanted to ensure I kept myself healthy.

All of us react to stressful situations by sometimes using our Protective Patterns. It is much easier to see Protective Patterns in others than in ourselves.

Protective Patterns and Stress

Life is full of adversity. Our stressors can include family and relationship challenges, health issues, workplace pressures, financial concerns, and our moods and attitudes. We may also feel stressed by community, political, or global concerns. How we deal with stressors impacts our emotional, mental, and physical health and those around us.

When a stressful event occurs—like a difficult phone call, someone getting upset with us, or bad financial news—our reaction can almost be automatic. We use this default reaction—**Protective Pattern**—to try to feel safer, but it takes a lot of emotional energy. When we react with a Protective Pattern, our emotions escalate, peak, and can take a long time to calm down. Often, we feel depleted afterward. (See Figure 3.) Many kinds of stressors can set off our Protective Patterns.

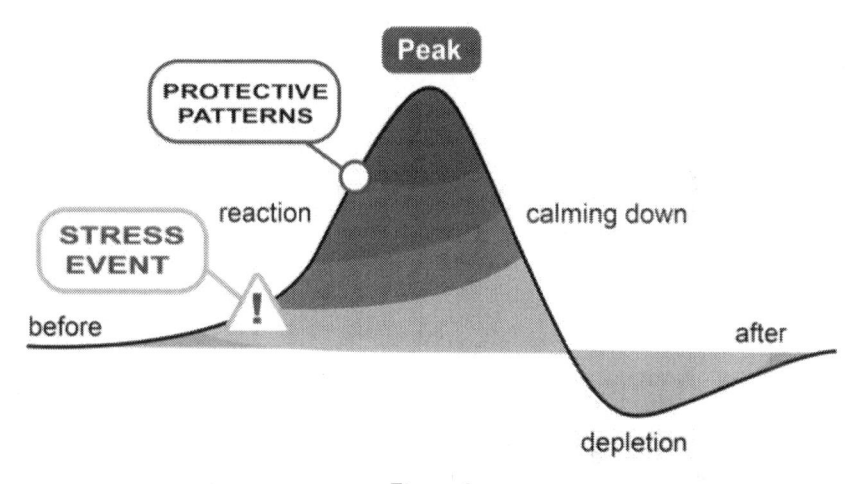

Figure 3
Adapted from hes-extraordinary.com/preventing-outbursts by Nicole Day

Meri—My Protective Pattern of *Attacking* emerged with that customer service rep because I felt my time was being wasted. How could I accomplish even half of what I needed to do when the rep was sucking me into a "customer service" vortex? Of course, after I launch into *Attacking*, I feel so depleted. My productivity also takes a dive from that.

We know that stress is not always bad, depending on its severity and duration. Some stress is healthy for us—it helps us perform at peak levels. (See Figure 4.)

- **Positive Stress**: This stress helps us focus on completing a project on time, achieving an important goal, or being vigilant and safe in a difficult situation. If our stressors are brief, we may have the skills to deal with them well, contributing to our ability to deal with stress over time. Dealing with brief emotional stressors builds our resilience, much like exercising our muscles strengthens our bodies.

- **Tolerable Stress**: Other stressors, such as a personal loss, might not feel good, but we can handle them if they are time-limited. To help tap into our resilience, we may need the assistance of others—a friend, family member, or other "buffering relationship." Even when the stressor is intense, as humans we are biologically hardwired to deal with it through extra surges of adrenaline and cortisol. These hormones are survival mechanisms that help us react quickly and effectively.

- **Toxic Stress**: However, if we have a prolonged period of stress or a traumatic incident, our stress response can damage us. Prolonged surges of stress hormones not only impair our emotional and mental health but can have a toxic effect on our physical body. We may need professional help to heal from toxic stress.

Stress Response Continuum

	Positive	Tolerable	Toxic
Severity & Duration	Brief	Time Limited	Extreme, Frequent, or Extended
Examples of Stress Triggers	Public Speaking	Personal Loss	Abuse, Neglect, Discrimination
Resilience Need	I can take care of myself	I need a buffering relationship	I need healing and regeneration

*Adapted from: Bucci M, Marques SS, Oh D, Harris NB. Toxic stress in children and adolescents. Advances in Pediatrics. 2016

Figure 4

How They Form and Why we use Them

We all have fundamental needs for safety: mental, emotional, physical, and social. We need to feel safe to feel like we belong and to thrive. When we feel vulnerable or experience stressors, we can become anxious or fearful. We instinctively react before we've had time to process a situation fully.

As children, this instinctive reaction might have been helpful to us because it kept us feeling strong, in control, or out of danger. As we develop and use these instinctive reactions more consistently, they evolve into default behaviors called **Protective Patterns**. We became comfortable using these normal human reactions when we felt vulnerable—even if we were not actually in harm's way. Our Protective Patterns are like a double-edged sword: helpful in some situations but harmful in others.

Some Protective Patterns are *pulling in* protective impulses while others are *pushing against*. When we distrust, avoid, or defend, we pull in to protect ourselves, like a turtle pulling into its shell. When we are *Hypervigilant, Hyper-Caretaking,* or *Attacking*, we defend ourselves by directing our energy outward, like a mama bear protecting her cubs.

Pulling In	*Pushing Against*
Distrusting	Hypervigilance
Avoiding	Hyper-Caretaking
Defending	Attacking

How Protective Patterns Help

- They can keep us safe.
- They help us deal with danger.
- They help us react quickly before thinking.

Protective Patterns lessen our sense of vulnerability and create barriers between ourselves and others—what Brené Brown calls "armoring up." These reactions can be vital for surviving a harmful or traumatic incident. They give us a certain level of **Reactive Resilience**, allowing us to react to danger quickly and feel safer.

Hilde's *Distrusting* pushed her to work on reforming the social system to ensure vulnerable children get the services they need. Meri's *Hypervigilance* means she is quick to call the doctor if she suspects her husband might have pneumonia. Chuck's *Defending* pattern keeps him from being too emotionally vulnerable.

How Protective Patterns Harm

- They can hurt our relationships.
- They can keep us stuck, so we don't take actions that can help us.
- They can make us afraid and exhausted.

While Protective Patterns can protect us from danger or difficulties, our reactions can be very harmful. If we react with our Protective Patterns in situations that do not require them, they can work against us. Chuck's Protective Pattern of *Hyper-Caretaking* backfired because Sandy became more upset when Chuck did not listen to her feelings. Meri didn't take proactive steps on her finances because she Avoided talking to her financial advisor. She got worse customer service when she Attacked the customer service representative.

If we react with our Protective Patterns whenever we feel vulnerable, they become self-defeating, preventing us from centering, connecting, or collaborating with others. Using Protective Patterns can damage our relationships, isolate us, and cause lost opportunities. They can hold us back and prevent us from taking necessary risks.

The key is to learn how to assess each situation and recognize when our Protective Patterns are helping or hindering us. With practice, we can improve at noticing our Protective Patterns and deciding whether to use them. Then, when our Protective Pattern is activated, we can shift from an old pattern to a new possibility by using our resilience skills and creating the safety we need inside ourselves.

Influence of Cultural Patterns

Protective Patterns can come from our families, what happens to us, our biology, or our personality. Our **Cultural Patterns**—passed down to us from our family and community—often influence our **Protective Patterns**. How our family members, particularly our parents, handled stressors is how we learned to manage stressors ourselves. If we grew up in a family where *Avoiding* or *Attacking* was normal, like Meri did, those are more likely to be our Protective Patterns. If our family and community taught us that nothing is trustworthy, then we are more likely to be *Distrusting*. If we were taught that caring for others comes first, we are more likely to use *Hyper-Caretaking*. If we grew up in a family or situation with a lot of fear, like Chuck did, we are more likely to be Hypervigilant.

Our families are not the only determining factor for our Protective Patterns, as life events can also shape them. Traumatic experiences, in particular, can cause different Protective Patterns to emerge. For example, those who have been physically or emotionally attacked or experienced others' victimization might become Hypervigilant. This might be essential for survival for a time, but we might have difficulty choosing an alternative resilience skill when that Protective Pattern is not serving us well.

Conversely, our children are watching how we behave. How we manage our stressors shapes our children's Cultural and Protective Patterns. Though we will never eliminate our Protective Patterns (nor should we—as they can be helpful in the right situation), trying to be healthy models for our children can motivate us to be more intentional about how we use them.

Centering Ourselves

There is hope when we can cope.

The good news is all of us have mindsets and skills we can use to help us make effective choices that serve us better. The We Are Resilient approach can help us practice these *Resilient Mindsets* and *Skills* more intentionally. We can learn to identify, understand, and be compassionate when our own or others' reactiveness creeps in. When we notice a Protective Pattern is not helpful, we can choose a Resilient Mindset or Resilience Skill instead. (See Figure 5.) The more we practice, the easier it is to make choices that serve us better. Over time, we can anticipate the skills and mindsets we need before a stressful event occurs. As we better understand these impulses in ourselves, eventually we can learn to support others experiencing their Protective Patterns.

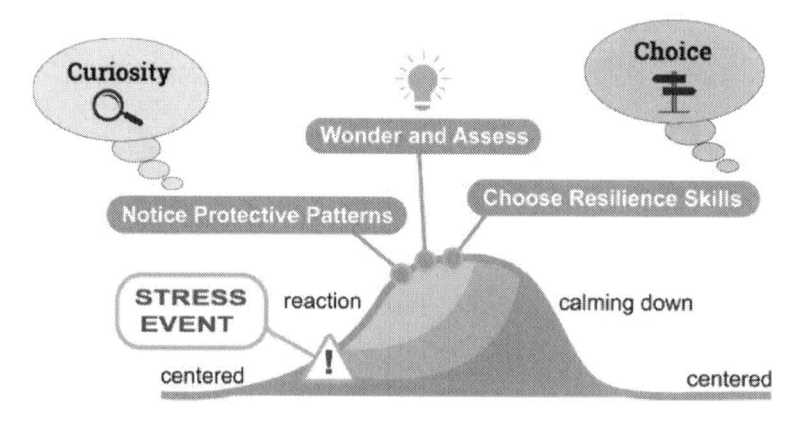

Figure 5. *The first step is recognizing when and how we use our Protective Patterns.*

As soon as we notice we are in a Protective Pattern, we can begin to move back into balance. Our **Resilient Mindsets** can help us:

- When we notice we are reacting automatically, we can become **Curious** about what our reaction is doing for us. In each situation, we can decide whether our Protective Pattern is harming or helping.

- By noticing our Protective Patterns, we can use **Choice** to shift ourselves. "Oops! I used my Protective Pattern, and it was NOT helpful. What can I do differently next time?"

- Then, we can lean into our values and use our **Courage** to make things right. What repair do I need for my relationships? (*See Chapters 15 to 18 for more information on Resilient Mindsets.*)

Anticipatory Resilience

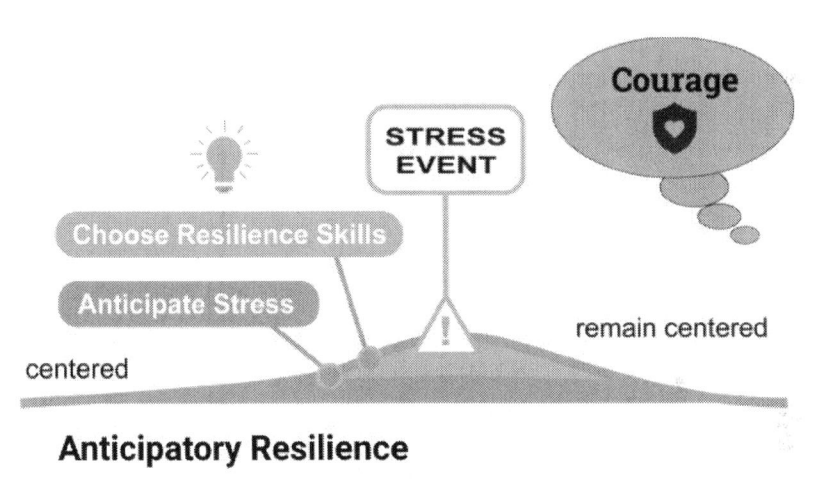

Figure 6

With **Courage**—listening to our heart—we can anticipate stress (see Figure 6) to choose the *Resilience Skills* we need to center ourselves, connect with others, and collaborate BEFORE a stress event occurs.

Chuck—The next Thursday, when I remembered it was trash day, I anticipated my wife's needs and let her know ahead of time that I'd have the trash out before dinner.

Meri—When I was cranky with the customer service person, fortunately, I was communicating by chat, so I could erase what I had written before sending it. After using my *Centering Skills of Noticing Myself* and *Breathing Mindfully*, I rewrote my comments to be clear, firm, and kind.

Our Primary Protective Patterns

Though we may use all of the Protective Patterns, many people have developed a primary emotional pattern or two that they resort to during difficulties. It can be helpful to think about how we behave in stressful situations. Are we more like:

- *Distrustful Deer,* who has to do everything herself because she doesn't trust others.

- *Hypervigilant Hare,* who worries about all the possible disasters.

- *Hyper-Caretaking Hen,* who spends so much time on everyone else's problems that her own needs seem to disappear.

- *Avoiding Armadillo,* who stays inside her shell to avoid her problems.

- *Defending Dog,* who justifies all his actions because he knows he is right.

- *Attacking Alligator,* who lashes out when things get tough.

The names and characters may seem silly, but they illustrate a more profound point: it is hard to move beyond our first reactions when they have become ingrained in our behavior. The following chapters will closely examine these six common Protective Patterns and help us consider when and how we use them. Think about how these Protective Patterns might operate in you. Then, we can look at new ways of dealing with stressful situations and explore the Resilient Mindsets and Resilience Skills that strengthen our resilience.

Chapter 5

Distrusting

> "Worry, fear, self-distrust bows the heart
> and turns [it] back to dust."
>
> ~ Samuel Ullman, poet

Meri—Half a block after leaving our house, my husband stopped the car. This had become so common that I didn't even comment. He was a little embarrassed, though, because he knew other people didn't routinely do this. "I am not sure I brought my jacket. Let me just check." He went to the trunk, rummaging through his suitcase, and found it right where he had packed it. Then he hopped back in, and we drove away.

My husband's Distrusting Protective Pattern often emerges when we leave the house. He doesn't trust himself to be diligent about preparing for wherever we go. In fact, he is right. About half the time, he has not brought the item that he doesn't think about until we are 20 yards from the house. So, stopping and going back is a useful strategy. This pausing after we leave the house actually prevents him from being disappointed later in the journey when he doesn't have something he needs. Unfortunately, it also exasperates me.

Steve is not alone in Distrusting himself. When we Distrust ourselves, it can bring on self-doubt or negative self-talk, especially when we are in new situations. For Hilde, when she was new as a social worker, she sometimes felt flooded by negative self-talk. "I don't know enough to make such important decisions… what right do I have to assess this family?" When she signed up to become a resource (foster) parent, negative self-talk emerged again, "I don't know how to take care of a baby! How am I supposed to handle their behavior?"

Kendra's Protective Pattern of Distrusting shows up in her work as a community college professor. She beats herself up when she thinks she has made a mistake with a student. She becomes Distrusting of herself, particularly when she has to handle racist or discriminatory situations in her classroom. Last month, she asked her students to share their work for peer feedback, a practice she has done for years. At the end of the class. Jemail, one of her Black students, handed her his paper with a racist comment from a peer. Kendra told him she would deal with it and get back to him soon.

After she had handled the concerns of the other waiting students, she quickly drafted a reply. She shared the draft with two college administrators to ensure it was complete. With their input, she emailed her response to Jemail, giving him choices on handling the situation. Unfortunately, Jemail never answered Kendra's email and stopped coming to class. "I wish I had handled the situation more quickly," Kendra said. "I should have dropped everything and handled it right then." She kept replaying her actions in her head, trying to create a different scenario so that Jemail would feel safe in her classroom. "He was already questioning his identity. This is his second time trying to take my class. I don't think he will come back to college now. It breaks my heart." Kendra's Distrust of herself has eroded her confidence in the classroom.

Like all Protective Patterns, Distrusting emerges when we feel vulnerable or unsafe. We might react with a Protective Pattern to something small or something important. It might be a little unsafe (I don't have my raincoat with me), or it might have much more impact (I am unsure how to handle a racist comment). Sometimes, we might not be unsafe at all—we just **perceive** a threat falsely (I see a look on someone's face that upsets me when it really has nothing to do with me). Protective Patterns are about how our emotions and bodies react, not what actually is happening.

When my husband left for our trip, he didn't feel prepared, so his Protective Pattern emerged. Hilde felt unprepared for her new roles as a social worker and a foster parent (resource parent). Kendra felt vulnerable because she cared so much about ensuring all students felt welcome and safe in her classroom.

For many of us, our Protective Pattern of Distrusting gets directed toward others. Meredith, from Massachusetts, is a life coach who practices mindfulness and meditation and enjoys mystery novels. She shared with us how she is Distrusting of the doctors who manage her husband Jorge's complex chronic lung condition. His previous doctor was all gung-ho and promised to make her husband feel better. He was supposed to be "the best" for this specific lung condition. The doctor prescribed medication and told her husband where to pick it up. That pharmacist told them the medication would be $8,000 per month. After recovering from sticker shock, they shopped around and found a pharmacy that sold it for $800/month. Unfortunately, Jorge's condition did not substantially improve. They felt the doctor had no clear plan for addressing Jorge's condition and seemed to be guessing about an effective treatment. When Jorge found new doctors who promised to help, Meredith was even more Distrusting. She had a "wait and see" attitude when they suggested a treatment. Meredith's Distrusting kept her from having too high expectations about the doctors' ability to help her husband.

A city employee, Hampton's Distrusting surfaced after he got a new manager, Miguel. When Hampton first met Miguel, Hampton was respectful. But Miguel was so complimentary that Hampton felt he was being buttered up, which triggered his Distrusting. Hampton responded, "Are you working me, Miguel?" Miguel backed off, saying he didn't have time for that. Over time, Hampton's seed of Distrusting grew. He realized that Miguel didn't have much experience. Miguel asked for cost analysis in situations where it was unnecessary. He didn't share leadership with those who understood the programs, instead bluffing his way through and making all the decisions himself. As Hampton's Distrusting grew, it fed his anger. He hated working for a boss he distrusted, so he eventually left the organization.

Nalda's Protective Pattern of Distrusting manifests in most aspects of her life. She was homeless by age four, and the adults around her taught her to lie and steal to survive. At age six, she was placed in foster care, and she lost contact with her sisters, who were her one source of family and belonging. As a child in foster care, she encountered physical and verbal abuse and felt rejected and lonely. It is easy to see how Distrusting became one of her Protective Patterns—her experiences taught her to Distrust relationships, community, and security because it all might be taken away.

What is Distrusting? There are two types: one inward and one outward.

Distrusting Ourself

- We have self-doubt, and we think we can't do something, or can't do it correctly, or that we are not smart enough.
- We are too critical of ourselves.

Distrusting Others

- We are cautious when feeling unsafe with someone. We may feel that we can't count on them or that the relationship could harm us.
- We may feel uncomfortable asking for help when we need it.
- We may be skeptical of what others say, question their motives, or be overly critical of them.

How it Forms and why we use it

For many, the Protective Pattern of Distrusting ourselves comes from feeling vulnerable to expectations—either our own or others'. Steve comes from a family with high expectations, and meeting them is difficult. Kendra wants to work for social justice, especially as a community college professor, and she Distrusts whether she can do that as well as she wants. For Hilde, becoming a social worker and a resource parent was outside her comfort zone.

Distrusting others develops when those close to us don't meet our needs or perhaps harm us. Even when trustworthy people enter our lives, it might take time to trust them. Trust is built through emotional vulnerability, honesty, and commitment over time.

Chuck—For me, Distrusting as a Protective Pattern started by not trusting my father. One of my earliest memories is when I was a young boy in Virginia, and my Uncle Red helped my dad lay a brick patio behind our house. I remember being excited about the huge pile of bricks, and I felt happy that my Uncle Red was there. He treated us kids with respect and loved to play with us. My dad was not that kind of person. I picked up a brick to carry over to my uncle, and my dad barked sternly at me to put the brick down. I was crushed. I'm sure it wasn't the first time he yelled at me, and definitely not the last.

My dad's alcoholism and emotional volatility in my early life were hard to bear. I learned that I couldn't trust him, but more importantly—I learned not to trust myself. His emotional abuse made me question whether I could do anything right. Was I fundamentally okay? Was I even loveable? Unfortunately, my Distrust of myself became ingrained.

I Distrusted my ability to succeed in school, so I didn't do my schoolwork. I went to ten different schools because we moved so much. I ran away from school in third grade when we lived in Peru, failed the sixth grade in Miami, and almost flunked out of high school in New Hampshire (my physics teacher gave me a D- so I could graduate). After two years, I dropped out of college because I didn't trust that I could make anything of it.

Kendra, the community college professor, also learned to Distrust from a young age, but her Distrusting came from her relationship with her younger sister, Jane. When they were children and teens, if Jane didn't get her way, she would lash out, scream, and yell, calling Kendra bossy and other names. Kendra would leave the house, walk to the nearby river, and sit down to calm herself. Her sister's outbursts might have been helped by mental health intervention, but at the time, Kendra and her parents didn't know how to deal with it. Instead, Kendra developed her Protective Pattern of Distrusting. She became skeptical of other people's motives and the possibility of being manipulated.

Anika's Distrusting didn't surface strongly until she was older. She had been in a 25-year marriage, which ended when her then-husband left her for another woman. Since then, she has been in a 10-year committed relationship with Fred. Even though Fred is loving and generous toward Anika, she is triggered by situations where she feels he isn't meeting her needs. Last year, when she learned her ex-husband was getting remarried, she asked Fred if they could do something fun and distracting that weekend. They planned a getaway. Then they realized that it was the same weekend as the Super Bowl, and Fred said he wanted to watch the game as part of the getaway. Anika's Protective Pattern of Distrusting kicked in, and she reacted immediately, feeling like she couldn't trust Fred to be there for her during a difficult time. She avoided the entire situation by taking herself on a weekend yoga retreat.

> **Distrustful Deer**
> has to do everything herself
> because she doesn't trust others

How it Helps

- When we Distrust ourselves, it helps us to **be careful**. We might take extra time to do something, so we do it well. Or not say something that could cause trouble. Steve took an additional stop to make sure he had everything. Hilde was super careful to get the information she needed to be a resource parent.

- Distrusting helps us **stay safe**. Maybe the people or situations we distrust could harm or cause us pain. Meredith, Hampton, Hilde, Nalda, Kendra, and Chuck all had those experiences.

- Being Distrusting helps us feel like we are **in more control** and can protect us from disappointment. Meredith didn't want to be disappointed again by a doctor's promise that he would make Jorge better. Anika didn't want to be hurt again by a partner who wasn't there for her. Hampton didn't want to work for someone he couldn't trust.

- Being Distrusting **helps us be cautious**. We take steps to prevent people from taking advantage of us and avoid going in a direction that will not serve us.

Meri—I grew up in a household without much money, so I am Distrusting of certain financial matters. Preparing my taxes makes me anxious, so I am very methodical and extra cautious about collecting and collating all the information. When I have to make a big purchase like an appliance or car, I spend a lot of time creating spreadsheets reviewing the pros and cons and the financial details. Distrusting myself in these situations helps me make the best decision.

Chuck—Distrusting my dad protected me from his wrath. I learned to stay away from him and to keep quiet. And, paradoxically, by Distrusting myself as a learner, I didn't feel so humiliated. I viewed myself as someone who wasn't made for school, so I stopped doing my homework—which gave me a good excuse for failing.

How it Harms

- Distrusting **hurts healthy relationships**. Being critical of others keeps them at a distance.

- It **robs us of hope** because we always fear the worst.

- Distrusting **keeps us from getting support** by preventing us from reaching out to others who could help us.

- If we are too careful, we can **get stuck** and not do something important. We don't take healthy and growth-producing risks.

- We might not take the difficult steps to help us grow or **miss good opportunities**. It might mean we:

  ◦ Won't take medication/get vaccinated/go to therapy

  ◦ Sabotage a job or placement interview or a date

  ◦ Keep running away

Chuck—Distrusting myself and others had a huge impact on me. I held myself back from my personal power in many contexts. As a child, in addition to holding myself back as a learner, I lied a lot because I didn't trust that I was okay, just as I was. I'd say I had done my homework when I hadn't touched it. I'd say I had done my chores and then run and do them before my mom found out. I kept myself socially isolated. As a young adult, the only place I fully trusted myself was out in the wilderness, camping or rock climbing. There, I could truly be myself. It took a long time before I could bring that "trusting me" into the rest of my life.

Influence of Cultural Patterns

Our Cultural Patterns, which we learn in our family and community and affect how we view the world, influence our Protective Patterns. If we see those around us as unsafe, as Kendra did with her sister and Nalda did with most adults, it is hard to trust ourselves or others.

Chuck—Like many alcoholic families, my family's Cultural Patterns were steeped in Distrusting because they were built on a pretense. It was not okay to talk about the drinking, the behavior, the emotionally frozen silence, and any semblance of healthy boundaries. Pretending that I didn't know what I knew was so ingrained in me that I did not realize I lived in an alcoholic family until I was a young adult.

Compounding the coverup of alcoholism was the fact that my dad was an undercover agent in the CIA. He pretended that he had other employers his entire career. I didn't know who he really worked for until I was in high school. So I learned to Distrust much of what I thought or felt might be true, as well as what others told me.

The construct of race can also create conditions for Distrusting. For Darius, as a Black man himself, he feels that Black families teach their children to be Distrusting to protect them. "Don't trust the government" was a useful family mantra because, historically, the American government has not protected Black families very well.

Hampton's experience as a Black man is slightly different. Hampton grew up in the military, so he was taught to obey those in authority. He is very respectful of the chain of command. At the same time, as a Black man, he recognizes that those in authority don't always have his best interests at heart. Hampton was Distrusting when Miguel micromanaged him at work, and he didn't feel safe enough with upper management to be transparent about what was happening. Since he worked in a primarily white environment, he felt that if he complained, he would be labeled an "angry Black man." Since he didn't want that target on his back, he felt leaving was easier.

Centering Ourselves

Centering Skills

When we find Distrusting is not helping us, we can make choices that serve us better. When Steve starts beating himself up too much because of his Distrusting, he uses the *Centering Skill of Breathing Mindfully* to ground himself. Kendra, the community college professor, mitigates her Distrust by using the *Centering Skill of Letting Go* of her negative self-talk. She recognizes that it's not helpful to look back and wish it was different. "I have to look forward to see if I can write a new ending to this story with Jemail," she added.

Meredith, the mystery-novel lover, copes with her husband's illness with the *Centering Skill of Noticing Myself*. Every day, she uses it as part of her mindfulness practice. She becomes aware of her emotions in her body. As she feels tightness or stiffness in her shoulders and her back, she focuses on relaxing them.

When Hampton's Distrust of his manager started affecting him, he leaned into the *Centering Skill of Nurturing Myself*. By doing the things he loved—performing and connecting with friends—he could reconnect with what was important to him and feel better about himself. Participating in a Dovetail Learning Resilience Circle also helped him process what was going on for him and strengthened his skills. Through these activities, he gained the confidence to find a new job where he didn't Distrust.

Chuck—I used other Protective Patterns and Resilient Mindsets and Skills to deal with Distrusting my father. Often, I used the Protective Pattern of *Avoiding*. I hated my father growing up, so I Avoided him as much as possible. The combination of Distrusting and *Avoiding* helped keep me safe. Sometimes, when I had to deal with his alcoholic rage, I would use the *Resilient Mindset of Choice* and *Centering Skill of Nurturing Myself* (though I couldn't name them at the time) to leave my house and go into nature to take care of myself. Our house in Virginia had a tall fir tree in the backyard. When I felt Distrusting, I would climb that tree to its tippy top highest branches where I could feel at one with the wind. It gave me a profound experience of the *Centering Skill of Breathing Mindfully*, but even more powerful was how connected I felt to the tree, the clouds, and the sky beyond my own life. I gave myself what I needed to feel whole and complete.

Deeper Insights

Chuck—Though Distrusting has certainly limited me, it has also opened up powerful opportunities for Resilience. By the time I hit middle school, I had suicidal ideation and didn't trust that I could handle being me at all. I was still a very poor student. I had repeated sixth grade, which made me feel a lot of shame. Even more significantly, during that time, I was being sexually molested. Ultimately, my Distrust and anger at my perpetrator gave me the personal power to choose to say, "Stop!"

> **"You never know how strong you are,
> until being strong is the only choice you have."**
> ~ Bob Marley, musician

The *Resilient Mindsets* had guided me. *Speaking Authentically* was an unconscious and significant *Choice*. It took the *Resilient Mindset of Courage* for me to stand up for myself and say what I knew was right in my heart. That act of *Courage* was one of the most powerful and resilient acts of my life. By choosing to speak up, my abuse stopped.

Now, as an adult, I use the *Resilient Mindset of Curiosity* when confronting my Distrust of myself. I lean into it and wonder, "What the heck is going on?" Since my Protective Patterns arise from early childhood experiences, I am continuously curious about how they all work.

Self-Discovery

- Where and with whom does Distrusting show up in your life?
- In what contexts might you not fully trust yourself? Not trust others?
- How do your Cultural Patterns influence your Distrusting?
- What might be the origins of your Distrusting, and how might you find healing from that?
- What helps you trust yourself or others the most?

Protective Patterns

Chapter 6

Hypervigilance 👁

"The natural state ... is to be somewhat on guard. However, in order to feel emotionally close to another human being... the brain needs to turn off its natural vigilance."

~ Bessel A. van der Kolk, *The Body Keeps the Score*

In December 2022, Meredith—the mystery-novel lover—and her husband Jorge, who has a lung condition, went to a small dinner party near Boston. To ensure Jorge would be safe, everyone tested for COVID before going. However, the day after the party, Meredith received a message. She learned that another guest had been exposed to COVID the day before the party. Just the thought of Jorge contracting COVID exhausted Meredith. Her Hypervigilance jumped up, and she couldn't stop worrying. "Who knows what could happen if he gets something on top of what he has?"

She already used enormous mental energy assessing every situation. "Is our household okay? Does Jorge have what he needs?" Every time they left the house, her Hypervigilance kicked in. Continuously scanning the environment, she asked herself. "Is this place safe? Are the other people wearing masks? Can they be trusted to understand our situation?" Though Meredith knew that her Hypervigilance drove her to catastrophize, the potential for additional trouble weighed her down heavily.

The close call with the party meant Meredith decided not to see her extended family over the holidays. She didn't want to feel the emotional exhaustion that comes from so much worry. It turned out her decision was a good one. Though no one had told her in advance, her brother's young granddaughter had a cold and a fever at the Christmas gathering. It reminded her that even her family didn't understand what might be dangerous to her husband.

Audrey is a runner who finds joy on the trails near her rural home. However, financial stress brought on her Hypervigilance. Her husband believed that "things will always work out," but Audrey did not. She wanted to know where the money was coming from before they took on debt. She watched the family's bank account to ensure everything was covered. At one point, they were teetering on bankruptcy. Audrey carefully timed all the bill payments, putting envelopes on the counter in the order she could mail them, and timed all their online payments. Her watchfulness and creativity prevented a financial disaster, but it was exhausting.

Chuck—My Hypervigilance made me feel like I had to do everything perfectly and always be on time. I have been a perfectionist and workaholic for much of my adult life. I just couldn't let go of doing, doing, doing. I would get up early to start work by 6 a.m. before leaving for the office. My workday often ended by 4 p.m., but I'd still be in my office at 6 p.m. I went to great lengths to make my work impeccable. Sometimes, I'd work on refining my presentation slide decks again and again. And my anxiety about being on time exasperated my wife. I would get anxious, upset, and very controlling. My pacing, jiggling of keys, questioning everyone's readiness, etc., created stress for everyone around me, especially my family. My Hypervigilance helped me get things right, but it came at a cost. Putting work above everything else meant losing time with my wife and children and upsetting them with my anxiety.

What is Hypervigilance?

- We are on constant high alert.
- We see potential danger in not handling things just right.
- We are anxious about what might go wrong.
- This constant worry impacts us and those around us.

How it Forms and why we use it

Like other *Protective Patterns*, Hypervigilance is our adaptation to perceived danger. Our brain keeps us out of harm's way by being highly alert to our surroundings. When we are in Hypervigilant mode, we see or anticipate potential danger or adverse outcomes in places they don't belong. While vigilance—being watchful about specific threats—can be helpful, it becomes Hypervigilance when high alertness, anxiety, perfectionism, or worry becomes the norm and harms us and our relationships.

Meredith's anxiety means she doesn't go to restaurants, travel, or spend time with friends who are not extraordinarily careful and thoughtful about her situation. Audrey's concern about her family's finances impacts her relationships with her family. Chuck's anxiety about getting things "just right" means he works too hard and misses time for himself, his family, and his friends. His concern about time makes others around him upset and defensive.

For some people, Hypervigilance manifests within more specific situations. Chuck's wife, Sandy, had a cat, Lily, the most affectionate, loving kitty imaginable. She would curl up around Sandy's shoulders like a warm winter shawl. As Lily grew older, though, she developed a nasal tumor and was slowly dying. Sandy became Hypervigilant about Lily's health. She went to extreme care to save her from discomfort and death. As the vet bills mounted, her fear of Lily dying caused her intense anguish. As the end approached, her Hypervigilance increased with her anxiety. Sandy's Hypervigilance gave her stomach pain and a sense of impending dread.

Carmen's Hypervigilance popped up at work. A manager, she was always looking for what could go wrong. Her Hypervigilance prevented her from being as productive as she wanted because she would get sidetracked by potential problems rather than focusing on her essential tasks. She also hurt her career by playing it safe and not stepping up to new growth opportunities for fear of not getting it right.

When we live in threatening situations, we may develop Hypervigilance as a Protective Pattern. Chronic illness or financial insecurity are often triggering, as they were for Meredith and Audrey. Sandy developed Hypervigilance in response to her mom's battle with breast cancer when Sandy was young. When her mom passed, the experience created a fear deep inside her that emerged as Hypervigilance with her cat.

A chronic illness also triggered Hypervigilance for Delphine. A recent college graduate and beach lover, she developed Hypervigilance when diagnosed with Graves' disease, a thyroid disorder most common in young women. She had been feeling very anxious. It was a relief to learn that her racing heart, panic attacks, and sweating had a physiological basis, but the treatment medication took months to reduce her symptoms. In the meantime, she struggled with simple errands. Her racing heart made her afraid she would pass out, even though she knew the opposite was true—low blood pressure and low heart rate caused passing out. Delphine became Hypervigilant, with a lengthy mental checklist on whether she would be okay in ordinary situations. She worried she would collapse when she went to the bank to deposit cash receipts from her job. How long was the line? Would the teller be quick, or would customers chat? Delphine knew her concerns were not logical, but her Hypervigilant self couldn't help but constantly assess for danger. She was exhausted and felt like her Hypervigilance was overtaking her life, and she couldn't even enjoy the beach anymore.

Chuck—My Hypervigilance started as protection from my dad's intense rage. I had to be Hypervigilant to stay safe. Where was he? What was his mood? Had he been drinking? If I did something "wrong," I was in danger of getting hurt emotionally or physically. Growing up, being late by one minute brought his contempt, humiliation, and shame. What could I do to avoid my father's wrath? I concluded I needed to be perfect. No mistakes, always on time. I grew to believe that if I do enough and do it well enough, I'll have earned my worth as a human being.

> **Hypervigilant Hare**
> worries about all
> the possible disasters.

How it Helps

- Hypervigilance helps us to **stay safe**. It can be the best survival strategy in certain environments.

- Hypervigilance helps us to **take steps early to avoid potential hazards**. We put defenses in place. In dangerous situations, we get ahead of everything that might go wrong.

- Our super-powered **spidey senses are "on" alert** to signal when danger lurks (real or perceived).

Chuck—My Hypervigilance protects me by helping me be ready and on time so I can feel confident and competent. I feel proud to do my work well.

Meredith knows that paying attention to her husband's health keeps her husband a little safer. Audrey knows her Hypervigilance saved their family from financial ruin. For both of them, however, that safety came at the expense of their peace of mind and potentially their wellbeing.

How it Harms

- Our fear of potential threats limits our ability to enjoy the present and to connect with others.

- We may overreact to situations that are actually safe. Our sense of fear may be unnecessary, and we fear things that won't hurt us.

- We might say no to something that actually would be a healthy stretch goal. We may impede appropriate risk-taking and avoid new opportunities that could help us grow.

- Hypervigilance can be exhausting when our fight-or-flight reaction stays turned on. It is tiring to always be on watch for danger.

The long-term activation of the stress response system and the overexposure to cortisol and other stress hormones can disrupt many of the body's processes, causing:

- Anxiety
- Depression
- Digestive problems
- Headaches
- Muscle tension and pain
- Heart disease, heart attack, high blood pressure, and stroke
- Sleep problems
- Weight gain
- Memory and concentration impairment

Like the other Protective Patterns, Hypervigilance can impact many aspects of our lives:

- Obsessive behavior patterns
- Physical and mental exhaustion
- Difficulty in relationships
- Problems in the workplace
- Avoidance of social situations

Chuck—Hypervigilance has also hurt me—primarily by keeping me from having quality time in important relationships. My wife used to say I was married to my work. Over the years, I only took a few vacations and didn't put my health first because work was number one. I was simply unaware of my Hypervigilance, which got in the way of caring for my own needs. Fortunately, as I've learned about how this Protective Pattern impacts me and my relationships, I've been able to shift it dramatically.

Influence of Cultural Patterns

Families and communities that experienced prolonged trauma, particularly racism, discrimination, and chronic violence, pass on to children the importance of Hypervigilance as a survival strategy. Many people become Hypervigilant from a traumatic experience or continued exposure to unsafe or unpredictable events. Being alert to unexpected threats can make the difference between life and death in those situations. Adrian developed his Hypervigilance as a child living in a wartime environment. He has difficult memories from that time: hearing the fighting, hiding in bomb shelters, and seeing the destruction from the attacks. This tense period in his life has contributed to his Hypervigilance.

Hypervigilance protects children in other unstable situations, even when the environment is not so dire. Vivienne, a social worker, also experienced trauma as a child. Her father had alcoholism, and Vivienne spent a lot of her time trying to protect her brother and herself from her dad's unpredictable outbursts. To this day, Vivienne often feels tense, expecting something "bad" to happen at any moment. When she enters a room, she does a scan, looking for danger, almost without thinking. She has difficulty relaxing in her environment.

Hypervigilance can become especially ingrained when adverse experiences occur in childhood or are long-term. Research suggests that those with trauma histories experience increased activity in their amygdala, the part of the brain that sends out the fight/flight/freeze signal. We can be overly sensitive to any activity in our environment, like Adrian or Vivienne, and not be able to accurately filter what is an actual danger. This part of the brain's limbic system can impede executive functioning. Hypervigilance kicks in before we can think rationally and ask ourselves: Am I really in danger? The problem is that it can be difficult to tame Hypervigilance after people are no longer in a dangerous situation.

Chuck—My Hypervigilance about timeliness is a Cultural Pattern from my father's family. Being on time was such a trigger for him. Growing up, I would be in trouble if I was not on time. My father's look of disapproval would cause me to shrink in shame. I might also get a "dressing down" that came with the fear of a harsh spanking. My dad absorbed this fear of being late from his military experience and because my grandfather had drilled it into him in his early life. My grandfather had been a general in Europe during WWI, fighting on the Western Front, and passed on Hypervigilance to his son. Many generations probably passed down this Cultural Pattern as my ancestors were generals in the army going back to George Washington.

Centering Ourselves

Centering Skills

When we find Hypervigilance is not helping us, we can make choices that serve us better. Though Delphine's Hypervigilance is triggered by her out-of-control body, which she can't escape, she uses the *Centering Skill of Breathing Mindfully* to regain her balance. She knows her breath will allow her to step back and go inward, giving her peace. She also practices the *Centering Skill of Letting Go*, which is still hard for her. She has to *Let Go* of her frustration that she can't go running because it increases her heart rate. She is *Letting Go* of the social pressure that she needs to do things for others. She focuses more on what she needs and can do for herself.

The *Centering Skill of Finding Gratitude* is also helpful for Delphine. At one point, Graves' disease was causing her to lose her hair. Now that she has her hair back, she is grateful for it. She is also grateful to have access to medication and good treatment. The whole process has reminded her that there is always something to be grateful for.

Chuck—To get relief from my Hypervigilance, I work at creating healthy boundaries. This begins with the *Centering Skill of Noticing Myself*. When I feel and see that I'm in my Hypervigilance, I use the *Resilient Mindset of Curiosity* to explore what's happening inside me. This helps me see what else is possible. My curiosity leads me to use the *Resilient Mindset of Choice*, and I often choose to use the *Centering Skill of Breathing Mindfully*. I take time away from what I'm Hypervigilant about and just breathe. As an introvert, I also use the *Centering Skill of Nurturing Myself* and give myself a lot of downtime to replenish my energy. When I don't, I get exhausted. *Noticing Myself*, being *Curious* about what I need, making a *Choice* for myself, and using the *Resilient Mindset of Courage* to act on my own behalf are some of the resilience superpowers that make all the difference.

Deeper Insights

Meri—For most of my life, I have been able to resist Hypervigilance. I had the privilege of being raised in a safe environment with parents who expressed their love for me and were able to provide me with comfort and security. Even though, as a child, my house was burglarized three times, I never translated that into a direct threat to be concerned about. My sister still chides me for not carefully locking doors. I have lived and traveled in situations that others view as sketchy, but I love the adventure of it. When I see others worry about unlikely threats, I find my life is more peaceful without those worries.

However, when my husband became ill with a rare tuberculosis-like illness, I suddenly moved into Hypervigilance. I was the one who first raised the need for more advanced care with his primary care doctor. I read all about the disease so his pulmonologist and I could have long discussions about the best potential courses of treatment. I noticed each time his coughing became too pronounced, likely signaling pneumonia. I was on high alert for anything that might endanger my husband. My Hypervigilance became like a guard dog working overtime. Sometimes, I barked at intruders, but other times, I barked at things that didn't pose a real threat, like leaves blowing in the wind. It drained me mentally, emotionally, and physically.

Now that my husband's illness has resolved for the time being, I can look back and recognize my Hypervigilance emerged only when I felt something incredibly precious to me was threatened.

Self-Discovery

- Where and with whom does Hypervigilance show up in your life?

- What's the impact? How does it hurt you, and how does it serve you?

- What Cultural Patterns did you learn that influenced your Hypervigilance?

- What helps you most to reduce your Hypervigilance?

Protective Patterns

Chapter 7

Hyper-Caretaking

> "Over caretaking ... means putting such a high level of attention on someone else's needs and well-being that you actually forget your own."
>
> ~ Martha Beck, life coach

Brenna's house was flooded. Her water heater had leaked all over her garage and kitchen, ruining the cupboards and the flooring. A single mother, Brenna could not get it repaired quickly. She lived in disarray for months while the moldy cupboards and bad flooring were removed, but nothing was replaced. When she contacted the contractor, he blamed supply chain issues and insurance inefficiencies. Brenna felt she had no choice but to live with this glacial progress. Simultaneously, Brenna jumped into assertive problem-solving mode with her daughter, who lived in an apartment a few hours away and had a rodent infestation. She helped her daughter move out to temporary housing and helped her to draft letters to the landlord to get out of the lease. She ensured he immediately covered all the costs of the disruption and her daughter's move into a safer building.

After Ximena's dad died, she was anxious and worried about her mom. She dealt with her anxiety by taking care of all the details of someone's passing. She wrote the obituary, planned the funeral, and took care of anything else she could think to do. It helped her mom and the whole family to have someone take care of all the details, and she did a good job of it. Ximena told herself she had to do it all, but, in retrospect, she realized she could have delegated some of the tasks to her siblings. That would have been better for them and better for her. Carrying the weight of everything left Ximena no time to deal with her grief. Her Protective Pattern of Hyper-Caretaking meant she neglected to care for herself and give herself time and space for her feelings.

Ximena and Brenna are like many of us. We will do anything for family members, even if that means not caring for our own needs. We have learned a Cultural Pattern that our first priority should always be someone else, as though we can continue indefinitely without caring for our own physical, emotional, or social needs.

Thirty-year-old Paxton worked for a small startup and loved watching football in his spare time. He shared that his Protective Pattern of Hyper-Caretaking emerged two years ago in his relationship with Toni. Rather than reflecting on how the relationship felt for him, Paxton spent all his energy trying to anticipate and take care of her needs. He meticulously cleaned his apartment and always tried to look his best. He gave her constant attention and took the lion's share of household duties. He deferred to all her choices in their activities and never allowed himself to relax around her. In the end, Hyper-Caretaking could not save the relationship.

As a nurse, Stella found herself reacting with Hyper-Caretaking all too often. She cared for hospitalized children waiting for spots in an inpatient mental health facility. Since her patients had psychosocial issues along with their physical ones, she wanted to heal their hearts along with their bodies. However, that was not possible in her limited time with them because they needed a higher level of care. Many of her coworkers struggled with the same issue, leading to high burnout on the ward. Eventually, Stella recognized that she wanted a different nursing position. The ward needed nurses with stronger personal boundaries who were not trying to find a solution to every problem, even when the problems were not theirs to solve.

Hyper-Caretaking often means trying to relieve another person's emotional distress to make ourselves feel better. Gideon, a school principal, struggles with Hyper-Caretaking. When COVID disrupted the global supply chain for his wife's job, the new reality became a massive stressor for Gideon. As his wife became more stressed, Gideon felt his Hyper-Caretaking getting stronger. He wanted to blame her colleagues and give her boss a "piece of his mind." Though he knew that would be inappropriate, he had to fight his strong urge to try to fix things for her.

Chuck—In my marriage, I'm an emotional Hyper-Caretaker. I'm quick to try to save my wife from emotional upsets or other discomforts. The other day, she was upset that the neighbors had built a new fence. I said, "Oh, don't feel that way. It's going to be alright." Later, I realized I was trying to soothe my own emotions because I feel upset when she is upset. I don't think of Hyper-Caretaking as giving up my needs for others. Instead, I push my needs underground and don't even know what they are.

Meri—I also used Hyper-Caretaking when my daughter was younger. She was sensitive to the pain and injustice in the world. Rather than validating her feelings and acknowledging their truth, I would try to take them away. "Don't worry about that. Don't be sad. You will be okay," was often my reaction. I was so uncomfortable when she was unhappy or in pain that I worked very hard to remove it.

What is Hyper-Caretaking?

- We take care of others so much that **we ignore our own needs**.
- We do something for others when **it would be better for them to do it** themselves.
- We try to **fix others' emotional pain** rather than accompanying them through it.

- We **protect others from the consequences of their behavior**. We enable them, limiting their ability to learn from mistakes. We might help someone so that it perpetuates a problem rather than solving it.

- We always **help others instead of meeting our own needs**.

- When we fail to meet our needs, it can make us **feel like victims**. We might become resentful.

How it Forms and why we use it

Most of us begin Hyper-Caretaking out of love and genuine caring. We want to ensure our family and close friends are okay. We want to be the solution for others who are in pain. These good and noble impulses help our world become a better place.

The challenge is when "caretaking" becomes a pattern of Hyper-Caretaking. When we work so hard to care for others that we do not attend to our own needs and feelings, especially when we do what others can do for themselves, we move into Hyper-Caretaking. Nariko experienced this when her father entered the hospital for uncontrolled bleeding from his mouth. As the oldest of six siblings, she felt she needed to take charge. Nariko ensured her parents and siblings were okay and did whatever she could to meet their needs. Her caretaking helped them, and she felt good about that. However, her hyper attention to their needs also meant she avoided her feelings and needs, and she never asked her siblings to help. By shouldering it all alone, Nariko elevated her stress rather than sharing the responsibility with others.

We know that our families, communities, and world need people who care for each other, attend to other people's needs, and sometimes put others' needs first. How can we determine when we have crossed the line from healthy taking care of others into Hyper-Caretaking? Like all Protective Patterns, this assessment is not something we do for others—it is something only we can determine for ourselves.

For many of us, it is easier to focus on others' needs rather than our own. When we focus on someone else's problems, we have more emotional distance, so the solutions can seem more evident. Plus, we don't have to think about our challenges and what we might have to change about ourselves. For Brenna, it felt overwhelming to deal with her flooded house and the tangled web of liability between the contractor and the insurance. It was easier to think about how to solve her daughter's challenges than her own. Ximena dealt with her father's passing by taking care of her mom and being so busy that she couldn't grieve. Stella also found focusing on her patients' problems easier than her own.

When we are emotionally Hyper-Caretaking, it is often because we feel upset when those we love are upset. We want to reduce their problems or sadness because it eases our discomfort. Chuck and Meri wanted to tell their loved ones to be happy rather than listen to them while they felt pain. By trying to solve others' problems (that are not ours to solve), we deny them their capacity to solve their own problems.

> **Hyper-Caretaking Hen** spends so much time on everyone else's problems that her own needs seem to disappear.

How it Helps

- We **feel good when we are helping** and contributing.

- We **feel valued by others** and connected to them.

- We like **feeling needed** by other people.

- Hyper-Caretaking can help us **feel like we belong** and are loved.

A high-school English teacher, Roberta encourages her students to delve into their lives in their writing. She often cries when reading their journals and papers because their lives are so difficult. One student, Joline, wrote about her abuse. Roberta started talking with Joline after class most days, and, sometimes, Joline would spend an hour or more crying. This extra time meant Roberta fell behind on her to-do list, but she knew she was the one person Joline confided in. Eventually, Roberta recognized that Joline needed professional support, so she connected Joline to the school counselor and other resources.

How it Harms

- We **neglect our own needs**.

- We hurt others by not encouraging their ability to take care of themselves. We are **not honoring their own capacity**.

- We are not helping others learn to take responsibility.

- Trying to fix others' emotional needs might feel good, but it often doesn't help them feel better or strengthen their emotional resilience.

- It can lead to emotional/psychological burnout as well as codependency and resentment of others.

Like other Protective Patterns, our Hyper-Caretaking may harm those we care for. Age 29, Ricardo was a fan of Latinx melodramas and passionate about supporting the Chicano community. Ricardo shared how he felt worn out by the Hyper-Caretaking of his mom, Rosa. Whenever Ricardo faced a challenge or needed something, Rosa would respond, "What do you need, sweetie? I got you!" Ricardo admits that his mother's constant focus on making his life easier felt reassuring as a child, but he became more irritated as he grew up. Even after he became an adult and moved out of his mom's home, Rosa wanted to take care of all his needs. "Let me do your laundry," she would say. To Ricardo, her Hyper-Caretaking felt like an effort to prevent him from growing up.

Finally, Ricardo had an authentic conversation with her. "Mom," he said. "I appreciate everything you do for me, but how can I go from being a boy to a man without some challenging experiences that I resolve on my own?" He also explained that his mom's over-involvement in his life made it more difficult to find a partner. Their conversation was difficult at first, but Rosa came to understand what Ricardo was saying.

Nurse Stella's son Jerry also confronted her about Hyper-Caretaking. A young adult, Jerry was trying to find his way, which included pausing his college education. Stella saw that he was floundering and was worried he was depressed. Her work as a nurse had exposed her to the danger of depression in young adults, and she had seen too many who had injured themselves. When Jerry said, "Mom, you have got to stop worrying about me. I am worried about you worrying about me," Stella realized her Hyper-Caretaking was not helpful. In the end, backing off helped them both. He got a job as a paraprofessional working with children with autism and discovered a whole new career track he is passionate about.

Influence of Cultural Patterns

Many families and communities value the group over the individual. They pass on to their children—verbally and through modeling—that their priority should be to the family, group, or community, and taking care of their own needs is "selfish." The children are taught to put the needs of others before their own. This Cultural Pattern shapes them into becoming helpers and creating caring communities. However, when "caretaking" crosses into Hyper-Caretaking, too often, it causes burnout and resentment while reducing others' capacity for growth and responsibility.

Rosa, a Mexican immigrant, learned to Hyper-Caretake as a Cultural Pattern in her family. When she had her own children, she always put their needs first. While Ricardo appreciated his mom's attention as a child, when he grew up, Rosa's Hyper-Caretaking began to feel suffocating.

This Cultural Pattern may be more pronounced in some cultures but can be found in many families. Maeve, who is Irish American, came from a family with ten children and was rarely allowed to have needs or wants of her own. To be "selfish" or "greedy" was one of the worst sins. She spends her life helping others—bringing little gifts, visiting those sick or dying, or running errands—and is embarrassed to admit the rare times she buys herself new shoes or a new coat.

For some, this focus on others through Hyper-Caretaking became a way to navigate a difficult family life. When Stella was young, her father had a disabling industrial accident, and her brother reacted by causing turbulence in the family. As a way of easing her mother's significant stress, Stella took on Hyper-Caretaking. She can see how that influenced her decision to become a nurse. After being trained in the We Are Resilient™ approach, she recognized how many of her medical colleagues also lean toward Hyper-Caretaking.

Growing up in rural California, Zelma also adopted Hyper-Caretaking to control her environment. In her family, her mom hit the kids even if they did not directly trigger the anger. As a young girl, she tried to avoid her mother's rage and protect herself by Hyper-Caretaking her family. She took care of everything for her three younger brothers. Now an adult, she still has trouble meeting her own needs. Even if she is exhausted, she tends to decline offers of help.

Chuck—I learned Hyper-Caretaking from my mom. My mother grew up in an era when women did everything for their husbands, including caretaking my father's difficult emotions. If he became rude or abusive at the dinner table, she would smooth things over by making light of it or changing the subject.

In an extreme version of Hyper-Caretaking, Eve's mother forced Eve to take over the role of parent when she was growing up. Her mother had an undiagnosed mental illness, which made her violent and angry. For twenty years, her mother forced Eve to provide all sorts of care. Eve was not allowed to have her own needs and sacrificed any hope for attention, comfort, and guidance. She knew she had to serve every whim of her mother if she wanted to stay alive. When children take over the role of parenting for whatever reason, they become used to caring for others at their own expense and often continue to do so. Reflecting on that experience now with her perspective as an 80-year-old author, Eve recognizes that Hyper-Caretaking is a response that can help us maintain safety and ensure survival.

Centering Ourselves

When we find Hyper-Caretaking is not helping us or others, we can make choices that serve us better. Understanding that other people don't want or need us to solve their problems is a big part of moving away from Hyper-Caretaking. People often just want to share their challenges and be listened to, seen, and heard.

For Zelma, one of the biggest challenges of learning not to Hyper-Caretake was stopping to try fixing the problems of those around her. When she sees her husband hurt by the behavior of his children, she wants to reach out to them and play peacemaker. She is learning that intervening inappropriately does not honor her husband's desire to handle their estrangement. She is working on honoring his wishes and capacities. When she sees herself falling into her Protective Pattern of Hyper-Caretaking, she steps back, uses the *Centering Skill of Noticing Myself* to understand how she is feeling, then moves into her heart and shifts to loving her husband precisely as he is amid his sadness about his relationship with his kids. She also uses the *Centering Skill of Breathing Mindfully*.

Stella, the nurse trainer, uses the *Centering Skill of Finding Gratitude*. When she wakes up, she wiggles her fingers and toes and thinks about how lucky she is to be able to get out of bed on her own. Stella also thinks about how lucky she is to work for a hospital that cares about a healthy work environment. Now a training nurse in her hospital, she is trying to help her fellow nurses reduce their Hyper-Caretaking because she knows it leads to burnout.

When Gideon, the school principal, was Hyper-Caretaking his wife, he used the *Centering Skill of Noticing Myself*. He realized that his Hyper-Caretaking energy was not only NOT helping his wife but also creating more destabilizing energy that strained their Relational Resilience. His wife's challenges were out of her control—not to mention Gideon's. Instead, he could use the *Resilient Mindset of Choice* and choose the *Connecting Skill of Empathizing*. Through Empathizing, he notched down his Hyper-Caretaking into "healthy caretaking" and did the grocery shopping, gave hugs when there were tears, and bought flowers. With empathy, he could acknowledge the new complexities of her job with, "I'm sorry, that sounds hard," or "You are doing a great job using the *Connecting Skill of Speaking Authentically* on your Zoom calls."

Chuck—I'm learning that instead of trying to fix my wife when she's upset, it is much better to listen to her and let myself know what I feel and need. When I feel myself attempting to take care of her emotions, I pause, then use the *Centering Skill of Breathing Mindfully* to regain awareness of myself. I also often use the *Centering Skill of Letting Go* to drop my impulse to take care of others when it denies what is true for them. I know people are capable of taking care of themselves. Lastly, by using the *Centering Skill of Nurturing Myself*, I can have compassion for myself and her. It helps me accept whatever is going on and just be myself.

Deeper Insights

Chuck—I have given up my needs throughout my life to gain love, acceptance, and belonging from others. Unfortunately, my Hyper-Caretaking almost killed me.

In 2017, I had a fabulous ski weekend in Tahoe with my daughter, Elissa. We had a blast, romping and playing to our hearts' content in the snow. On the chairlift, we had ice crystals all over our face masks because it was so cold and exhilarating. After a wild wipe-out, I was totally plastered with snow but still had a huge grin. It was pure joy and a deep connection with my daughter.

That Monday, my thigh muscles were weak and rubbery. It was weird, but I chalked it up to overtaxed muscles from the awesome ski trip. A little later in the day, I walked from my office into the foyer, and my left leg collapsed under me. I rolled onto the floor and bounced back up to a standing position. Our receptionist was shocked, and I said, "Wow, I wasn't expecting that! I guess I'm more out of shape than I realized." Again, I chalked it up to skiing and gingerly walked back to my office. I walked very carefully for the rest of the day.

That night, the muscles in my legs became excruciatingly painful from my feet to my hips. The pain was so bad my wife, Sandy, took me to the emergency room. Hours later, after several consults, X-rays, an MRI scan, and armed with pain medications, I went home. There was no resolution, but I had an appointment the next day for more MRI scans. That very tough night turned into two weeks of such intense pain that by the end, I could barely crawl to the bathtub to soak my legs in scalding hot water, which was the only way I found to relieve my pain. During those two weeks, I had many rounds of consults, three MRIs, and sequentially more powerful narcotics, which gave me no relief from the pain and still no diagnosis.

Thankfully, friends encouraged me to see a neurologist, who found I had no knee-jerk reflex at all. He diagnosed me with a rare autoimmune disease called Guillain-Barré Syndrome. He sent me directly to the hospital for a week of blood plasma transfusion to rebuild my immune system, which had essentially been attacking itself.

I had a long recovery, with much physical therapy and strong medications for nerve pain. Somewhere inside, I knew that this illness, which seemingly came out of nowhere, was connected to something deeper in me. As a transpersonal psychologist, I was intensely interested in the connection of the body/mind, so I started a deep internal inquiry with the help of a somatic therapist. Through that process, I discovered clear connections to my early childhood trauma. Not only did my father's emotional abuse lead me to deny my own needs and use Hyper-Caretaking, but it came back to haunt me through my body. Denying my emotions and over-prioritizing others' needs had led to my immune crisis. My story was not uncommon, as there is a very high correlation between a lack of emotional boundaries and autoimmune disorders.

> **"Hyper-Caretaking is often associated with codependency, where the caretaker's sense of self-worth becomes tied to approval and validation."**
>
> ~ Anna Drescher, NHS assistant clinical psychologist

Understanding the emotional costs of deeply rooted trauma not only brought me face to face with my past but also how I was replicating that trauma in the present. My body forced me to recognize that I needed some profound emotional healing. This discovery was a significant step in my journey of resilience.

At the time of my Guillain-Barré, I was avoiding an ongoing emotional trauma. Seven years earlier, I had joined the founder of Dovetail in its initial startup. The work was profoundly fulfilling and engaged my lifelong desire to help children. However, my relationship with the founder echoed the traumatic patterns I had with my father. Too much of my focus was on Hyper-Caretaking his emotional needs, and I gave him all the credit for my work, thinking my humility was a good thing. As unhealthy as our relationship was, I believed in our work for children and gave my all to help Dovetail succeed. My conflicting feelings signaled that I knew something was wrong in that relationship, but I didn't let myself see the whole truth until my body forced me to. When I finally started letting in my awareness about how I was stuck in extreme Hyper-Caretaking, I became anxious and woke up with panic attacks in the middle of the night. I had depended on this unreliable and toxic relationship for my livelihood. My immune crisis showed me I had to have stronger boundaries and extricate myself from my Hyper-Caretaking.

Self-Discovery

Impact on yourself

- Where and with whom does Hyper-Caretaking show up in your life?
- Are you trying to alleviate someone else's pain—i.e., fix it for them—rather than listening, empathizing, and accompanying them through it? Are you using emotional Hyper-Caretaking because you are uncomfortable seeing them sad or in pain?
- Are you avoiding your feelings or losing your boundaries through Hyper-Caretaking? How can you ask for help or set boundaries to meet your own needs?
- How do your Cultural Patterns influence your Hyper-Caretaking?

Impact on others

- Have you asked the other person if they want you to do something for them? Have you assumed their desires and needs?
- Do your actions honor the other person's capacity to do something for themselves? Do your actions impinge on others' needs for healthy risks and growth?
- Are you encouraging others to Contribute Intentionally and thus reap its benefits (a sense of purpose, confidence, and competence)?

Chapter 8

Avoiding

> "The best way to avoid criticism is to do nothing,
> say nothing, and be nothing."
>
> ~ Elbert Hubbard, American philosopher

Meri—I felt a buzz from the phone in my pocket. Then another one. I quickly glanced at my phone and noticed my sibling group was hot. When I saw the word "mom" as part of the chat, I put my phone down. It wasn't *something* I wanted to deal with now!

My mother had Alzheimer's disease for six years, and my siblings and I shared supervising her care. We organized in-home care as well as all the finances, legal issues, and daily needs that emerged with our elderly mom. Until my stepfather passed 18 months before, that also included trying to meet his needs. Incidents popped up regularly, from the true emergency—an ambulance call due to a severe fall—to the merely annoying, like more cockroaches in the kitchen. Often, the texts came through during the workday, so I was also juggling meetings, trainings, or other situations requiring focus. But even when those texts came in the evenings or weekends, I might Avoid them. I could be relaxing, cooking dinner, or trying to do just about anything else. I knew I regularly used Avoiding because I didn't want to deal with my mom's situation. While I treasured the occasional moments I spent with her when she was lucid and could follow the conversation, there was very little joy and a lot of heartache and headache in dealing with the logistical, financial, and health aspects of her care.

Avoiding has been one of my top Protective Patterns for as long as I can remember. Sometimes, it worked out well for me, like when I Avoided talking about my pain when some junior-high "friends" iced me out of a long-planned end-of-the-year party. When we returned to school in the fall, I could smooth over the rift and resume friendships with those girls as if nothing happened. Other times, Avoiding helped me feel safe in the moment but was not a successful longer-term strategy. When my dad left when I was 12, I never mentioned it to anyone outside my family. If anyone asked about him, I said he was away on a business trip. I had so much shame around it and no skills to deal with it. Only after many months, when my best friend's mom talked to my mom, did the whole ugly truth come out. That added the shame of hiding from the truth to the shame of my dad leaving. I felt miserable. Looking back, I could see that I used the Protective Pattern of Avoiding as an important resilience strategy. It helped me feel safe.

Many of us use Avoiding because we don't want to confront something difficult. Football fan Paxton was looking forward to living with his girlfriend Amelia for the first time. For Paxton and Amelia, evenings could be challenging the first few months they lived together. Amelia came home exhausted from work. Paxton would ask Amelia, "Do you want to go out? Or maybe play a game?" Amelia responded, "I am tired. I just want to watch a TV show again." While she was a morning person, Paxton was a night person, and he had the energy and desire to do more. He didn't want to complain, but he didn't like watching shows he had already seen. Though deferring to her was not working for him, his Protective Pattern of Avoiding emerged. He didn't want to have a hard conversation with Amelia when she was tired. Even as this pattern dragged on week after week, and he got increasingly frustrated, he still Avoided the conversation.

Renée, an executive coach, learned how destructive it could be to Avoid tough conversations, as this pattern contributed to her divorce. "I would pretend nothing was wrong. I tiptoed on eggshells," she explained. Like Meri and Paxton, Renée found she could Avoid only for so long. Eventually, her frustration exploded into the Protective Pattern of *Attacking*. Avoiding damaged her marriage. She added, "I didn't have the skills to have honest, productive conversations to problem-solve with my ex." She recognizes now that this period around her divorce was the hardest thing she'd ever been through. In the end, Avoiding caused more problems for her than it helped.

Like many people raised in the age of cell phones, Levi, a college student, regularly used Avoiding to navigate his social life. Since he didn't want to hurt anyone's feelings by saying no, he used Avoiding by not committing when he received invitations. He was invited to a friend's birthday party, but another friend had already mentioned a different get-together. It felt like one of the friends would get chosen and the other left out. He wanted to appease both friends, so he considered whether he could do both, but that didn't work in the end. His friend with the birthday felt snubbed when Levi didn't come.

As a family doctor in a short-staffed office, Rose found Avoiding was crucial to getting through her workdays. In addition to being a mom with young children, her day was so crammed with patients, meetings, and writing up charts that she had no time to deal with her own emotions. When her patients were in emotional turmoil, or she felt terrible about not getting enough work done, she shut down her feelings. As a faculty member overseeing residents, Rose also Avoided the conflict of dealing with a resident who was not getting work done. This resident kept calling in sick. She had so many absences that she ran out of time off and fell behind in charts. Rose noticed how her internal voice about Avoiding the conflict started as minor background noise, then became nagging and, eventually, a siren. When the resident dropped the ball on essential patient matters, she knew she could no longer Avoid the conflict.

What is Avoiding?

- We **ignore** something that needs attending.

- We **numb our emotions** by staying busy, overeating food, spending too much money, or spending too much time working, watching TV, or on social media. Many people avoid by misusing drugs or alcohol.

- We **avoid certain people** who make us uncomfortable.

- We pretend everything will be fine—with "**toxic positivity**"—when we know deep down something is wrong.

- We **emotionally withdraw** from someone or a situation.

- We **pretend something is not happening** or to be more or less than we really are.

How It Forms and Why We Use It

Shame is a common reason for developing Avoiding as a Protective Pattern. When something feels shameful, we will do almost anything to Avoid the situation and our feelings. Very few of us can admit all of our problems to ourselves, let alone to others. We have an overriding need to be "normal." For Meri, as a seventh grader, when her father left the family, it meant Avoiding the fact that she no longer had a "normal" family with a mother and father at home.

For Hampton, a city employee, shame was the big reason he Avoided dealing with his health. He knew he had a higher risk of developing diabetes because he was an African American male. Fifteen years earlier, he could tell he had symptoms, but he avoided going to the doctor. He didn't want to become one of those classic Americans who developed diabetes due to a poor diet. Avoiding the truth didn't change it, and, eventually, he was forced to deal with his diabetes. Even now, the mighty wound of shame prevents Hampton from caring for his health. He knows that he must check his blood sugar to prevent getting worse, but he is afraid of the results, so too often he Avoids taking the test. At one point, a pharmacist reprimanded him for failing to care for himself. He felt like responding, "You are not helping! I am already so down on myself. You can't think worse of me than I already feel." His shame and disappointment in himself makes him Avoid dealing with his feelings and his health issues.

Often, we use the Protective Pattern of Avoiding because we don't want to feel uncomfortable emotions, especially around conflict. Paxton had been in a previous relationship where he deferred to the woman, so he was more comfortable Avoiding than initiating a challenging conversation with Amelia about their evening time. Levi values his friends and doesn't want to hurt one friend by choosing another's social activity. Rose didn't want to deal with the resident who was underperforming.

Delphine, a recent college graduate and beach lover, was learning to navigate life as a young adult. Delphine used Avoiding when dealing with one of her roommates, Tara, who never seemed to help. Her other roommates even called Tara lazy behind her back because she did not do the dishes or take out the trash. Rather than having a potentially challenging conversation with Tara, they decided not to unload the dishwasher and see how long it would take Tara to do it. This little game helped them shift the blame onto Tara so they could avoid a hard conversation with her and their own responsibility for not creating agreements on chores.

Avoiding Armadillo stays inside her shell to avoid her problems.

How it Helps

- We may need to Avoid someone to **stay safe** from their hurtful behavior.

- It provides time or space for us and others **to calm down**.

- It gives us **time** to develop a way to resolve the issue.

- It can help us **prioritize** more essential issues.

If a situation is heated and we choose not to deal with it right away—either physically or emotionally—it gives us time to cool down. We can Avoid taking things personally and being hurt by what is happening.

Sometimes, we use the Protective Pattern of Avoiding because we are not ready to handle the situation or our feelings. Many people find Avoiding helpful in their work environments. Rose experienced that as a family doctor, and so did Elsie, who is also a busy medical provider moving from crisis to crisis without any time to attend to her feelings. One moment, Elsie may be counseling a woman who is being harmed by intimate partner violence, and the next moment, she is called to help a woman going into premature labor. Elsie can only handle these issues effectively by avoiding her own feelings.

Meri—Lack of confidence in our ability to handle problems is another reason we protect ourselves using Avoiding. There were so many problems that came up with my elderly mother's care. Many of them were new to me, and they took me down a rabbit hole when I tried to solve them. How do I get a handicapped car placard for someone whose driver's license has expired so I can use it when I drive her? Why did her Medicare fees suddenly increase? I didn't know who to ask for help, and I ran out of energy to deal with them. By Avoiding dealing with her issues immediately, I could wait until I had time and energy to be more creative about solving her problems.

How it Hurts

- We may be **ignoring our emotions** and our **needs**.

- We may **make the problem worse** by not addressing it.

- Avoiding **prevents us from creating lasting solutions**.

- If we numb ourselves with addictions, we are likely to hurt ourselves and our most important **relationships**.
- It can lead to **loneliness**.

Chuck—When my alcoholic father went into a rage, the whole family used the Protective Pattern of Avoiding to get through it. No one talked about it, and the hidden message was, "Shut down anything you feel. This isn't happening." Feeling and expressing emotions were not okay, so I learned to shut my emotions into a box. I learned not to cry, get angry, or even care. I learned to wear a mask that hid my emotional truth from others.

Influence of Cultural Patterns

Like many people, executive coach Renée learned growing up in her family to keep her inner judgments to herself and Avoid talking about her honest reactions and feelings. Now she can recognize, "By being silently judgy, I avoided being vulnerable." In remaining silent, she didn't risk how others might react to her thoughts and feelings. Avoiding protected her self-esteem in a family that did not appreciate her gifts. She kept the Avoiding pattern in her marriage. "If I keep it to myself, I can go along in my marriage without the risk of blowing it up and losing the relationship." Now she realizes she tried to keep herself safe from any potential conflict and thus lost the potential for real intimacy.

Chuck—In my family, we were taught to avoid emotions altogether. My mom's admonition to me was, "Don't feel." When I expressed a strong feeling like, "I hate school," my mom responded, "Oh, don't feel that way, honey." My mom would try to convince me everything was okay when it clearly was not. She learned to Avoid feelings from her family, where secrets were buried and never shared. Emotions were taboo for our whole clan—my aunts, uncles, and cousins. It's sad, really, to see how much we missed from lost authenticity and intimacy.

Food is the love language for city employee Hampton. He likes to share all the foods he grew up loving: ribs, mac and cheese, etc. On the other hand, these foods contributed to his diabetes and thus to his shame. It feels like his way of showing love is bad and harmful. Hampton is working on untangling his Cultural Pattern of eating unhealthy food so he doesn't pass it on to his son. His desire to help his son gives him the courage to stop Avoiding.

For so many, Avoiding crops up in "always being busy." If we are always busy, we don't have to reflect on how we feel, what we need, or how to have difficult conversations. Rose, the pediatrician, grew up in a family with this Cultural Pattern. They were "doers" who didn't have time for, and thus Avoided, feeling. "I have difficulty slowing down due to this family pattern of always being busy. At night, I tend to stay busy instead of sitting with my husband."

Many of us use the Protective Pattern of Avoiding for problems that seem too big to take on. If we are worried about food, shelter, and the other basics of survival, Avoiding going to the doctor can be helpful prioritization. Since doctors can give bad news, the Protective Pattern of Avoiding bad news can become a Cultural Pattern of avoiding the doctor. Family therapist Renata is grateful that her father, John, broke their Cultural Pattern and went to the doctor when something felt wrong. Though the doctor diagnosed him with prostate cancer, it was caught early and could be treated. Not only was Renata grateful for the positive outcome for her father's health, she also learned the value of exploring her Cultural Patterns to see which might be limiting her.

Centering Ourselves

Centering Skills

When we see that Avoiding is not helping us or others, we can make choices that serve us better. For Renée, the executive coach, it was helpful to learn that Avoiding is a Protective Pattern that sometimes supports her and is part of normal behavior. Knowing that everyone uses Protective Patterns and that they can be helpful, as well as limiting, reduced Renée's shame and helped her have more self-compassion about Avoiding. Now, she uses the

Centering Skill of Noticing Myself to pay attention when she might be Avoiding vulnerability. She uses her *Resilient Mindsets* and chooses vulnerability when she feels ready for connectedness.

College student Levi is learning how the *Resilient Mindsets of Courage* and *Choice* may be more helpful to him than the Protective Pattern of Avoiding to navigate social situations. Last summer, his old high-school friends wanted to visit a mutual friend in the Midwest. He Avoided talking with them because he was trying to arrange a trip to Europe with his college friends instead. The Europe trip would be more fun, but it was uncertain, and the Midwest trip seemed like a good backup. But he waited until the last minute to bail on his high-school friends, and they were hurt. After everyone returned, Levi realized he needed to clear the air with them and apologize. He learned his friends are more hurt by Avoiding than just being upfront with his dilemma. Six months later, when his friends planned a ski trip, Levi chose to commit to the trip.

Social worker Hilde felt a lot of judgment from her extended family, so she Avoided them for a long time. Even after she told them she didn't want to talk politics, they still brought it up every time she saw them at family events. This estrangement bothered her parents, and they wanted to mend it. Last Halloween, her dad asked to bring her children to her relatives' house for trick-or-treating. She thought about Avoiding the situation, which had been her pattern, but decided she could use the *Resilient Mindset of Curiosity* to see if limited interaction could work. She chose to go with her dad to the relatives' house. By staying for a short time and talking only about Halloween, she realized that minimal contact could be okay.

To reduce her reliance on the Protective Pattern of Avoiding, family doctor Rose uses the *Centering Skill of Nurturing Myself.* She is *Letting Go* of her to-do list to take better care of herself and get that extra hour of sleep. She dove into new creative pursuits to energize her optimism as solace for her hard days in the clinic. The *Centering Skill of Noticing Myself* motivated her to return to therapy to face herself openly and clearly.

City employee Hampton knows that for too long, he Avoided dealing with his health and shared his unhealthy eating habits with loved ones. As a dad, he knows this impacted his family significantly. His son also adopted cooking as a love language and likes cooking for other people. Seeing that ripple effect has motivated Hampton to make changes. Hampton uses the Resilient Mindset of Courage to Choose to face the issue rather than Avoid it. He wants to make better choices and model better behaviors. He tells himself, "You are a talented cook, Hampton. You can make other things that are way better for your family. You can make some very healthy options that are delicious."

Deeper Insights

Chuck—When we consider all that is going on in our lives—our emotions, health, family, community, and the world—it is no wonder we use Avoiding to cope. I would be overwhelmed thinking about politics, climate change, or world conflicts on a regular basis. I have to avoid these topics at times, intentionally, to stay centered and balanced. Like most people, I need to avoid and pretend on a daily basis to function well.

The mental trick of pretending helps us Avoid the complexity of reality. While pretending can help us stay focused so we can function, Avoiding reality can prevent us from being our best authentic selves. We might imagine we are more significant than we are or act like we are less than we are. Pretending can block our ability to know what we care about or neglect what is true for those around us. Ultimately, Avoiding can help us forget that we are responsible for our own attitude, behavior, and wellbeing!

I fall into all these traps. I sometimes Avoid my limitations by thinking I can do it all. When I began as managing director of Dovetail, I took on every challenge and thought I had to do it all—including making every organizational decision. Whoa! I was Avoiding so much—my limitations, my needs, my relationship responsibilities, and the skills and brilliance of my talented teammates. The cost of Avoiding due to my grandiosity was my own burnout, as well as not inviting and fostering our team's important contributions and talents.

At the same time, I pretended to be less capable than I was by Avoiding owning my abilities and skills. I gave the founder recognition rather than honoring my own significant role in our success. Even more importantly, by Avoiding my authentic leadership, I created silos of thinking (stay in your lanes). I was inattentive to what mattered most—the brilliance of the people working with me and their capacity to contribute collaboratively. Only by inviting everyone to one table could we excel. The cost of my pretense held us back organizationally and damaged my health. Pretending was at the core of my autoimmune disease, Guillain-Barré Syndrome.

The most significant cost of Avoiding came in pretending I was not personally accountable for my own attitude, behavior, and wellbeing. I wasn't taking vacations and was overworking, overeating, overdrinking, and acting as if my overblown dedication to work was a source of pride. By not nurturing my wellbeing, I avoided taking care of my health. This almost cost me my life when I had a major heart attack, followed by triple bypass surgery. Those events were a blessing in disguise, as they were the wake-up call I needed.

Self-Discovery

- Where does Avoiding show up in your life?

- In what contexts might you Avoid, and in which are you more likely to face what needs to be faced?

- Do you avoid deep feelings and emotions?

- What do you pretend is or is not true?

- How do your Cultural Patterns influence your Avoiding? What did you learn about avoiding from your family of origin, ancestors, and Cultural norms?

- What helps you most to not avoid things in yourself, others, or life?

Chapter 9

Defending

> "Self-defense is … a state of mind,
> and it begins with the belief that you are worth defending."
>
> ~ Rorion Gracie, Brazilian Jiu-Jitsu master

In rural California, Zelma's husband, Nash, couldn't find a tool he needed to fix a leaking pipe. He confronted Zelma, "Where did you leave my wrench?" Zelma responded, "I didn't take it. I don't know where it is. I had nothing to do with it." Rather than pacify Nash, Zelma's defensiveness seemed to frustrate him more. He kept insisting that Zelma had taken it. At Nash's angry tone, Zelma felt her Defending Protective Pattern coming out even more. The more he blamed her, the more she insisted, "No way! I didn't do it!"

When we are blamed by someone, especially someone close to us, the Protective Pattern of Defending can rear up quickly. Paxton, the football fan, worked for a small startup company, which meant he and his boss Ricardo had to wear many hats. Too often, they were in conflict about their roles. One day, Paxton asked Ricardo for a conversation to clarify their roles. Paxton laid out all his tasks and asked Ricardo to take on business development. Two weeks later, Ricardo called Paxton, saying, "You need to do business development. It should be your priority." Paxton felt like Ricardo was saying he was not pulling his weight and putting one more thing on his overfull plate. Paxton felt attacked, and his Defending Protective Pattern reared. Instead of listening, he pushed back.

Even when we are wrong, we might jump to the Protective Pattern of Defending. Spouses Jonah and Ariana were across the country from each other, catching up by phone on things they needed to do. Ariana, a retired tech executive, wanted their quarterly income taxes paid early because she has a strong Cultural Pattern: "I always pay my bills on time." So Ariana asked Jonah, "Can you make sure to pay the taxes a week early, on January 11, by certified mail?"

On January 11, Ariana texted Jonah, "Did you pay the taxes?" He immediately called her and said that he had not paid the taxes, explaining that she said she would do it. Jonah's calm comment just escalated Ariana into the Protective Pattern of Defending. She said, "I didn't say I would do it! You are supposed to do it!" Ariana knew she was right and Jonah was wrong. It was his fault, not hers, that the taxes had not been paid!

An hour later, Jonah forwarded Ariana a copy of a text she had sent the day before. The text said, "Don't worry about paying the taxes. I will pay them because I have the tax voucher here." With this stark evidence, Ariana realized she was totally wrong and called Jonah to apologize. Her Protective Pattern of Defending had gotten the better of her. She was so focused on being right she had not been Curious about his perspective.

Sometimes, the Protective Pattern of Defending can have big consequences. When Jon, an entrepreneur, was younger, if someone at work had a contrary opinion, he would say no, that's not how it is and defend his position like a rock. Since he was right, he felt no need to be curious about other perspectives. At one early start-up, Jon was an integral team member, and the company depended on him to do an enormous amount of work. He thought he was indispensable. When a new senior manager who didn't have the same level of experience was hired, Jon dug in his heels on several issues. His new boss finally said, "It's clear we don't see eye to eye—and I'm not leaving." Jon's Protective Pattern of Defending caused him to lose his job and face a major career setback. It was a crushing blow.

Chuck—My Protective Pattern of Defending emerges when I feel bad about myself. I have a typical volley of Defend—Attack—Defend with my wife, Sandy. One day last week, the conversation started calmly. She tried to create some healthy agreements about who does what around our house and yard. I immediately felt bad about myself and dug into Defending. I named everything I do around the house and how hard I work at helping out. My defensiveness triggered her Protective Pattern of *Attacking*. As Protective Patterns do, we escalated from there. The more I felt attacked, the more I wanted to defend myself. As usual, when I am Defensive with Sandy, it leaves me feeling awful. I don't want to be that kind of person, especially with someone I love.

What is Defending?

- We respond as if we are being judged or criticized.
- It is a counter-response to prove we are right.
- We dig in our heels rather than listening to the other person.
- We feel like we need to protect ourselves.

How it Forms and why we use it

Like other Protective Patterns, Defending emerges when we feel vulnerable. The Protective Pattern of Defending is more likely to form if we grew up in situations where we felt attacked. When we feel attacked, it is normal to want to Defend ourselves, and protecting ourselves can be important.

We might use Defending if we think our character or behavior is being attacked. Paxton felt his boss Ricardo was complaining about his work ethic when Paxton felt he was already doing the best he could and that Ricardo didn't see the work stress he was already carrying.

Chuck also felt like his wife was demeaning him as a good partner. His contribution is a matter of pride to Chuck so he felt vulnerable when his wife brought it up.

We are more likely to use Defending if we feel insecure or anxious about a situation, especially if it is important to us. Ariana was afraid that something important to her—paying her bills on time—would not be honored, and she felt vulnerable because she thought she had to rely on Jonah to do it. Those feelings were so strong that her Protective Pattern of Defending emerged before she remembered that she had already promised to pay the bill herself.

At Jon's first start-up, he felt he needed to prove himself. He was so afraid of failure that he thought he had to know everything. He had a Cultural Pattern against asking questions. He didn't engage his Curiosity Mindset about what his new boss might be thinking because he felt that would show weakness and vulnerability. Instead, he learned the difficult lesson that sometimes, Defending actually weakens him. In this case, he was fired.

> **Defending Dog**
> justifies all his actions because he knows he is right.

How it Helps

- Defending can feel like we are **standing up for ourselves**.

- It can help us **explain our point of view**.

- It can create a **sense of power**.

- It may help **prove that we have been right**.

As a school principal, Doris is often attacked by parents who feel the school is not doing right by their kids. Usually, Doris tries to listen and acknowledge the parents' fears while explaining how she and the educators involved are trying to help their children. With one set of parents, however, Doris felt like they were attacking her to prove their worth to each other and had forgotten about the child involved. She crafted an email Defending all the actions her school team had taken and said the parents were welcome to enroll in another school if they preferred. Defending and setting boundaries may be our best option when the attacking person is not interested in an authentic conversation.

How it Hurts

- It can **make a conflict worse**.

- When we interrupt others, we **shut down our ability to listen** to them.

- We may **harm our relationships** by holding being right over being in a relationship.

When Paxton looked back at his conversation with his boss, Ricardo, he saw that Ricardo was just trying to present the company's needs so that Paxton could prioritize his work. By defending his position instead, Paxton lost an opportunity to have a productive conversation with his boss.

Chuck—When I get defensive with Sandy, I harm our relationship. When I jump immediately to prove I'm right, I completely miss the opportunity to let her know that I hear her and care about her needs. My Defending pattern has caused a lot of discord in my marriage.

Influence of Cultural Patterns

Growing up in her family in rural California, Zelma learned she might be attacked anytime. To this day, she feels vulnerable and retreats inside when someone asks her about something. If she doesn't know the answer, she feels insecure. Since her parents criticized her for asking questions, she has to work on using the *Resilient Mindset of Curiosity* when stressed. Defending is deeply ingrained.

Jon, the entrepreneur, was raised to believe that Defending his positions showed he was strong. His mom cultivated his strong sense of ego by telling him, "You're smart, and you need to be successful because you have so much privilege." His grandfather also drummed in the message that he needed to be successful. Every holiday, his grandfather told his grandkids they needed to outshine the generation before them. This expectation of success gave him a tremendous work ethic and a big fear of failure. He compensated for his anxiety by feeling he needed to do everything right and using the Protective Patterns of Defending and Hypervigilance. These Protective Patterns damaged his relationships and created a workaholism that destroyed his marriage. He said, "As I became less connected to my wife, I tended to fill that void with more work. Not surprisingly, this started an accelerating downward spiral."

Music lover Adam is a young twenty-something who feels his Protective Pattern of Defending comes out in his relationship with his sister, Piper. A few months ago, he and his sister got into it while cooking dinner and playing music in the kitchen. As Adam sang along, Piper corrected him on a lyric. Adam didn't want her to correct him, and he definitely didn't want her to be right. As they argued, Adam realized he might be wrong but didn't want to admit it. He left the room when she started looking it up on her phone, hoping the subject would change. When Adam got back, he refused to agree that she was right. He felt humiliated. Adam realized that his vulnerability relates to his desire to impress his parents by showing them how smart and mature he is. This vulnerability pushes him to use the Protective Pattern of Defending even in ridiculous situations where he knows he is wrong.

Meri—My Protective Pattern of Defending comes out most with my mother-in-law. She will ask a simple question, "Do you know where the book is?" or "Who changed the laundry?" and I jump right into, "Not me! I didn't do it!" My mother-in-law is asking a simple question, but it triggers the little girl in me. Growing up, if someone did something "wrong" (like eating dessert meant for the family dinner), my mother would line us up and accuse us. She hated lying and was trying to get someone to confess to the deed. As a committed rule follower, it usually wasn't me who did the deed, and I hated being lumped in with those (one of my siblings) who did. I still have that little girl inside who wants to please others, and Defending pops right out if there is any fear of me being labeled "one of the bad kids." So if my husband does something I fear is a transgression in his mother's eyes, I move into Defending. I don't want to be linked to his "bad" deeds.

Centering Ourselves

When we find that Defending is not helping us or others, we can make choices that serve us better. Zelma has learned to use the *Centering Skill of Noticing Myself* when she starts to spiral, which helps her relax. Nash's frustrated tone might still trigger her, but she can use *the Centering Skill of Breathing Mindfully* to calm down. Eventually, Zelma uses the *Connecting Skill of Heartfelt Listening* to hear what is underneath Nash's frustration. She recognized that Nash was angry because he needed help quickly because the kitchen was flooding. She used the *Centering Skill of Letting Go* of her defensiveness to say, "I acknowledge your pain, and I'll help you look for the tool." She knew she didn't have to agree with his angry statements, but she could at least acknowledge his feelings. Letting him know he was being heard and listened to shortened the time she used her Protective Pattern of Defending.

Chuck—With Sandy, my defensiveness is tied to our familial roles and how much we both care. Fortunately, we have been working on this for a long time, so even though I still get caught in Defending, I can use the *Centering Skill of Noticing Myself* almost immediately. My skills in Relational Resilience can stop the volley, create a connection with her, and sometimes end in laughter. When we use the *Connecting Skill of Speaking Authentically* about what we each need and want, we can be Centered in our Relational Resilience.

Deeper Insights

Chuck—I have some of my earliest memories from age three when I lived in the Philippines. I remember swimming to cool off from the hot tropical sun. I was so happy running to the end of the diving board and jumping in, even though all I could do was dog paddle. Unfortunately, one of my most traumatic memories also occurred there. My mom and older sister contracted polio, and my mom's treatment included several months in an iron lung. My dad described how being in a foreign country with his wife and daughter both in iron lungs was the most traumatic experience of his life. I can't imagine how hard that must have been!

My experience left me feeling distraught and alone. My mom was my deepest anchor and the one person from whom I felt unconditional love. Her prolonged absence from my life, along with my sister, left me with my father, who was frightened and stressed. This abandonment had a huge impact on my early development. I learned to cope by developing my Defending Protective Pattern. I defend myself to prove that I'm okay. It only takes a milli-second for my Protective Pattern to be activated as a pushback against feeling shame, low self-esteem, or lack of confidence in how I handle something. In elementary school, I became the class clown to compensate for my failures in school. Over time, that eventually turned into my knee-jerk reaction of Defending that I am right about something when challenged.

When I notice I am using my Protective Pattern, I now have great self-compassion, knowing my early trauma. Using my *Resilient Mindsets* makes the most difference. With *Curiosity* I can catch my wave of Defending as it emerges and become more conscious of what is happening. With *Choice,* I can step back, sometimes immediately, and say, "Oh, wow, I just got caught in my Defending. I'm so sorry." And with *Courage*—listening to and following my heart—I gain the wisdom to make things right.

Self-Discovery

- Where and with whom does Defending show up in your life?

- In what contexts might you be Defending yourself?

- What would happen if you used Curiosity when you felt yourself reacting?

- What might help you most to move beyond Defending?

- How do your Cultural Patterns influence your Defending Protective Pattern?

Chapter 10

Attacking

> "Fear nothing; attack everything."
> ~ Eric Berry, NFL Player of the Year (2015)

Meri—I asked my husband to wash the front door in preparation for painting it. I gave him a bucket of soapy water and a scrub brush. Then he grabbed some paper towels and some rags. "What do you need those for?" I asked.

He responded, "I need to keep the water from dripping down the door because it is leaving a trail." "Steve," I raised my voice. "When the water leaves a trail, you need more water, not less! The dirt trail is a sign the door is still dirty!" Steve was somewhat surprised that I yelled as he cleaned the door, but it was an old pattern. I asked him to do a job, and he started to do it, and then I got mad at him when I felt him going "off track."

Esther, an artist who works at home, had the mixed blessing of spending much more time with her husband Rowan, when his office closed during the pandemic. Even though she loved him dearly, she felt him encroaching upon her territory. Esther was used to having the whole house to herself during the day, and now he worked out of a bedroom.

Rowan came out at random times for a snack. "One day, he rearranged my tea drawer without asking me. I blew up and verbally attacked him." The kitchen had been "her domain," and she felt he had crossed a boundary. "This simple incident triggered all my anger over the big change in my life. I was so upset, and it came pouring out. I could feel my heart pounding and my blood pressure rising." Esther knew her attack was overblown and had hurt Rowan's feelings. He thought he was being thoughtful and doing her a favor by organizing the tea. After calming down and reflecting on what had happened, she felt ashamed.

Many of us feel shame after we attack someone we care about. When Levi was a junior in high school, his friend Quinn sided with someone else against Levi in an argument. Levi felt hurt by Quinn's actions. Everything that Quinn did started to bug Levi. Finally, at lunch a week later, Levi's emotions came to a head, and he started attacking Quinn. She said something, and Levi started berating her. He used some confidences she had shared with him against her—that she felt lonely and her friends didn't like her. Levi told her she was right, and they all had reasons not to like her. At the time, launching his attack felt so good that he didn't worry about the consequences. Later, Levi felt embarrassed and regretted lashing out. He hated that he had tried to make himself feel good by making Quinn feel bad.

When retired tech executive Ariana feels vulnerable, her Protective Pattern of Attacking can emerge. Ariana and Jonah were visiting Ariana's mother in Massachusetts when Jonah's 4-year-old truck began making weird noises. Ariana was particularly attuned to potential car problems because after they had driven across the country with their other car, they had a $3,000 repair bill. The truck's weird sound happened going uphill, so it was potentially a transmission issue, which would mean another big bill. She asked Jonah, "Can you make the appointment with the mechanic when we get to Mom's house?" He agreed it was a good idea.

The next day, she heard the noise again while returning from an errand. She walked into the house and said, "Did you make the appointment with the mechanic?" As soon as he said no, she angrily launched into him. "You said you were going to make an appointment! You forgot to do it!" She ramped it up with, "This is another example of you not following through on a timely basis. You don't do stuff on time!" Feeling the anger continue to build, she walked away.

School principal Gideon uses Attacking when he thinks he needs to protect others. A few months ago, Gideon entered a room where his two daughters and wife sat. His 9-year-old, Josie, was crying. No one was saying anything. When Gideon saw his daughter crying, "The Attacker" in him looked for something or someone to fight. He felt this visceral rush in his central nervous system. All sorts of thoughts rushed through him: "Do I need to take her to the hospital?", "Who is responsible?" and "She wouldn't be crying if it wasn't serious." When he asked, "What happened?" his wife calmly responded, "It's fine." This was unacceptable to him, so he made a face and gestured with his hands toward Josie with a shoulder shrug and WTF body language. His wife said, "Just stop!" That's when he aimed "the attack" at his wife through a barrage of questions. He punctuated his attack with, "When my daughter is crying . . . I have to be involved!"

Ramona, a juvenile justice worker, also uses Attacking to protect her family. Her 21-year-old daughter Sherelle and Sherelle's one-year-old son live with Ramona. Sherelle is very protective of her son and works hard to be the best mother she can be. Still, Ramona has a lot more years of experience and wants to share that with Sherelle. It doesn't always end well. A few months ago, when Ramona tried to advise, Sherelle felt attacked as a parent and got very upset. Their conversation escalated, and Ramona's Hyper-Caretaking morphed into an attack on Sherelle.

What is Attacking?

- We **blame, criticize, or judge** others.

- We use a **harsh voice** or yell. We may sound mean, look mean, or act mean.

- We **use our bodies to show power** over the other person.

- We use Attacking against ourselves, **blaming** and **criticizing ourselves**.

How it Forms and why we use it

Like all Protective Patterns, Attacking emerges from the amygdala, the emotional part of our brain designed to keep us safe. We protect ourselves by acting aggressively. For many of us, "the best defense is a good offense," so we attack before we can be attacked. We try to be the strongest or smartest and push threats away before they have a chance to harm us.

Through attacking, we can put the focus on others and what they did wrong, rather than reflect on our part. It also can make us feel more powerful. Rather than listening to the cues that anger gives us—what value has been violated?—we send anger's energy outward toward another.

Meri—My *Attacking* often emerges when I am trying to get something done, and my progress is interrupted. Unfortunately for my husband, he is usually the interrupter. He might even be trying to help, like when he washed the door, but I attacked him for "doing it wrong." This goes south fast because he feels I shouldn't attack him if he uses an approach different from mine, while I feel like he should welcome my guidance.

We often attack if others don't respect our authority, feelings, or property. Esther's *Protective Pattern of Attacking* emerged when she no longer controlled her kitchen domain. Levi, the college student, felt he had lost an ally when Quinn sided with someone else, triggering his feelings of vulnerability. For retired tech executive Ariana, her Hypervigilance fed into her *Attacking*. She was anxious about the truck failing and stranding her on a dark, wintry road. The idea of a looming bill made it worse. She anticipated a potential problem and catastrophized about it. Gideon and Ramona expressed their Hyper-Caretaking by Attacking anyone who threatened their family—even when it was other family members.

Attacking Alligator lashes out when things get tough.

How it Helps

- Attacking can give us a **sense of power** when we feel wronged.
- It can **make us feel stronger** if we put someone else down.
- We may need to **protect ourselves** from emotional or physical harm.

How it Hurts

- When we Attack, others may **Attack us back**.
- We **hurt other people** by Attacking them.
- Attacking **harms our relationships**.

Marcia, an expert in organizational effectiveness, felt powerless and weighed down by responsibilities she never expected. Her husband, Isaac, has been a brilliant therapist and the love of her life. She cherishes him, and she knows he has dramatically improved the quality of her life over many years. However, Isaac has had Parkinson's now for a while. As his capacity to care for himself has decreased, Marcia has had to care for him in ways she never anticipated. "I have so much grief about who I've lost as a friend and how much I have to do that I never expected. My frustrations tip me into Attacking him all too easily. Just last week, I was helping him shower, and the water started getting cold, so he told me it was too cold. It felt like he was criticizing me. I yelled at him that I don't deserve this." Marcia admits, "Attacking him is the last thing I want to be doing. It gives me so much shame."

Influence of Cultural Patterns

Growing up, Marcia's mother had unexpected bursts of anger. Marcia fought back with her own Attacking. "I was the eldest and got the brunt of her meanness. I felt a deep sadness because I knew I didn't deserve it. I blew up to prove that I'm a good child, not a bad child. When I don't deserve someone's meanness, it triggers my Attacking." When something hits her wrong, she just blows up and starts yelling.

After Esther's mother died when Esther was 18, she used her Protective Pattern of Attacking more frequently. Both she and her father felt lost without her mother. He dealt with the loss by dating immediately and marrying a much younger woman within a year and a half. Esther's new stepmother had two sons, 11 and 13, and the older one was confined to a wheelchair by muscular dystrophy. When this stepfamily moved in, Esther's dad rearranged everything to accommodate their needs. Esther felt she no longer mattered and had no place in her home. To this day, she is very protective of "her space" and either gets anxious or attacks when her boundaries are crossed.

Renée, the executive coach, realizes now that she learned her Attacking Protective Pattern in her family. Though she used the Protective Pattern of Attacking a lot, most of her Attacking was silent because she held it inside. Since she kept it hidden, others didn't react to her Attacking. However, Renée could only keep her Attacking inside for so long after she married. She started verbally blowing up. Her sudden Attacking made honest communication difficult, and it hurt her marriage.

Luz, a Mexican immigrant, often gets accused of Attacking when she uses a loud voice. She feels like her passion is misunderstood as Attacking because she is not angry. Her family and community have a Cultural Pattern of using loud voices and lots of passion to express themselves, which can feel like Attacking to others. She knows others from different communities can feel intimidated by that passion.

Centering Ourselves

When we find that Attacking is not helping us or others, we can make choices to Center ourselves that serve us better. Of course, like all Protective Patterns, it can be challenging to modify ingrained behavior even if we notice we are activated. Practice helps, as does being open to the feedback of others—though most of us have trouble listening when other people tell us we are off-center.

For Gideon, the school principal, his daughter was crying from disappointment about not getting her way when his wife held a healthy boundary. Like most of us, especially when we are Attacking, it was hard for him to admit he escalated the problem. He was using Attacking to protect himself from negative self-judgment, that he wasn't a good father if his daughter was crying. Because he was scared and worried, along with Attacking, he was Hyper-Caretaking—taking on his daughter's challenges as his own rather than respecting her capacity to handle them herself. His questions could have been answered if he had used the *Resilient Mindset of Curiosity*. Most importantly, he could have used the *Centering Skill of Breathing Mindfully* to calm himself before pressing the issue. Eventually, after all his huffing and puffing, he used the *Connecting Skill of Speaking Authentically* with his wife and daughters about what he could have done differently.

For Ramona, the juvenile justice worker, she admits that she didn't handle the situation with her daughter well. She could not Center herself until after their explosion. After she removed herself from the situation, she took a moment to use the *Centering Skill of Breathing Mindfully*. Then she apologized to Sherelle for not using her *Centering Skills* before exploding. She moved to the *Centering Skill of Finding Gratitude*, feeling so grateful that her daughter, Sherelle, does have her grandson's best interests at heart and is trying her best. Ramona is also grateful to still have her daughter with her. "Last year, Sherelle was in a bad place after she had lost a friend." Ramona knows that no matter the disagreement, she can have a profound moment of gratitude for her daughter.

When someone else is Attacking us, it is helpful to remain Centered. Jonah was able to keep his cool while Ariana attacked him. When she returned to finish the conversation, he could explain that he had not yet made the appointment because he had thought about their plans. They both needed a vehicle for the next few days, and if the truck was in the shop, one of them would be stranded. Ariana immediately recognized the wisdom of his perspective, and she apologized for attacking him. She also recognized that she could have avoided escalating the situation if she had used the *Resilient Mindset of Curiosity* and asked why he had not made the appointment.

Deeper Insights

Meri—I grew up in a yelling household. My parents were stressed trying to raise four children on one income with a tight budget. They married young and didn't strengthen many of their Resilience Skills until they were older. I have two older brothers, and I learned to attack to defend myself from them. I couldn't compete with them physically, but I could use logic, a quick mind, and a loud voice to communicate my point.

This Protective Pattern served me well in school, as most of my classes were male-dominated. Well-timed attacks demonstrated that I could keep up with them and even be a leader. I also used Attacking in my personal relationships. Having grown up in a world where too often women were subservient, I thought it was the only way I could maintain my boundaries.

About six months into my relationship with my now-husband, I suddenly realized I could lessen my Attacking. Steve would respect my boundaries and be there for me, even if I didn't use Attacking. Because I felt less vulnerable, my relationship with him allowed me to notice my Protective Pattern and use it a lot less.

Having been together almost 40 years has changed both of us for the better, though I still do Attack occasionally, mainly him. His questions about how to use simple technology launch my attacks. I use a harsh voice to tell him everything he should do and ask why he hasn't done that. My underlying issue is difficulty identifying healthy boundaries for myself. On the one hand, I don't want to leave him stranded when he needs tech help to do his job. On the other hand, I believe if he works at it, he can learn how to solve his own problems. Since I haven't yet learned how to resolve this conflict, my inner turmoil comes out in my raised voice.

It also crops up occasionally in other situations. A few years ago, a colleague and I met with a partner organization. One of the doctors was making a case for something I greatly disagreed with. Over a few minutes, our conversation heated up, and I moved into Attacking. It felt like a familiar role, and I made my case very well. I felt powerful at the end. After the conversation was over and we were walking back to the car, my colleague asked, "What happened there?" Only then did I realize I may have crossed the line. I had Attacked without realizing it.

Sometimes, while using the Protective Pattern of Attacking, I use the *Centering Skill of Noticing Myself* to assess whether it is helpful—usually, it is not! Then, I use the *Resilient Mindset of Curiosity* to ask myself, "What is really bothering me about this situation?" When I am Centered, I recognize my part in the problem: I feel anxious about something not going how I think it should.

Self-Discovery

- Where and with whom does Attacking show up in your life?
- In what contexts might you Attack, and in which can you use Curiosity?
- How do your Cultural Patterns influence your Attacking?

Chapter 11

Our Evolving Protective Patterns

"One can choose to go back toward safety or forward toward growth. Growth must be chosen again and again; fear must be overcome again and again."

~ Abraham H. Maslow, pioneering American psychologist

As human beings, we naturally grow and change over time. Thus, our use of Protective Patterns also changes over time. Some of those changes are forced upon us because we encounter new situations or are going through transitions. When we become parents, move, or get a new job, our Protective Patterns can be heightened. New stressors may impact us, or they may occur more frequently.

When she became a parent, Laila experienced a new Protective Pattern. Laila's baby was fussy. She was a very attentive mother, but all the feeding, changing, and holding weren't comforting him. As a new mom, she thought she was responsible for his emotions. Laila had to learn that after she cared for all his needs, her complete focus on trying to stop his crying could cross the line into Hyper-Caretaking. She realized that some of his fussy crying was signaling that he was uncomfortable and he had to work it out himself. Only then was she able to recognize that her Hyper-Caretaking wasn't helpful to either of them.

Meri—When my children were young and sick often, I was Hypervigilant about trying to keep them healthy. As they grew and became healthier, and especially after they became independent and moved out, that Protective Pattern moved into "hibernating." Recently, my husband got very sick, and suddenly it emerged again.

Francesca's job was going along well until she got a new boss. This boss was a micromanager, so Francesca suddenly felt all her work was under a microscope. Francesca started using *Distrusting* in a way that she hadn't before. She distrusted that her boss would treat her fairly and give helpful feedback, and she distrusted that she could do work the boss would accept. This *Distrusting* helped Francesca keep her boss at arm's length but made her work situation very stressful.

When we encounter new situations that require different Protective Patterns, we can recognize that all Protective Patterns come from the same place: we feel vulnerable or unsafe. It is helpful to remember that while our Protective Patterns can be beneficial, if they are not serving us, we can look for other choices.

Reasons They Persist

Since Protective Patterns can be harmful, especially to our most important relationships, why is reducing reliance on them so difficult? First, we need to recognize our nervous system is wired to protect us. When we face threats—real or perceived—our amygdala (the emotional part of our brain designed to keep us safe) reacts. These reactions are often described as "fight, flight, or freeze." Our Protective Patterns are a more specific way of describing these reactions. (See Figure 7.) Since they are hardwired into us for our protection, we will always have them, though we can be more intentional about when and how we use them.

Responses to Stress

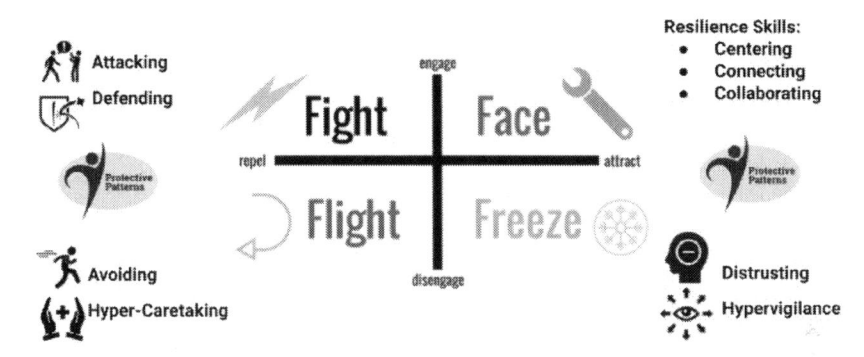

Attacking
Defending
Protective Patterns
Avoiding
Hyper-Caretaking

engage
Fight | **Face**
repel ──────── attract
Flight | **Freeze**
disengage

Resilience Skills:
- Centering
- Connecting
- Collaborating

Protective Patterns
Distrusting
Hypervigilance

Modified from Grace LaConte Consulting (2017)

Figure 7

Sometimes, we are too discouraged and feel we **can't** change. Other times, we think that our Protective Patterns are helping us and that we **don't need** to change. They can also become so familiar that they feel like a part of us—our personality and identity—that we **don't want** to change.

We feel discouraged.

When we are in a loop of using a Protective Pattern, it is hard to see there is a different way to approach situations.

Meri—When Steve was really sick, my Hypervigilance was on such high alert that I was exhausted. It was hard to see a way out. Even though I wanted to return to my usual resilient self, I felt my Hypervigilance was necessary. My fatigue prevented me from seeing any other options.

We feel protected.

Our Protective Patterns can help us feel safer and less vulnerable.

Chuck—I tend to use Avoiding when I haven't finished something I said I would do and have a nagging feeling of being incompetent.

Instead of using the *Centering Skill of Noticing Myself* about how bad I feel not getting it done, I often fill in the gap by doing something else I can feel good about. Since I love splitting wood and being outside in nature, I split some wood for our wood stove when I want to Avoid writing a report for work. By Avoiding writing the report, I used the *Centering Skill of Nurturing Myself* to gain more energy to write a better report later.

We feel comfortable.

Our Protective Patterns can be so ingrained in us that they are like a comfortable blanket that keeps us in familiar territory.

Chuck—Too often, I use the Protective Pattern of Defending when my wife tells me something I don't want to hear. Sometimes, I don't want to admit the truth of what she's telling me. Defending myself is just automatic. It's too uncomfortable to face my limitations. It is easier for me to move directly to resistance and resentment rather than take in what she says or see that she shares from a place of care, love, and concern.

We identify with them.

Our Protective Patterns can become part of our personality.

When school principal Gideon moves into Attacking mode, it is as if the energy in his body is calling for an outlet or grounding rod for lightning to dissipate. Even his wife and children have noted that they can *feel* it. Since he played rugby as a young man, "Rugby Gideon" is a term they all use to identify when Gideon feels out of sorts.

Intentional Practice

We can transform when and how we use our Protective Patterns over time. The crucial first step is to focus our attention on our behavior and assess whether it is serving us.

Chuck—I initially thought that Defending was my primary Protective Pattern. I saw myself regularly engaging in Defending with my wife, Sandy. As I've learned to use the *Centering Skill of Noticing Myself* and understand my Protective Patterns better, I use Defending a lot less because I now catch myself almost immediately. That's not who I want to be.

For a long time, I thought I only used Hypervigilance as a child. I stayed on high alert around my dad to ensure I didn't do anything wrong to trigger his emotional abuse. Over time, I've discovered how my Hypervigilance about doing things right is the source of my tendency for perfectionism at work.

In my forties and fifties, I worked as the Director of Counseling and Human Development at a prestigious independent school. During that time, I also worked a second job as an adjunct faculty member, which required staying up late many nights mentoring graduate students worldwide. Somehow, my need to DO enough still wasn't fulfilled, so simultaneously, I remodeled our 1912 craftsman-style bungalow.

This pattern of working long hours seemed normal to me, but it was to my great detriment. I missed quality time with my wife and kids, and I often coped by eating or drinking too much. I was blind to how workaholism and perfectionism were impacting my life. At the time, I was part of a network of school counselors who met monthly. Most of us complained a lot about being overworked. I remember being perplexed by an older, experienced counselor with plenty of time for vacations and creative activities like canoeing and artwork. Seeing his freedom was intriguing and challenging for me. I didn't realize I could use the *Resilient Mindset of Choice* to make decisions to care for myself.

Now, I know I had adopted the Protective Pattern of Hypervigilance to cope with my early childhood trauma, and as I grew, it morphed into a feeling that I had to work all the time and be perfect to feel okay about myself. As I learned to recognize these patterns and connect the dots between my Cultural and Protective Patterns, I took much better care of myself. I use Hypervigilance less, and I have a much better work-life balance. I take vacations and finish projects when they are "good enough" rather than compulsively working toward perfection.

"Rugby Gideon" has been using Attacking as a Protective Pattern for as long as he can remember. When he felt emotionally unsafe, it would be triggered automatically, and off he would go. Gideon's Attacking is part of his Cultural Pattern about how "a man" is supposed to be in the world—passed down through family and community norms. Because it was so much a part of his identity as a teen and young man, he has ambivalent feelings about changing it. When he was younger, he was often rewarded for his brash, "alpha male" aggressive nature, like when a newspaper journalist wrote about him for winning a wrestling tournament, or a coach said he was "relentless," or when he won a college national championship. Now, as an older man, it is a challenge for him to shift his identity and keep the honorable, good elements of being a teammate/leader/"brave" friend while reducing the arrogance/ego-driven jerky behavior that the Protective Pattern of Attacking can bring with it. Because he is proud and fond of those times and part of him doesn't want to let them go, intentionally trying to use less Attacking feels like trying to jump while standing on his own hands. Even with these conflicting feelings, becoming more conscious of his Attacking and Hyper-Caretaking has reduced his use of these Protective Patterns. Knowing his behavior came from Cultural Patterns makes it easier to be gentle in his judgments of himself and have self-compassion.

Meri—In the past, I also used Attacking much more frequently, raising my voice when I was frustrated with something. More often now, I notice it creeping in, and I can stop it when it harms more than helps.

Reading about, studying, and practicing the *Centering Skill of Noticing Myself* when our Protective Patterns emerge is in itself a healing process. As psychiatrist Dan Seigel says, "When we name it, we can tame it." We encourage you to talk about your Protective Patterns with those close to you. When we are vulnerable about the truth of who we are, we can have profound, nurturing, and healing conversations with others.

Our Protective Patterns can "get in our way" and show us we need greater resilience. Cultural Patterns can also hinder our access to resilience. Learning to notice when, and how, our Cultural Patterns affect our perspective is critical to strengthening our resilience.

In the following chapters, we will explore the benefits of examining our Cultural Patterns and how essential this work is to creating the world we want.

Chapter 12

What are Cultural Patterns?

> "Until you make the unconscious conscious,
> it will rule your life, and you will call it fate."
>
> ~ C.G. Jung

Hank, a music teacher, grew up in a small town in the rural South. "It was the most classist, sexist, bigoted, and prejudiced place I have ever experienced. Two days out of college, I left and never went back."

While Hank thought he rejected those values from his hometown, he hadn't realized how the values impacted the way he saw himself and the world. For many years, his college girlfriend Liz tried to wake him up to these ingrained Cultural Patterns—the perspectives Hank unconsciously absorbed from his community. "I didn't think I was classist or prejudiced. However, I behaved in ways that gave the message that '*you are less, don't forget it, and I have a million ways to prove it to you.*' I was stuck in thinking I was superior to others. Liz couldn't handle me acting like that, so she ended our romantic relationship."

They remained friends, and many years later, Hank was on a phone call with her and started to give her advice. She interrupted Hank and said, "That, right there, is why I couldn't be with you." This time, Hank recognized his behavior. "All of a sudden, I became 'the advice giver.' I moved into my privileged place. Smart, white, male, and spiritually elevated. What an asshole I had been, not even knowing I was doing it."

Hank is now more able to notice these patterns in himself. "At age 68, I can feel in my body the part of me that resists equality. I know it is my issue—a superiority thing. It keeps me feeling powerful. I know I don't have to act on these patterns because I've gained some ground, but it's so frustrating that they are still there."

Hank is not the only one who struggles with his Cultural Patterns. For all of us, they can lead us down pathways that don't serve us. Meri struggles against her Cultural Patterns in another way.

Meri—Every year, as December approached, I vowed to make THIS holiday season better. I wanted more joy but had difficulty finding it. For some reason, for most of the last 35 years, I felt compelled to "Do Everything Christmas." Oh, my!!!

- ✓ Create 150 Christmas cards with personal notes
- ✓ Cut, set up, and decorate a fresh tree and decorate the house, inside and out
- ✓ Make crafty, homemade ornaments with my kids for family and friends
- ✓ Make family photo calendars for both sides of the extended family
- ✓ Bake and deliver dozens of cookie plates with 7-10 varieties of cookies
- ✓ Buy and wrap presents for needy families
- ✓ Attend church services, children's concerts, holiday parades, etc.

- ✓ Buy and wrap presents for family and friends
- ✓ Make delicious holiday meals
- ✓ Travel to see relatives on Christmas

All while carrying on with life—working, helping kids get to their activities, and all the everyday life chores. I am exhausted just remembering it! What was I thinking? Or, more precisely, *why was I NOT thinking, "This is so ridiculous?"*

When we wonder why we act in ways that hurt us, understanding the concept of Cultural Patterns is helpful. It gave me a better awareness of my unconscious behavior. Cultural Patterns are ingrained messages about the "right thing to do"—what we should or should not do—passed down through generations of family, community, the media, etc. When we understand how they help or harm us, we can work toward changing what doesn't serve us. Clearly, my vision of "Christmas," created by my Cultural Patterns, was on overdrive. It stressed me out and wore me down.

I let go of some of my expectations when I realized my overload made me and my family unhappy. The *Resilient Mindsets of Curiosity, Choice,* and *Courage* helped me intentionally choose a different type of holiday behavior that aligned better with my values. My holiday season wasn't perfect (another Cultural Patterns trap!), but my Resilience Skills helped with the bumps.

Like Meri, whether it is for holidays, events, work, or everyday life, many of us feel overwhelmed and sometimes buried by expectations of what we "should" do. One of the ingrained Cultural Patterns of modern society is that we try to do too much and often try to do it "right."

Both Hank and Meri discovered that they had Cultural Patterns that were making them and those around them unhappy. Once they realized that they could alter their perceptions of what was "right"—adjust their Cultural Patterns—they began to find a way through the morass of hidden beliefs underlying their behavior. Noticing Cultural Patterns is the first step in coming to terms with them. When we notice and understand their influence, we have opportunities for different choices.

Cultural Patterns: What are They?

It is easy to believe that our way of seeing and thinking about the world is the only valid way. However, when we look closely, we realize that people see through very different lenses.

Our Cultural Patterns are those intergenerational beliefs, attitudes, and behaviors passed down to us. They come from people who have modeled to us how we should behave. They come from our ancestors, family, community, and experiences growing up.

Cultural Patterns shape how we view the world and ourselves. They are similar to gravity in that they shape everything we do, but we are usually unaware of them. Here are some key influences of our worldview:

- Ethnicity
- Language
- Racial Construct
- Gender Identity
- Sexual Orientation
- Religious Tradition
- Socioeconomic Status
- Disability Construct
- Political Affiliation
- Family Experiences and Stories
- Community Norms
- And many more

The norms we learn from these important contexts form our Cultural Patterns. Cultural Patterns enrich our lives and are crucial to our identity and belonging, but they can also significantly limit us and harm others. Cultural Patterns cause misunderstandings and conflicts because we don't understand—*"How can those other people even think that?"*

We don't have a choice about the Cultural Patterns handed down to us. As Brits, Huxley's parents passed on the Cultural Pattern of wanting to look like a perfect family. They valued "keeping up appearances," which meant Huxley should not display emotion, particularly if upset. Any display of emotion was weak. Huxley resisted this Cultural Pattern because he was a deeply feeling person and wanted more authentic conversations with his parents and siblings. When he asked family members, "How are you feeling?", they were uncomfortable. The family message was, "We don't talk about feelings. We don't have conversations about personal things." He had two dozen friends who would discuss sensitive issues with him and knew him better than his family. He felt they didn't actually see him for who he was.

This clash of Cultural Patterns became even more apparent when Huxley brought his American girlfriend, Sadie, home to meet his family. Huxley's parents would immediately change the subject when she brought up vulnerable topics, like her father's health crisis or her eating disorder. Huxley knew he wanted a different type of Cultural Pattern in his life. The openness and vulnerability of Sadie (and her family) helped Huxley to be eager to marry her and build a new family pattern.

Cultural Patterns can also feel restrictive in the workplace. As a professional woman, Isabella sometimes felt constrained by the gender norms that are ascribed to Latina women. She felt she was expected to juggle many difficult things while remaining compassionate to others' work stress. Isabella also felt she was supposed to "lean in" to take on more responsibilities whether she wanted to or not. When Isabella was assertive, she was labeled by others as aggressive. When she set standards for her staff and expected them to meet the standards, she felt others saw her as "lacking compassion."

Huxley and Isabella were constrained in their behavior by their Cultural Patterns. That is true for all of us. We decide to do—or not do—certain things based on whether we learned it was appropriate or not.

The good news is that our Cultural Patterns change over time. We have a different perspective on the world than when we were eight or 18. We can be intentional about exploring our worldview. Hank and Meri chose to explore their Cultural Patterns and are working on modifying them. Huxley decided he wanted a different Cultural Pattern for sharing feelings, and marrying Sadie helped him make that shift. While it is not easy, intentionally exploring and altering our Cultural Patterns is a lifelong journey that helps us expand our possibilities and understand others better.

How Cultural Patterns Form and why we use Them

No matter who we are, Cultural Patterns are ingrained in all of us. Culture is not something "other" people have. These patterns can feel "inherited" because they are passed down from generation to generation. They are passed to us through stories, conversations, media, and modeled behavior. We receive messages—about what is and is not okay—from society, people around us, and our family.

Meri—Growing up in the 1960s and 1970s, I received conflicting messages about appropriate female behavior. On the one hand, I read books by Laura Ingalls Wilder and Louisa May Alcott, with female heroines who were strong and a little rebellious but stayed within the restricting lines of 19th-century American womanhood. My mom volunteered and campaigned for others, but her primary roles were wife and mother. Some of my male teachers put down girls and told us what we could not do. My parents taught me I could "be anything I wanted to be," but what did that mean without empowered female role models? I scoured books to try to find examples of women in history or literature, looking for alternative Cultural Patterns without knowing it.

My younger sister was much more willing to do her own thing. Five years younger, she came of age while my mom was working and returning to school. Women were more prevalent in the workforce and politics. While my sister is a wife and mother, she is also a corporate attorney, filled with determination. Her Cultural Patterns mean she is less of a people-pleaser and fiercer about fighting for what she wants and deserves.

While family, early experiences, and society influence our Cultural Patterns, each person develops their own unique blend of Cultural Patterns, as Meri and her sister did. Even in the same family, everyone's distinct personality, gender, expression of sexuality, skin color, and the different ways their parents react to them shape their specific Cultural Patterns.

Whether we are aware of them or not, our Cultural Patterns affect what is important and what gives us meaning. They shape how we see the world and how we behave. The better we understand them, the more we can see how our Cultural Patterns can be both helpful and harmful. Intentionally exploring them strengthens our Cultural Resilience.

> **"You think you're thinking your thoughts. You're not. You are thinking your culture's thoughts."**
>
> ~ Jiddu Krishnamurti, Indian philosopher

How Cultural Patterns Help

- Give us our **core values**.
- Help us feel we **belong** to a group of people with whom we feel safe.
- Shape our **thought patterns** and **habits** for navigating the world.
- Provide **opportunities for shared meaning and celebration**.

When we see how Cultural Patterns help us, we can appreciate how they enrich our lives. We can also see how other people's Cultural Patterns, which may differ significantly from ours, help them.

Core Values

Our Cultural Patterns give us our core values, which are intimately tied to our identity. Sometimes, those values are expressed directly. Tatiana's dad wrote her letters when she was a college freshman and in graduate school. In them, he shared what was important to him—his values—of giving back to the community and putting relationships first. Tatiana tries to live out those values in her work as a social worker and in her family life with her husband and young daughter. Since her dad has passed away, Tatiana treasures those letters as a reminder of his values.

Luz has an Our Lady of Guadalupe pendant that symbolizes her family's values. When Luz was two years old, she was very sick. Her mother promised God if He saved Luz's life, she would pledge her child to Our Lady. "Some schools did not want me to wear a religious symbol," Luz said. But it was too important for her to give up.

"Our Lady inspired the Aztecs, whom the Spaniards had oppressed," Luz explained. "She represents my culture and my religion. She gives me strength and faith, and she motivates me." Luz also has a large framed portrait of Our Lady in her living room. Though her children are annoyed by such a large image, Luz wants to pass on the Cultural Patterns symbolized by this cultural and religious icon.

Our Cultural Patterns and values are often passed on through our actions—how we model what's important to us for others. Martha's parents grew up in challenging situations—her mom in a high-crime, low-income neighborhood in Los Angeles and her dad in segregated Texas—but they modeled for her the importance of giving back. The family didn't have much money, but they were generous. When people needed help, her parents opened their home. Guests would live on the sofa or in the garage while they were getting their lives together, sometimes for months at a time.

Martha described her family's Cultural Pattern as, "How do we care for other people while caring for ourselves?" This value propelled Martha to become a pediatrician who serves low-income families in a community where she has deep roots. This community matters to her because her grandparents lived there, and her parents went to school there. Martha's values also motivate her to run marathons to raise money for charity.

Tatiana, Luz, and Martha all have clear Cultural Patterns that shape values which enhance their lives. Knowing our values helps us use the *Resilient Mindsets of Choice* and *Courage* to stay aligned with what is most important to us. Sometimes, our values are more hidden. We may have to think about it. Do I value "getting a deal" more or "saving my money"? Exploring where these more unconscious values came from can help us clarify what will serve us best.

Chuck—My family taught me the importance of preserving nature. My dad was an ornithologist, and when I was growing up, we traveled far and wide to see specific birds. Once, we took our small family boat into the Florida Everglades to find a rare Scarlet Ibis, and I was the one who saw it first. It was so exciting. My parents were active in the Appalachian Mountain Club and supported groups like the Nature Conservancy. We did lots of camping, hiking, and canoeing. These experiences fostered my love of the wilderness and influenced my first career as an Outward Bound instructor. Environmental care and climate restoration are important to me.

Chuck's friend has different Cultural Patterns. While he was raised to hike and mountain bike and values being a steward of the land, he opposes governmental policies to mitigate climate change. He believes climate change has nothing to do with human behavior. The Cultural Patterns of Chuck and his friend have given them opposite views of "the truth."

Sense of Belonging

Wanting to belong is a common human impulse, hard-wired into us. Shared Cultural Patterns give us a sense of belonging with people we feel safe with. Katia found her people by playing and coaching softball. The women in Giovanna's family share "chisma" (gossip) through a family chat. That chat strengthens the matriarchy and helps Giovanna feel connected. Jiawei loved being at a guitar conference because everyone there could talk about music together. For Celeste, her Black hair bonnet helps her feel connected to the broader Black community. Since the bonnet protects Black hair from damage while sleeping, for Celeste, it represents the care that "we as Black women must give our hair." These kinds of shared experiences and common Cultural Patterns help us feel like we belong.

We may feel a sense of belonging due to our family, ethnicity, religious tradition, or political affiliation. We adopt the group Cultural Patterns without question. Mio speaks Spanish, so he feels connected with other Mexican Americans. Their shared sense of humor in Spanish gives him a sense of belonging. On the other hand, Carmen struggles to fit in with some groups of Mexican Americans. Though she is a fluent Spanish speaker, she has yet to learn the double entendres and other jokes in Spanish. Though she finds many things funny in English, "In Spanish, I feel dry, like I have no sense of humor," she explains, so she feels excluded when people joke in Spanish.

Sometimes, we find the people we belong with because we are different from the mainstream. For instance, Darius shared how Black people in a predominantly white space may acknowledge each other with a slight nod. Due to historical racism, they are more likely to have a shared perception of the police. When Black people get together, they can make jokes or "laugh at shared pain" in a way that might feel offensive if non-Black people were doing it. As a Chinese American, Mei feels connected when others mention a grandmother who stores dishes in the oven or dishwasher since this habit is more common in Asian families.

Talking about our Cultural Patterns can create indelible bonds. Family stories connect us to each other. For children of immigrants, family stories illuminate a world and Cultural Patterns that profoundly affect them, though they may not have experienced it personally. Growing up, Arjun heard many family stories about India. Since he only visited India three times, these family stories constructed his connection to his ancestral land and shaped Cultural Patterns such as the need to work hard to climb the ladder. Though raised in a different time and place, he is motivated by an ambition to make something of himself like his ancestors were.

The flip side is that when we are with people with different Cultural Patterns, we might not feel safe. Huxley went to a sports academy that he described as "bro-ey," meaning a homophobic and racist group of privileged white, straight men. Since the school culture prioritized sports, rugby-playing boys were seen as the most manly. The school had no opportunities for theater and few in music. Though Huxley was also a straight, white male, he secretly wanted to sing, play the piano, and be in theater. Even thinking about those activities felt embarrassing and unmanly. He felt the school's Cultural Patterns would never value his true self, and he wanted to fit in, so he adopted a bravado persona and hustled to make people accept him.

Huxley moved to London for college, hoping to find a group of people with Cultural Patterns similar to his own, and he did. He auditioned for an improv troupe the first week he arrived and discovered his belonging there. During that first audition, "I breathed out, and my shoulders lowered. I felt funny and interesting, and it felt like a different me. It changed my brain chemistry," Huxley recalled. "Everyone I needed was there. I learned to trust that I was enough. People would accept me."

Thought Patterns and Habits

Our Cultural Patterns help us understand how to behave. Our learned thought patterns and habits about navigating the world help us know what we "should do." Polina grew up in a small town where everyone knew each other. So, when someone died, the Cultural Pattern was that everyone would attend the funeral. Growing up, she went to many funerals, and it helped her realize how much death is part of life. After she moved to the Bay Area in California, she encountered the opposite Cultural Pattern. Most of her friends did not have their children go to funerals. Polina sees they don't know how to access comforting rituals or community connection when someone dies. Polina believes her Cultural Patterns would help others deal with the reality of death, so she encourages friends to go to funerals.

Having very different Cultural Patterns from others is a common cause of conflict. Differences in how we communicate are often tied to Cultural Patterns. Ivy grew up in a family with an "ask culture," where it was okay to ask for anything at all, knowing that sometimes they would get a "no." Her sister-in-law Eileen grew up in a family with a "guess culture" where she learned to avoid asking unless she was pretty sure she would get a yes. Ivy thinks Eileen forces people to read her mind by not asking for what she wants, and Eileen believes Ivy is rude with her direct requests.

When Ivy hosted a wedding shower, she invited everyone she thought might like to be included. She was not offended when some declined to travel to the event. For Eileen, inviting those who lived far away felt manipulative, like a "present grab." Like other Cultural Patterns, "ask culture" and "guess culture" describe two valid yet opposing ways of interacting with the world. Though she still prefers being direct, Ivy has more empathy for Eileen after seeing that her Cultural Patterns created her communication style.

Different Cultural Patterns also mean we develop different coping skills. Fatima was taught to rely on faith when she had burdens. Her thought patterns and habits include wearing a saint bracelet and lighting candles when she wants more clarity and confidence. Fatima is following in the footsteps of her immigrant parents, who had many hardships acclimating to the U.S. and struggled with finances. Their faith gave them courage.

Jonah's Cultural Patterns are entirely different. Though he was raised Catholic, his parents were not very religious. For Jonah, when he hears people talk about biblical beliefs, the beliefs seem not guided by logic. The stories seem so absurd that he questions their judgment or mental capacity. He prefers to base his behavior on what he sees as good common sense.

Our Cultural Patterns inform what we think is dangerous and thus what behavior we curtail. When Jaya grew up in India in the 1970s, most parents felt pressure to marry their daughters off by 25. By that age, unmarried girls were seen as undesirable and a burden to their parents. They also viewed girls as vulnerable to prevalent sexual harassment, so they were prohibited from dating, attending a late show, or emigrating to other countries to pursue a career. When Jaya and her friends passed by a group of boys, the boys would catcall. Jaya stewed inside at this sexual harassment. Though angry, she had no skills to deal with it other than by sticking with other women for protection.

When we recognize that Cultural Patterns shape our thought patterns and habits, we can decide if we want to continue being influenced by those Cultural Patterns or if we want to modify them. Polina appreciates the habit of going to funerals, so she encourages others to do it. On the other hand, Jaya is reforming her Cultural Patterns. Jaya wants to pass a different Cultural Pattern to her children so her daughter has the skills to deal with harassment and boys know that harassment is not okay. Chuck is practicing jumping into rapid discussions with more ease.

Shared Meaning and Celebration

Our Cultural Patterns promote the joy of being together. Connecting with others who have shared Cultural Patterns gives us strength, belonging, and a sense of "knowing who we are."

Meri—Though my family suffered upheaval for several years after my father left, my mother continued to give us a sense of family. She passed on a Cultural Pattern of celebrating all birthdays, holidays, graduations, and other milestones together. My extended family has gathered together monthly—sometimes more often—for decades. Even as my mother declined through Alzheimer's, I know these family traditions will continue because they are Cultural Patterns that the children and grandchildren value.

Sometimes, we have special objects that remind us of our shared Cultural Patterns and strengthen us. Ricardo honors his Chicano heritage through the art that he collects. Giovanna connects with her ancestors by carrying her babies with a rebozo, a long cloth. Giovanna's grandmother used the same rebozo to carry her mom and aunt as babies. Since Giovanna's mother immigrated from Mexico at 11 years old, Giovanna treasures the rebozo as a link to her family stories from Mexico. Ruth's menorah serves as a link to her Jewish religious practices. "When I was young, we stayed with my grandparents and uncles for one year. I remember my grandparents lighting the candles. While I stopped attending religious school, I remember the prayer for the candles. Even though we no longer celebrate as a family, I will continue to light the candles with my dog, as I want to carry on the tradition."

The celebrations in Meri's family, Ricardo's art, Giovanna's rebozo, and Ruth's menorah all strengthen their resilience by connecting them with their unique Cultural Patterns.

How Cultural Patterns Harm

Chuck—If I talked back to my father, he would lash out angrily and shout, "Don't interrupt me when I am talking to you!" Because of this, I developed a habit of waiting my turn to talk. At work, I had three colleagues from families that constantly interrupted each other. They rapidly spoke over each other in meetings, interrupting often and enjoying what felt like a creative and generative conversation. Because of my family pattern, I felt left out, and it was harder to stand up for a different point of view. When I learned to name my Cultural Pattern for myself and our team, the others left more space for me to talk, and I practiced interrupting on purpose so I could be more fully in the conversation.

When we explore Cultural Patterns, we also begin to recognize how our Cultural Patterns can harm us and others because they filter our understanding of how others view the world. Since we haven't grown up in other people's cultures, had their families, or lived their experiences, we often have difficulty imagining life from their perspective—their way of seeing the world.

Our brains naturally create patterns and associations that help us have order but also block some areas in our awareness. These blocked areas of understanding, which occur at an unconscious level, are called "mind gaps." Our Cultural Patterns have these mind gaps, which shape the lens through which we see the world. We have thoughts, beliefs, and attitudes about ourselves or others that we would see differently with a greater perspective.

Our Cultural Patterns can:

- **Distort** our self-image
- Distort **our view of others**
- **Exclude others** because of differences
- Create **inequitable structures**

Cultural Patterns prevent us from being who we want or need to be in our families, communities, and the world. Noticing the harm embedded in some of our Cultural Patterns is the first step to changing them.

Distort Our Self-Image

We all have things we don't know about how we operate that others might see. Our Cultural Patterns have mind gaps that prevent us from seeing truths that could help us grow and engage better with others.

Meri—Growing up, my mother liked to organize things, so I learned to organize things too. I felt calmer when things were organized. During the first year of my marriage, I insisted I knew where everything in our new apartment should go, and I chastised my husband if he got it wrong. It took me several years to recognize I needed to moderate my expectation that everything had to be organized. After I had a baby, visiting relatives who came to help put dishes back in the "wrong" places. I quickly learned I needed to modify my Cultural Pattern and let go a bit if I wanted their help. If I wanted my husband to feel comfortable caring for our children (and I did!), I needed to let him do things his way.

Chuck—I grew up with the Cultural Pattern of believing I had a "perfect" family. Everything I was told by my parents and in our family stories was that our family had it all together. This mind gap became apparent when I later learned the truth about my alcoholic family, which included incest and emotional abuse. I had a long journey of gaining a more complete picture of myself, my family, and our distorted Cultural Patterns.

When Riya was growing up in India, her community's Cultural Patterns had gender bias that held a limited view of what women could do. Indian girls weren't allowed to become scientists but could become pediatricians. This Cultural Pattern determined Riya's career path—she became a pediatrician—and she knew that she needed to marry before emigrating to the U.S. Now that she has lived in the U.S. for decades, she sees how her Cultural Pattern limited her view of herself and what she could have done.

Exploring our Cultural Patterns can help us fill in our mind gaps, unravel our internal stories, and create new perspectives that serve us better.

Distort Our View of Others

Because our mind gaps also cause unconscious or implicit bias, we all have Cultural Patterns that give us inaccurate views of others.

For Keiko, a Japanese-American pediatrician, too many people perceived her through Cultural Patterns that limited their ability to see her as a doctor. When people saw Keiko in the hospital, they would address her as if she were a nurse or a maid. Some of her patients had to alter their understanding before they could see her as an authoritative source of healing for their families.

As a design enthusiast and a Chinese American whose family has been in the U.S. for decades, Emilia didn't experience much racism growing up in her primarily Asian community. But sometimes, she faced awkward judgments even if they weren't meant to be hurtful. Her middle-school PE teacher would mock Asian languages with weird sounds and say random Korean words to her. He also told Emilia, "I had this good Asian food—spring rolls," even though she wasn't Vietnamese. During a recent Uber ride in Los Angeles, the driver talked about how Asians are so smart and Emilia's family is so intelligent. Emilia knew her family fitted the model minority stereotype because her parents are doctors, but she didn't like being put in that box.

With a Mexican-American father and an Irish-American mother, Julia usually felt privileged to grow up with a dual identity. Her heritage exposed her to different approaches to the world. Growing up in Los Angeles with her Mexican-American relatives nearby, her family would eat Mexican food such as carnitas, guacamole, and salsa to celebrate the Fourth of July. She looked Irish, however, so acquaintances would say derogatory things about Mexicans in front of her. Sometimes, she would respond to the slur, "You know, I am Mexican." They often sputtered that she didn't look Mexican. Julia continued, "Well, you are stereotyping. Mexicans come in different colors." These interactions showed Julia how Cultural Patterns created mind gaps that prevented people from accurately seeing her.

Sometimes, it is language that limits our perspective and connection. Fatima saw this with her parents. "As immigrants from Ecuador, my parents felt like they could never make themselves truly understood in English." She says many people underestimated who they were and what they could do because of their broken English.

Yande, a pediatrician, works to overcome how language Cultural Patterns can be a barrier in her work. When a grandmother brought a child to her office, though the grandmother didn't speak English, Yande still spoke right to the grandmother rather than ignoring her. By addressing the grandmother directly, she hoped to convey that she appreciated the grandmother's concerns and knew how vital the grandmother was for healing the child.

Meri—Because of an incident that happened to my grandfather long before I was born, I grew up with a Cultural Pattern of not trusting wealthy people. On my first day of college, when I saw another young woman dressed up and driving a fancy car, I thought she was probably snooty and planned on keeping my distance. Over time, I discovered that she was a creative, thoughtful, and caring person, and she became one of my closest friends. This type of surprise—a disruption of my Cultural Patterns—has become one of my treasured joys in life.

Exclude Others

Our Cultural Patterns can cause us to be unable to see the truth about other people's lives, leading us to assume that people who are different from us are inferior. When we judge others as threatening or find another reason to exclude them, we hurt them and ourselves. Because our Cultural Patterns create a mind gap, we may not know how they impact others. Our Cultural Patterns can lead to bias, discrimination, and racism.

Growing up, Martha battled racism. Fellow students at her high school asserted that her success was due to affirmative action rather than her hard work and talent. They would tell her that, of course, she could get into Stanford because she was a Black woman. They chose to ignore how hard she worked or that she was smart and had a lot to give to the world. Their attitudes isolated Martha from these peers.

As a 10-year-old Indian girl living in downtown Detroit in the 1970s, Jaya faced discrimination. She was picked on and called names. She smelled different. When she walked home, people bullied her and yelled "Indian" at her. She was so traumatized by the discrimination that when her parents offered her a chance to return to India to live with her grandparents, she gratefully accepted. When she was 15, she tried living with her parents in Michigan again. She remembers that experience as easier, perhaps because she was not as young and tenderhearted. Still, she moved back to India at the end of the school year and finished high school, college, and medical school in India. She did not return to the United States to live until she married.

When Jonah grew up near Boston, his community was divided between the Italians and the Irish. As an Irish man, he grew up hearing Italian jokes. His dad would make racially stereotypical jokes. He now looks back and realizes they were dehumanizing. Jonah knew his limited contact with Black people growing up gave him racial bias. When he was in Washington DC or Atlanta—cities with a high Black population—and saw many Black people, it felt normal, like they belonged. On the other hand, when he was in his home community, the northwest area of Boston, he noticed when fellow drivers were Black. Jonah was also aware that he had never seen affluent Black people in TV shows or books, so he noticed when he saw an affluent Black person. He knew his Cultural Patterns shaped this stereotypical judgment. He didn't like it but acknowledged it as real and tried not to act on it.

> **"Prejudice saves us a painful trouble, the trouble of thinking."**
> ~ Rabbi Alfred Bettelheim

Hector was born in the U.S. but spent his childhood in Mexico before returning to Los Angeles for high school. After graduating from USC in three years, he wanted to study medicine, but it was the early 1950s and medical schools were not widely accepting Mexican Americans. Hector argued his case directly with the dean of his first-choice medical school, successfully persuading him that he was worth a chance. With a heavy accent and as the only person of color, Hector had to work extra hard to be accepted and succeed in medical school.

After his residency, he served in the Navy for two years. Upon his return, no one would rent an apartment to him. Even in uniform, being a Mexican meant doors were closed. Eventually, he practiced medicine in the Mexican American community. Though his fellow doctors practiced in more prestigious areas, he wanted to give back and serve his community.

Like Hector, many people face obstacles because of others' Cultural Patterns. Cultural Patterns are the most insidious when they lead us to create and enforce policies and structures perpetuating disproportionate access to education, healthcare, or wealth-building strategies. Exploring our Cultural Patterns can be an essential first step in dismantling these policies and structures.

> **"No one is born hating another person because of the color of his skin, or his background, or his religion. People must learn to hate, and if they can learn to hate, they can be taught to love, for love comes more naturally to the human heart than its opposite."**
>
> ~ Nelson Mandela

Understanding Cultural Patterns helps us open our hearts and minds to what has influenced us and others. By exploring our own unconscious bias, we can build strong Cultural Resilience, empathy, and compassion to create the world we want to live in.

Chapter 13

The Power of Exploring our Cultural Patterns

"Mindfulness is the bedrock of breaking bias. It is the act of noticing or becoming aware of what is happening in the heart, mind, and body at the moment of contact with another person."

~ Anu Gupta, psychiatrist

As a child, Huxley didn't know his poor eyesight was a genetic condition that would worsen. Though his parents knew he would have increasing sight loss, they chose not to tell him until he was 21. Instead, they became helicopter parents. "They protected me like bubble wrap," Huxley said. "It made me fearful, like I couldn't handle things alone." Huxley believes these unspoken messages from his parents—that he needed to be protected for no apparent reason—contributed to his anxiety as a teen. His anxiety became so intense that sometimes he threw up multiple times a day.

His parents' silence also shaped a Cultural Pattern: his condition should be kept hidden. Even as a young man, Huxley continues to conceal his poor eyesight. Because others do not easily notice his condition, Huxley is "able-bodied passing." Unfortunately, when the light is low and he bumps into things, people feel free to make hurtful comments. "When they see me in a dark room or a bar, they laugh at me and say that I am drunk," he admitted.

Huxley also absorbed the Cultural Pattern that a disability meant he was weak. His rational mind said, "That's crazy. I would never say that about anyone else." Yet, years of living with a secret conditioned him to reject the label of disability. "In a perfect world, no one would know I had a disability. Why would I give myself the label when I didn't want anyone to know?"

Hiding his truth affected how he thought about himself and interacted with others. "I labeled myself as a 'hermit' who doesn't like dancing, bars, or going out," he said. Thankfully, when Huxley found his community—friends he could be honest with—they gave him the courage to explore his Cultural Pattern around the construct of disability.

He also explored his Cultural Pattern—his ingrained view of himself—that he would crumble under challenging situations. He now has a new mantra: "I can handle things." And while he is not quite ready to carry a white-tipped cane, he is considering it for the future. He realizes it would be a helpful signifier for others. And he is venturing out further. "I realized I DO like dancing—in a safe space. If it's 5 pm and bright, I am among the first people out there!"

Maya is also exploring her Cultural Patterns. She grew up in Puerto Rico, where most people were from her ethnic group, so she had little exposure to other types of people. Her view about people of other ethnicities was limited to the media's stereotypes. When she moved to the United States, she met different kinds of people: British, African, Indian, Italian, etc. Through these friendships, Maya learned how limiting those stereotypes were. She recognized how many similarities we all have and that individual experiences shape everyone.

Noticing Our Cultural Patterns

Huxley and Maya realized that becoming Curious about their Cultural Patterns would help them create a better version of themselves. First, they had to see that they had Cultural Patterns—perspectives about themselves and the world—that they had learned and could be modified.

Too often, we see "disability" as fact, a description of how challenges in the body limit someone. We actually have a "construct of disability"—a Cultural Pattern—about how someone with that body would function in the world, a construct that may not recognize that person's potential. Once Huxley started modifying his Cultural Pattern of how he thought about his disability, it was no longer so limiting. He learned that he could be and do more.

Maya, too, modified her Cultural Patterns regarding different ethnic groups and gained a broader view of herself. She realized she could be friends with many types of people and learn about their view of the world.

We can learn so much when we ask questions like: *Why do I think about things in a certain way? What are the stories I tell myself about who I am? Where did I learn that? Where did I get my values? Why do I think about money/food/body image in this way? Where did my ideas about gender roles/ethnic identity/construct of race come from? How does all of this influence why and how other people are the way they are?*

Noticing our Cultural Pattern is the first step of exploration. Then, the *Resilient Mindsets of Curiosity, Choice,* and *Courage* can help us better understand our Cultural Patterns and thus ourselves. Mind gaps may be blocking our ability to connect with others. Looking closely, we can better understand beliefs and attitudes that harm ourselves, our relationships, and our communities. We can clarify conflicting parts of our identity. We can explore how our Protective Patterns are related to Cultural Patterns. We can begin to understand why other people see the world so differently from how we do.

Resilient Mindsets Bring Insight

(Resilient Mindsets)

Chuck—Recently, I realized that I had a Cultural Pattern that had subtly damaged my relationship with my wife for all of our 45 years of marriage. I was floored when I came face to face with this perception. My Cultural Pattern was rooted in my privilege as a white male psychologist: I thought I knew what was true for my wife, and I had a right to tell her. This powerful Cultural Pattern—believing I had superiority of insight—was demeaning and deeply hurtful to my very best friend. How did my Cultural Pattern develop? Why had I acted that way?

I used the *Resilient Mindsets of Curiosity, Choice,* and *Courage* to look at this deeply. For six days, I went on a desert retreat, camping in the wilderness and meditating on my emotional truth. A trusted guide, an elder in this work, and a close group of friends supported my exploration. One night, I sat up all night with the stars, fasting and feeling my deep feelings of hurt, surprise, and awareness. I had to feel my tears and the difficult realization that I was replicating the way my father treated my mother. Difficult—yes. Liberating—absolutely! My heart shifted when I saw how I was like my dad. Our humanity mingled, and I found empathy for myself and compassion for my dad. He had impeccable reasons for behaving exactly the way he did. I had mind gaps passed down through generations of patriarchy. Seeing my Cultural Patterns gave me space to make different choices that aligned more with my values. I can see so much more is possible for me and my relationships. I can use my courage to dance through life rather than struggle so much.

Celeste, a fan of Kendrick Lamar, is a Black woman whose family comes from Mississippi. Curious about the Cultural Patterns passed down by her family and community, she realized many were critically important for safety. Understanding where these Patterns came from and their original purpose helps her as she sifts through them and tries to shed those that no longer serve her.

Luz, a devotee of the Virgin Mary, did all the work for family gatherings. Once she recognized she was living out a Cultural Pattern shared by generations of women, she became curious about it. Luz realized this Cultural Pattern was connected to her Protective Pattern of Hyper-Caretaking, and the imbalanced workload reduced her desire for family get-togethers. Now, she wants to make a different choice to sustain her energy and create more equity in her family. Change is difficult because she has to rally her family, so they take on more tasks. But changing her Cultural Pattern, unlearning generations of behavior and ways of seeing the world, is the hardest part. She needs courage to silence her "you should be doing this" voice.

As a Latina woman, Isabella is influenced by the Cultural Patterns of Marianismo—which is the counterpart of Machismo. Like Celeste, she uses the Resilient Mindset of Curiosity to sift through these Cultural Patterns. Isabella aspires to uphold some of these Cultural Patterns in her life—to be a matriarch and a source of strength for the family. However, she is also aware that Latinas are harmed by some of these Marianismo Cultural Patterns, such as the pressure to be self-sacrificing, virtuous, and chaste. These Cultural Patterns can oppress women and negatively impact their health and wellbeing, like accepting intimate partner violence to uphold the ideal of family harmony. Isabella wants to reform those Patterns.

As a Black woman and superhero fan, Imani had the Cultural Pattern that her hair had to be styled a certain way to be acceptable. Growing up, all the women in her family—her grandmother, mother, and aunts—repeatedly discussed whether letting their hair go natural was okay. In her twenties, she used the *Centering Skill of Letting Go* of her fear of stigma and embraced her natural hair. Because it is such an ingrained Cultural Pattern, the issue still comes up inside her, even today. By embracing her natural hair, Imani is choosing courage to fight societal expectations and her expectations of herself. When she drives down the highway, she thinks, "Are my locks okay? Will a cop stop me because I look unruly (and, therefore, dangerous)?" Imani's ongoing tussle with her Cultural Pattern around hair exemplifies the recurring battles most of us have and the courage we need to free ourselves of Cultural Patterns that no longer serve us.

Ximena, a vegan, is also using her courage to change a harmful Cultural Pattern: the stereotype of a "strong, Black woman." She wants her family—and the world—to recognize that Black women have feelings and that this stereotype fails to recognize that they require emotional and psychological support. Black women are women who shouldn't have to bear the weight of the world to survive.

Similar to our Protective Patterns, when we notice how our Cultural Patterns influence our thoughts or behavior, we can use the *Resilient Mindsets of Curiosity, Choice,* and *Courage* to explore how to handle them. When we are curious, we begin to understand other perspectives, opening up new possibilities for ourselves. Can we learn something about ourselves from this Cultural Pattern? Do we want to shift the practice? Adapt it? Do we reject it outright? We might need to Choose different Cultural Patterns to create new beliefs, attitudes, and behaviors that give us a different way of looking at ourselves, others, and the world. Modifying our Cultural Patterns requires Courage, but it is a powerful step toward creating the life we want. Chuck, Celeste, Luz, Isabella, Imani, and Ximena are all on the journey. The Choice to change Cultural Patterns that don't serve us anymore is often a process of personal healing.

Revealing Our Mind Gaps

Our curiosity can help us uncover mind gaps created by our Cultural Patterns that cause us to judge others. Zainab, the daughter of Pakistani immigrants, had a mind gap about education. In her family, people who did not attend college were considered inferior. When Zainab became curious about this Cultural Pattern, she realized that not everyone has the same opportunities and that attending college is a privilege. Many good, intelligent people don't have a college education. After recognizing her mind gap, Zainab chose to open her heart to people without a college degree. Her wider lens helped Zainab change the Cultural Pattern that had limited her relationships.

Emilia, the design enthusiast, also had a mind gap based on her privilege. She had believed that if she studied hard in high school, she would get into whatever college she wanted. This equation that hard work guarantees success made her college application process very painful. Even with her stellar credentials, several colleges rejected her. Now, as a college student looking back, she recognizes it was a privilege to focus on studying without caring for family members or working for survival. Emilia now understands that people carry unequal burdens in their quest to survive and get ahead. Exploring her mind gap has given her more compassion for her peers who were not high achievers.

Hank, the music teacher, had a different set of mind gaps. As a white boy in a small town in the rural South, Hank developed a Cultural Pattern that people should be self-sufficient and not rely on anyone. This Cultural Pattern made him feel superior and limited his ability to work well with others. As a younger man, he had founded a community center to teach world music. It was a lively place with many classes, student performances and a sense of community. He was proud of this studio he created, and as the center grew, it became his livelihood.

Other people wanted to teach there, but the thought of expansion threatened Hank. His Cultural Pattern dictated that he had to control the center. When Olivia, a fellow musician and gifted teacher in her own right, wanted to teach a class, Hank blocked it even though others had requested her teaching. When Hank moved away and others took over, the music center flourished and quickly expanded. Looking back, Hank realized the mind gap in his Cultural Patterns had caused him to miss a major opportunity. Including Olivia and welcoming her to teach would have helped him experience the benefits of letting go of control, and the power of collaboration and nurturing an inclusive and supportive community.

Julia, with mixed Mexican/Irish heritage, had mind gaps around political attitudes. An empathic person, she wanted to help struggling people and transform systems to uplift those on the margins. She appreciated the Democratic party's emphasis on social justice and ensuring people have resources to improve their lives. She was frustrated by Republican policies, which she felt hurt those on the margins.

Julia's political views made her feel isolated in her family. Her siblings, who are Republicans, called her a "do-gooder." She wonders how they grew up in the same house and yet became such different people as adults. For many years, she felt frustrated with their lack of interest in helping others.

Julia became curious about her Cultural Patterns around political parties and discovered gaps in her own awareness. She realized that many Republicans, too, want to "take care of others"—just with a different emphasis. For example, while her parents don't support governmental policies for helping people experiencing poverty, they generously help those in need directly. Her mom has an envelope of money in her car and hands it to needy people. Her father is a doctor who treats many low-income families for free. Acknowledging her old assumptions and embracing the full complexity of her family's Cultural Patterns has improved Julia's relationship with her family. She recognized that people are much more than their bumper stickers.

How other people see the world is just as valid to them as our perspective is to us. Like Zainab, Hank, Emilia, and Julia, we may believe falsehoods that paint a picture that limits us and prevents us from connecting fully with others. We may have been taught to assume that people act or think in a certain way and discover that it's not true. When we become curious about our Cultural Patterns and choose to discuss them with others who may have different ones, we gain a broader lens that serves us better. We can find things in common with people who appear to be very different than us. Recognizing our mind gaps can help us connect with others better.

Clarifying Identity

Being curious about our Cultural Patterns can help us better understand our identity as well as how others see us. We may be exposed to conflicting Cultural Patterns about how we should be in the world. Exploring our Cultural Patterns can help us sort out those identity questions and choose who we want to be based on our values.

When she came out as gay, Izzy was forced to choose one part of her identity. Her deeply religious parents said she could not discuss her lesbian identity with her Spanish grandmother because "Spanish people don't accept lesbians." Izzy accepted this limitation because her Cultural Patterns led her to "believe what family says." However, as a lacrosse player, when she traveled to Spain to play in an international tournament, she discovered many lesbians among the Spanish lacrosse players. This revelation helped her reclaim the Spanish part of her identity. She could be both! Izzy reconciled her Spanish and lesbian identities while recognizing that her parents' Cultural Patterns had limited their perspective. She broadened her understanding of herself and the world by being curious about her Cultural Patterns.

In ninth grade, Julia had to confront her Cultural Patterns about her mixed Mexican/Irish heritage when she was invited to a special weekend retreat. Her high school had a history of ethnic tension involving the mix of Black students bussed in from south central LA as well as Latino and white students. The purpose of the retreat was to diffuse tension by building commonalities. The organizers began the retreat by telling participants to sit with the group with whom they most identified. Most people knew where to sit, but Julia and a half-black/half-white peer were left standing in the middle. Julia was very uncomfortable being forced to choose part of her ethnicity. Ultimately, she realized most of her close friends were white, so she sat with the white kids. Later, she realized she had also chosen privilege because, in her neighborhood, most Latino children were poorer. The experience pushed Julia to examine how her Cultural Patterns from her mixed heritage affected her behavior and how she saw the world. While she still viewed her ancestry as a gift, she realized that sometimes others only saw one aspect of her heritage.

Julia was again confronted with her Cultural Patterns in college when she applied for an internship at the *Los Angeles Times*. One interviewer asked her why she hadn't applied for the Hispanic internship. Julia said that she felt like she didn't deserve it. She came from a privileged background and the internship was for those who needed it. The interviewer replied, "You don't know how often you have been discriminated against because of your name. When you send your resume around, people judge you." He added, "You should join the Chicano Media Association."

Despite this suggestion, Julia struggled to find common Cultural Patterns with other Hispanic journalists. "I don't speak Spanish," she explained. "And I have blue eyes and Irish-colored skin." Julia gradually learned how to integrate both cultures better into how she presented herself. Later in her career, she intentionally chose her maiden name as her middle name in her byline. She wanted readers to know her connection to the Mexican community.

Tala, who loves the Sierra Nevada Mountains, also grew up with conflicting Cultural Patterns about who she should be. Her great-grandmother was a powerful Indigenous woman in Alaska who married a white pioneer. He was a very successful storekeeper who moved the family from Alaska to Berkeley in 1890. "When my great-grandmother settled in a big house in Berkeley, she told everyone they were Russian, not Native," Tala explained. "They had to keep it secret because California had been legally committing genocide against Native peoples since 1860." Tala's family began a Cultural Pattern of hiding their Native heritage. "We are Native, but don't tell anyone" was the message they carried.

Like many bilingual, bi-cultural people, Tala has worked at unraveling her Cultural Patterns. Being both a person with White privilege and a Native kid, growing up, she felt the dissonance of two opposing cultures. Like too many Native families, her family experienced trauma and had little income. Some relatives still live on the edge and are vulnerable to substance abuse, untreated mental illness, and arrests. In some ways, Tala feels her internal self is still in the Native community. "My great-grandmother is always with me. She helps me cut through the privileged perspective, to see things as they really are and to see the 'fenced-in people' in our reservations, ghettos, barrios, border areas, etc. Our collective enculturated privilege conditioned us to not see them and ignore their suffering."

On the other hand, because she had a white parent and could look and act White, she could more easily escape the trauma-laden community and become a successful professional. Tala feels uncomfortable that her White privilege opened doors that were closed to other Native kids. "I am embarrassed by how my White privilege has helped me achieve the pinnacles of my career. It can be confusing having ancestors who had been both colonizers and those who had been colonized."

Being curious about her Cultural Patterns has helped Tala see things from multiple perspectives and be more rigorous about her unconscious bias. She reconciles the opposing messages in her Cultural Patterns with a career working with historically marginalized people and a call to serve social justice. She also has found self-acceptance. She's become more adept at moving back and forth between the two cultures and using the advantages of both to accomplish her mission. This sense of "two-eyed seeing" empowers her to make a difference in the world.

Like Izzy, Julia, and Tala, many of us grew up with mixed feelings about different, perhaps conflicting, parts of our identity. It is essential to be curious and pay attention to those feelings. What do they tell us about how we view ourselves? How do we view others with those Cultural Patterns? They may reveal our mind gaps—like Julia's belief that no one would discriminate against her even with her Mexican last name. As we explore our Cultural Patterns, we can make choices about our identity that align with our values.

Connecting to our Protective Patterns

Our Cultural and Protective Patterns are often connected, as they are both passed intergenerationally through our families. Exploring our Cultural Patterns can help us see our Protective Patterns, and vice versa. Understanding both sets of Patterns helps us see how they impact us and which ones we want to modify.

Isabella was the daughter of Latino immigrants. As newcomers to this country, her family felt it was essential to be skeptical about other's intentions. She was taught, "Don't open the door. Don't talk to strangers."

Isabella's family used the Protective Patterns of Hypervigilance and Distrusting to feel safe. Isabella knows these Cultural Patterns have made her too cynical about others. She spends too much time figuring out their hidden agendas, making it more difficult to develop healthy relationships.

Ricardo, who collects Chicano art, knows he learned the Protective Pattern of Avoiding from his dad. Having grown up in a traumatic, dangerous environment, Ricardo's dad Avoids conflict at all costs. Ricardo has found himself Avoiding conflict, even when it would serve him better to address the problem directly.

For Giovanna, as a Mexican-American woman, her Cultural Patterns mandated clear gender roles, which included the Protective Pattern of Hyper-Caretaking her family. Growing up, she saw her mother trying to "do it all." Now that she is married, she also feels she must "do it all." Though her family taught her that "a mom never gets tired," she knows that's not true. As a therapist, she sees how this thinking is unhealthy. She knows her white husband has different Cultural Patterns and is open to dividing up family chores. Exploring her Cultural Patterns has opened her eyes to how her Protective Patterns hurt herself and her family.

Like Isabella, Ricardo, and Giovanna, once we notice which of our Protective Patterns are connected to our Cultural Patterns, we can have empathy and compassion for ourselves and our family members who passed them along. Deeply ingrained Patterns can be hard to modify, but noticing them is the first step. We can then practice the *Resilient Mindsets of Curiosity, Choice,* and *Courage* to shift them when they are not serving us.

Revising Our Cultural Patterns

Ruby can see how her Cultural Patterns are both helpful and limiting. Her grandmother and mother were strong Black women, handling whatever life threw their way and raising her to do the same. However, Ruby also feels the impact of Cultural Patterns that emerged from intergenerational trauma. Her grandmother lacked a home, and her mother was adopted, creating a legacy of feeling unrooted. Moreover, since the family immigrated from the Caribbean, they didn't identify as "African American" which reduced their connection to the Black community in the U.S. They never asked for help when needed and thought it was important "not to depend on anyone." Ruby is committed to passing on reformed Cultural Patterns to her children. She wants them to be strong but also to have a community and ask for help when needed. She is trying to model these new Cultural Patterns for them.

Marla is also working on reforming her Cultural Patterns and using the *Centering Skill of Letting Go* of intergenerational trauma. In her family and other families that she works with, she sees intergenerational trauma show up in Protective Patterns like Hypervigilance, as well as increased anxiety, insomnia, and other self-destructive behavior.

For Jaya, her husband Kahaan helped reform her Cultural Patterns. Growing up, Jaya felt pressure to live within community norms, with a voice in her head that said, "What will other people think if you do that?" Kahaan marched to his beat, using the Resilient Mindset of Courage to live from a place of, "I will do what is true in my heart." He looks at the whole context and makes the best decisions for himself and his family.

When Jaya was growing up, her Indian parents hovered over her to keep her safe. No one dated, especially when they were students and supposed to focus on studying. Her husband helped her see that dating was normal for her children's generation. He also helped her accept when her son and his girlfriend moved in together as a step toward marriage. When her daughter wanted to study abroad and travel with a friend, it was totally outside of her comfort zone. Jaya learned to reframe it for herself: "If there is a lesson for my daughter in this experience, she will learn it." She realized that even when she disagrees with her children, she can still respect them. Jaya has modified her Cultural Patterns for the good of her family.

If we fail to explore our Cultural Patterns, we will likely put the weight of our ancestors' patterns on our children. Sometimes, that history needs to be passed on to protect our children, as some Black American families teach their children about their history with law enforcement so they understand how to act safely. On the other hand, too often our Cultural Patterns pass on intergenerational trauma that limits our children in unhealthy ways, as Ruby's family did by never asking for help and Marla's did with Hypervigilance and anxiety.

Like Ruby, Marla, and Jaya, many of us are motivated by our children to reform our Cultural Patterns. We want a different world for them—one with less fear, less anxiety, and less discrimination and racism.

Creating a New Sense of Belonging

Examining our Cultural Patterns can force us to explore very personal ideas and concepts intimately connected to our identity. Our Cultural Patterns give us a sense of who we are. When we start altering our Cultural Patterns that no longer serve us, we might experience a sense of loss. When we change our views, people in our community may have difficulty with our new perspective, or we may feel like we don't belong to groups with which we were once close.

Darius grew up in predominantly Black communities in Baltimore and Pennsylvania. Language with his peers often included slurs against those in the LGBTQ community. As a child and teen, Darius didn't think about how this language impacted others. However, as he grew older, especially after moving to California, he realized that language was hurtful. Darius deliberately changed his homophobic Cultural Pattern. Now, when he spends time with his friends from his old neighborhoods, he cringes when he hears those words. Darius has grown away from those friends as they no longer match his values.

Libby noticed, "My Korean husband's family is very huggy. Since I live close to them in California and see them a lot, my Cultural Pattern has changed, and I am huggy too. When I return home to my family of origin in Virginia, I find it off-putting that my family doesn't hug me. It takes some getting used to."

Ximena knew that her family's favorite foods, like many of those delicious fried or heavy-fat foods passed down through Black families for generations, contributed to poor health outcomes. To improve her health, she changed her Cultural Patterns around food and became a vegan. Her mom initially saw Ximena's choice as "a phase." Her family did not change what food they served, which meant salad was her only choice at most family gatherings. Ximena felt frustrated because she loved eating her family's heritage foods and felt left out. Finally, after eight years, Ximena's mom realized that her daughter had changed and she needed to change too. Now, Ximena's mom makes delicious family food, like black-eyed peas, which she has altered to be vegan.

Darius, Libby, and Ximena recognize that their modified Cultural Patterns impacted their sense of belonging because they no longer fit in with their old friends and family. They don't want to go back to their old ways of thinking, but there is some cost to broadening their perspective. They are using their courage to reimagine how and with whom they belong.

Riya, who was raised in India but immigrated to the U.S. as a young woman, has tried to blend Cultural Patterns from both cultures into her identity. She said, "I want to wear both a sari and a sexy dress." Each culture has strengths that she enjoys.

Like Riya, for many people, especially as we mature, the Cultural Patterns of any one group can become too restrictive. We may become uncomfortable with one or more habits of the group. When we can't find one group that celebrates all of who we are, we can choose various groups to belong to. Ultimately, many of us form an identity that is a blend of Cultural Patterns—those passed down to us and those we adopt because they fit who we are and serve us better.

Spotlights

Cultural Patterns affect many aspects of our lives and are at the root of many misunderstandings and conflicts. We have chosen two types of Cultural Patterns to spotlight because they affect us profoundly every day, yet we usually don't think of them first when we think of our Cultural Patterns: money and food.

Money

Money brings up complex feelings that impact our relationships. In the U.S., financial disagreements contribute to 20-40% of divorces. Whether those disagreements are about too little money, too much money, or different spending patterns—they almost always emerge from our Cultural Patterns. Our Cultural Patterns around money can impact so many of our interactions—with family members, work colleagues, friends, and even those who perform a service for us. Exploring our Cultural Patterns around money can help us understand them better and communicate more effectively with our loved ones.

Audrey and her husband, Niles, exemplify how differing Cultural Patterns around finances can create conflict. The values that Audrey's family passed on to her include being prudent, paying off debts as quickly as possible, and communicating with those involved if there might be a shortfall. Her family tells a story about her grandfather, who started a shoe store right before the Great Depression. Early on, there was a time when he didn't have funds to pay his suppliers. He wrote to one of his main suppliers and explained the situation. The manufacturer appreciated his honesty and told him to pay as he could. Using this strategy of integrity and honest communication with his customers, Audrey's grandfather built a very successful business that is still thriving almost 100 years later.

Niles came from an immigrant family with a different ethic. Niles is an optimist with a "can do" belief that "it will all work out." Rather than careful tracking and transparent communication, Niles believes in taking on what he considers appropriate debt as a path to success. So if solar panels or a new car are priced right, Niles sees those as suitable investments. Niles also sees himself as an excellent provider for his family, and anything that tarnishes that image feels shameful. When Audrey and Niles recognized how they handled money derived from their Cultural Patterns, it prevented them from viewing each other's money habits as deliberately damaging their family. They became more curious and less judgmental, and they could talk about it more calmly with each other.

Meri—After exploring the concept of Cultural Patterns, I realized that my distrust of "too much money" was probably passed on from my grandfather to my dad. As a small boy, my grandfather lived in an orphanage and hoped to live with his older sister and her new husband. When the couple refused to take my grandfather, the story he created and passed on to my father was that "wealthy people can't be trusted." That Cultural Pattern impacted my choice of career, and it affected my marriage. If my husband wants anything I think might put us in the "wealthy people" category, I become uncomfortable and anxious, and my Protective Pattern of Attacking will likely emerge. Becoming more curious about this Cultural Pattern helps me keep my Protective Pattern at bay.

Some couples have financial Cultural Patterns that align well. Liam's dad grew up with very little money, but he passed a Cultural Pattern of careful money management to his son. He taught Liam the value of a savings account, paying bills on time, and understanding how much one saves vs. spends. He also stressed the value of accumulating savings to care for aging. Liam's wife has a Cultural Pattern of trusting her husband to handle the money, and they have remained on the same page throughout their two decades of marriage. Even now that his wife has her own business, she still has delegated him to run the books.

Money also can be a "love language." Who we spend money on, why, and how much can signal what we value. Gift-giving is often something friends, particularly couples, have to learn to negotiate with each other.

Otis' father had little money growing up but became a well-respected medical specialist with an income to match. He loved showering his family with gifts at Christmas. As a child, Otis sometimes felt overwhelmed by excessive gifts. As an adult, Otis had complicated Cultural Patterns around gift-giving. On the one hand, he had learned from his dad that "gift showers" were how love was expressed. However, Otis didn't want to ask for presents and talked about his discomfort with too many. It took him a while to tease out how to get the connection he craved from gifts so he could receive what was given with joy.

Hilde, a social worker, shared how gifts can have unintended consequences on foster youth. While they appreciate presents, these gifts remind them of what they lack: a stable family who knows them and can provide what they long for without asking.

Our use of credit cards can also be a Cultural Pattern. In Meri's household, they are a pragmatic tool, a way of paying for goods and services. For others, they can represent a way to "get what I deserve" or shopping as an avoidance strategy.

Ruby's family loved to collect souvenirs wherever they went. She recognizes that this is probably connected to the fact that her family had few material goods and had to fight for whatever they could get. She thinks the lack of financial resources created a Cultural Pattern in that they held onto everything dearly. This has created more material and emotional baggage than feels good to Ruby now.

For Audrey, Niles, Meri, Otis, and Ruby, exploring their Cultural Patterns around money is powerful. Being curious about their reactions, and knowing that their frustrations and fears are a learned perspective that can be modified, helps them think about what they want money, gifts, credit cards, and souvenirs to mean to them.

Food

Our Cultural Patterns affect our attitudes about food. Many of us have special foods that tie us to others. For Cristiano, his family shares coffee and the Mexican sweet pan dulce around the kitchen table. The tradition makes him feel like he belongs. Meri's family loves ravioli and enjoyed sharing it when they gathered for her mom's funeral. Luz recalls all the special cooking her mother did for Good Friday. "There are so many traditional foods that she cooks," Luz explained. "I feel so connected to my mother when I think of those foods." For Isabella, the New Year is symbolized by eating green grapes. "We eat 12 grapes to symbolize the good things that will come our way or for our loved ones in the New Year. We shove them in our mouths at midnight, trying to eat all the grapes," she explained. Sometimes, she buys extra grapes to ensure everyone has enough because she doesn't want to miss out on this happy tradition.

Juana treasures a little basket with a cloth she got at her aunt's wedding. The basket keeps tortillas warm, reminding Juana of the importance of eating together. Her family cares for people they love by cooking for them and eating meals together. These meals help everyone decompress from the day and share with each other. Juana wants to pass on these Cultural Patterns to her children so they know and understand their traditions.

Carmen's family also values preparing food. When Carmen started her first professional job, she planned on buying her lunch because she had the Cultural Pattern that professionals purchase their lunch each day. Her mother reminded her of another Cultural Pattern: she was taught to prepare food with care. Bringing her lunch would connect her to her roots and save her money. This lesson helped Carmen be mindful of what she needs and spends. Sometimes, she buys lunch, but it is a treat.

What we eat, how we eat, with whom we eat, and when we eat are all traditions passed down through families and communities. Most of us probably have a mix of happy and unhealthy Cultural Patterns around food, so exploring those patterns can guide us in improving our lives. For some, dieting is a way of life, and many types of food are connected to shame. After years of talking about and struggling with their own diets, some mothers wonder why their daughters have unhealthy body image issues. Maeve grew up drinking Diet Coke regularly. While it symbolizes the Cultural Pattern of "treat," and eliminating it is challenging, she realizes it is harmful and is trying to cut back.

Imani, a superhero fan, has also Let Go of some of her Cultural Patterns around food. While Imani loves the history and heritage of Black food, she wants to defy the statistics of poorer health and shorter lifespans for Black people. For her health, she has chosen to become a pescatarian. Her mother now knows how to serve her "greens without the meat."

Chuck—After my heart attack, I realized my Cultural Pattern of eating the all-American diet had almost killed me. Meat and potatoes were the rule. My mom made a sandwich she called the "Fisher Special." It was a grilled tuna sandwich filled with mayo, cheese, and Thousand Island dressing, and it was oh-so-horribly good. Our family salad was a slice of iceberg lettuce with white sugar on top. Breakfast was frosted flakes with extra spoonfuls of sugar to ensure it was sweet enough. No wonder my arteries became clogged, and I have heart disease! My heart attack forced me to face my Cultural Patterns. I have learned to recognize that my food is medicine and have drastically changed my diet.

Mei, a social worker, explained that foster children often do not have consistent Cultural Patterns around food. For many of them, whose early family life was disrupted, home mealtimes were not regular, there was not enough food, and meals were rarely a time for decompressing or sharing stories. Foster families must recognize that their foster children may not understand why they are expected to participate in scheduled meals if they are unfamiliar with them from their family of origin.

Sometimes, we change our culinary Cultural Patterns when encountering new friends or communities. Darius grew up noticing that most African Americans love their meat cooked really well done. He understood these Cultural Patterns developed because enslaved people got leftover meat parts, and they were unsafe to eat unless cooked well done. He never ate sushi because "sushi was for white people." When he moved to the West Coast for college, he finally tasted sushi. He thought it was terrific.

Like Maeve, Imani, Chuck, and Darius, being curious about our Cultural Patterns around food can help us be more intentional about which ones we want to keep and which we might like to modify. Then, we can use our courage to strengthen our Cultural Resilience.

> **"Who in the world am I? Ah, that's the great puzzle."**
> ~ Lewis Carroll, *Alice in Wonderland*

Chapter 14

Creating the World we Want

"Yesterday I was clever, so I wanted to change the world.
Today I am wise, so I am changing myself."

~ Rumi, 13th-century Persian poet

What is Cultural Resilience?

Chuck—Between ages 3 and 8, I lived in the Philippines and then Peru. My earliest memories are of being comforted by my Filipina housekeeper. In Peru, because my mom was busy with her social circuit and mostly unavailable, our Peruvian cook, Rosa, lived with us and became my surrogate mom. The local Peruvian kids made me feel safe and that I belonged, even though we had different cultures, socioeconomic status, and skin color.

Returning to "the States" after living abroad was like going to a foreign country. I had to figure out my world all over again. In seventh grade, I moved to Virginia and became part of forced desegregation. Since majority-Black schools needed more whites, I was bussed to an all-Black junior high. Though my father was appalled, my mom thought it was a good idea. For me, it just seemed normal. I loved being in class with my Black peers, roughhousing in gym class, and once again, feeling that I belonged. I thrived being with children in a non-white culture.

Meri—After I started living abroad, I realized my previous view of the world was extremely limited. Though our family hosted foreign exchange students throughout my middle- and high- school years, my perspective broadened while studying in France during my sophomore year of college. I was shocked and overwhelmed by how completely differently people lived. Everything was new—from wall sockets and cooking supplies to greetings and emotional expressions. So much to learn, and all in another language! Eventually, I leaned into the adventure, and soon I was thriving. I loved the excitement of always learning something new about the people around me. Over the last several decades, I have lived and worked on four continents. Every move brought a tough transition, followed by the exhilaration of learning. Each new place uncovered more about my own Cultural Patterns and touched my heart. In China, our friends defied the government to celebrate "tomb-sweeping day," illuminating that respect for one's ancestors comes in many forms. Our "brand new" apartment in India included many old parts that routinely broke down, reminding me that what is on the surface doesn't necessarily match what lies underneath. In very simple homes, our friends in West Africa regularly had huge gatherings of friends and family, reminding me that my favorite entertainment is conversation with loved ones.

For both Chuck and Meri, these formative experiences with people vastly different from themselves helped them develop Cultural Resilience.

Cultural Resilience *is the ability to acknowledge and understand our own beliefs, values, norms, and social practices, as well as to be curious and humble about the multiplicity of*

others' experiences. Strong Cultural Resilience limits the perpetuation of bias, racism, and discrimination.

The Impact of Others' Cultural Patterns

One doesn't have to live in a foreign country to strengthen Cultural Resilience. Using the *Resilient Mindset of Curiosity,* we strengthen our connection by noticing other people's Cultural Patterns and empathizing with them. When those patterns are harmful, we can take a stand against them. By recognizing the Cultural Patterns of others, we learn much more about ourselves and develop our Cultural Resilience.

Seeing Others' Truth

When we see other people's Cultural Patterns, it can transform our relationship with them. Sometimes, that means seeing another person's truth with sensitivity and letting them know it. Without working at it, Darius could ace his elementary and high-school tests. He knew he was seen as "smart for a Black kid" and did just enough to be at the top of his class. Finally, Darius had one teacher who did not just see him as a "smart Black athlete," but as a person. This teacher realized he was not working to his potential, so she motivated him to work harder and learn more. By circumventing the Cultural Patterns at his high school and genuinely seeing him, she helped him learn how to succeed on a bigger stage.

Cristiano, who loves pan dulce, sees how his Latina mother feels a need to be a Hyper-Caretaker. When he called his mom because he didn't make it home for Easter, she came up with all sorts of other ways she could take care of him. Even though he is a 36-year-old married man, his mother wants to care for him. Understanding her Cultural and Protective Patterns helps Cristiano have empathy and understanding for his mom rather than feeling controlled by her.

When design enthusiast Emilia was younger, she didn't understand how sexual identity and orientation could be difficult to navigate. At her high school, homophobia was hidden, and it seemed LGBTQ-friendly, like everyone was accepted. When some students came out as trans or with a different sexual identity after COVID, they were immediately accepted. Emilia herself identifies as pansexual—she is attracted to people because of who they are, regardless of their sexual identity. She pondered what her life would be like if she switched her sexual identity, and she talked about it with her boyfriend. He is "so straight" and told her he is only attracted to women. At first, Emilia was upset with this idea. Why would he not be attracted to her if she identified as a different gender? Then Emilia realized that he had a different Cultural Pattern than she did. He was who he was, and she understood it was okay to be attracted to only one gender. Her empathy kept her heart open to him.

When Darius' teacher, Cristiano, and Emilia examined the Cultural Patterns of the people they cared about, they could see their whole truth. Understanding and being able to relate respectfully to people with other Cultural Patterns is essential to stronger Cultural Resilience.

Taking a Stand Against Harmful Cultural Patterns

Sometimes, Cultural Resilience involves reforming harmful Cultural Patterns.

Chuck—In eighth grade, we were selling our house in preparation for moving again. When a family called for an appointment to see our house, my dad excitedly invited them to come over (he was selling without a realtor). When the family drove into our driveway and got out of their car, my dad almost had a hemorrhage. They were Black people. My dad told me, "Chuck, go out and tell them someone else just made an offer, and the house has been sold." His bigotry made me sick to my stomach. I felt deeply ashamed speaking to this family while my father hid behind the living room curtains. I began to see bias all around me in a way I never had before. My eyes were opened to racism and discrimination. I resolved not to be like my father. Now that I see how Cultural Patterns are passed down, I can see where my father's white privilege came from and how he learned to fear "others." I can better understand people who judge or want to harm others.

Sometimes, we can see how others' Cultural Patterns harm us and others. Reforming these Cultural Patterns can be a powerful force for healing ourselves and improving our world. Luz wants to reform the Cultural Pattern of colorism in Latino culture. She sees how the color tones of children's skin are compared. Those who have fair skin and light eyes get more attention. With four siblings, she saw these preferences in her family of origin. When she was born, with lighter skin and hair with a slight wave, all the attention shifted from her sister to her. When she had children, she saw the same colorism. People would say, "Look how light your kids are. Their dad must be light." Those comments made her feel "less than," like there was something wrong with her skin. Luz is inspired by her mom's response, who modeled how to let the cruel comments go and gave Luz's sister positive attention to compensate for the rudeness of others.

Like Luz and Chuck, recognizing the Cultural Patterns around us helps us identify which stories and concepts give us strength and resilience and which limit us. We can name, acknowledge, and move away from Cultural Patterns that promote inequities and contribute to "othering" people who are different from us in our communities and world. We can choose to be anti-racist and anti-discriminatory.

Strengthening Cultural Resilience

When Liam was a young boy, the family next door to him only spoke Spanish. Though younger than those children, he played with them a lot. After his family moved to a new house, his dad continued to hire the oldest son, Bobby, to do yard work. Through this Spanish-speaking family, Liam's eyes were opened to a different culture, and he learned how to interact with people even when their shared language was limited.

When Liam became a teenager, his family hosted six foreign exchange students—from Japan, Spain, Germany, and Norway—over several years. From these students, Liam learned more about people with other Cultural Patterns. These two experiences fostered his Cultural Resilience. When he fell in love with a Colombian woman, that Cultural Resilience gave him the courage to marry her and move to Colombia to be with her family.

Arjun developed his Cultural Resilience in another way, as the one who "was different" than his peers. He grew up in a small midwestern town that had only one other Indian family. Arjun had to "whitewash" himself to fit in. His peers were racist and homophobic, and he felt uncomfortable. Those attitudes seemed normal, though they did not feel good.

"When I went to college, I unlearned my racism and homophobia very quickly," he explained. What was more surprising to him was his reaction to other Indian Americans. His university had a huge Indian American community, mostly from the large Indian communities in Texas, New Jersey, and the Bay Area. He would meet other Indian American students who had very similar life stories—same birth order, parents with the same profession, and who heard the same stories of perseverance growing up. Yet, they related to each other differently than he was used to. They were formed in this tight community with lots of communal pressure, so they focused on breaking out of that mold. They were more comfortable as Indian Americans but didn't know how to be "uniquely themselves." When Arjun tried to be "Indian" with them, it felt like he was putting on an act. He made some friends but didn't do group activities with them because the dynamic felt odd.

Arjun realized that his Cultural Patterns had given him Cultural Resilience. Though he did not feel entirely at home in either group, he had insight into both his white high-school peers and the Indian Americans at university. He had become comfortable enough with himself to be unique and do things differently. Though it can be a challenge growing up, "being different" can be our most incredible resource in developing Cultural Resilience.

The Power of Empathy and Compassion

Chuck—Sometimes, my Protective Patterns bring out the worst in me. I will have a knee-jerk negative reaction, being quick to judge and blame, rather than showing care and concern. *What? How can they say that? That #!** just cut me off at the exit!* Other times, I am just as likely to empathize and be filled with compassion. I recognize the person very likely has a history of being hurt from trauma, and their Protective and Cultural Patterns generate aggressiveness. They unconsciously throw all that hurt back at others.

What makes the difference? In me, it occurs as fear vs. understanding. If the situation brings up fear or vulnerability in me, I am quick to judge. If I am centered and have some perspective and understanding, I can think about how Cultural Patterns may have affected them. I can understand how someone feeling oppressed or vulnerable impulsively attacks others because I know my impulsivity works the same way. When I see the truth behind someone's behavior, my heart opens, and I find room for empathy and even love. It is the best way to build our Cultural Resilience.

The Value of Diversity

Born in New Mexico, with a Hispanic mother, Anna's father was a university linguistics professor who raised his family in Romania, Bulgaria, and the Soviet Union. Anna studied Russian culture, language, and literature in college, and through her study and experiences, she came to recognize a Cultural Pattern common in Eastern bloc countries with repressive governments: people tend to form very tight inner circles of belonging with those they trust, and they tend to be rude, abrupt, reluctant to share, and suspicious with people they don't know well.

Understanding this Cultural Pattern is helpful in her job as a County Commissioner in Oregon. She interacts with a broad range of people across the political and socioeconomic spectrum, from university professors and judges to blue-collar workers and those in minority populations of Chinese, Guatemalan, or Arabic. She recognizes that when people feel vulnerable, they often come off as brash or rude.

At county meetings, attendees display considerable bias around language and communication patterns. The professors and lawyers who attend often portray a Cultural Pattern of "I'm right, I know, I have accumulated wisdom and knowledge." Those from the agricultural and timber communities speak from their own experience. When her colleagues pay less attention to those who speak a lower level of English, she is sensitive to this Cultural Pattern. She looks for the competency and skills beneath a person's communication skills. Anna wants to hear the diverse voices of all her constituents.

Cultural Patterns that are political or related to disability, socioeconomics, gender identity, and age all show up in her work. "We've gotten better about addressing diversity in our health department," she explained. "But many of the underserved don't have citizenship, are not voters, or are not represented well. Fortunately, we have many bilingual and bicultural staff who reach out to those who need it."

Anna is part of a growing group of people who understand the value of diversity and are working to advance issues of equity and inclusion. The concept of Cultural Patterns can help us have the difficult conversations we need to have as we navigate our assumptions about each other. Strong Cultural Resilience helps us promote diversity, equity, and inclusion with more grace.

Building Bridges

Many of the conflicts in our world emanate from a struggle of Cultural Patterns. Strengthening our Cultural Resilience by recognizing how Cultural Patterns play out in others' lives helps us build bridges of understanding.

> "Working in San Francisco as a paramedic is like being in a war zone. I get so upset by how homeless people act when I'm trying to save their life. After learning about Cultural Patterns, I feel different now. Like they can only be who they are."
>
> ~ Nicolas Hansen, San Francisco Fire Department

Meri—I will admit it. Watching and reading about the January 6th Congressional hearings made me angry. As I have learned by practicing the *Centering Skill of Noticing Myself*, anger signals that one of my values was violated. So true! My fear for our country also brought out my Protective Pattern of Attacking, as I am sure my friends noted in a recent Facebook post.

When I paused and noticed my judgments, I appreciated the clash of Cultural Patterns fully displayed in these hearings. For many of us, clashing Cultural Patterns usually remains in the muted background of daily life because the people we spend time with have similar Cultural Patterns. While our colleagues or friends might have some significant differences in family or life experiences, the values they express overlap enough with ours that we feel comfortable.

The January 6th hearings, on the other hand, displayed a clash of Cultural Patterns in all its messiness. First, I was shocked and saddened at seeing Cultural Patterns that were so different from mine. But when I looked deeper, I also saw conflicting Cultural Patterns in the participants, by how they made decisions:

- Demonstrate loyalty to my leader
- Listen to my conscience
- Hold onto political power
- Uphold the Constitution
- Remain true to my "team"
- Treat others well
- Fight for what is important to me, taking up arms if necessary
- Refrain from violence

When I listened to the participants in the January 6th hearings, I was reminded that their ancestors, families, and communities have given them the lens through which they see the world. When I paused my judgment long enough, I could use the *Connecting Skill of Empathizing* to recognize that they might feel that they had very tough choices regarding the events of January 6th.

Understanding Cultural Patterns and thinking about how they influence my own and others' behavior doesn't mean throwing away my values and thinking that everything is okay. It does help me recognize the humanity in other people and see the importance of our maxim: "Everyone has impeccable reasons for being exactly who they are." It allows me to see THEIR truth so that I can build a better bridge between my world and theirs. These bridges are essential to Dovetail Learning's vision: Creating a World of Kind Connected Human Beings.

**Since our world includes all of us,
we need to learn to live with and learn from each other,
even those who seem very different from us.**

Mindsets and Skills

So often, harmful Cultural Patterns are passed on because of fear. It takes courage to move beyond that fear. It can feel unsafe or threatening to examine our Cultural Patterns. It can force us to explore very personal ideas and concepts intimately connected to our identity. We might feel sad or angry when we look at some of the stories and experiences that have contributed to our Cultural Patterns.

In the following chapters, *Resilient Mindsets* and *Resilience Skills* offer us a path to help us notice, acknowledge, and manage ourselves in the face of our Cultural Patterns, our Protective Patterns, and all that life throws at us.

Practice, Model, Coach

Practice

- Recognize when a difference in Cultural Patterns creates a conflict. Try opening up an authentic conversation by naming the conflicting Cultural Patterns without blaming or shaming.
- What is the impact on me and others?

Model

- Share when I notice my Cultural Patterns influence me.
- Let people around me know when I feel empathy and compassion for others' Cultural Patterns so others can learn from me.

Coach

- Share examples of how and when Cultural Patterns operate in the world.
- Recognize others' Cultural Patterns and help them see the impact on themselves and those around them.
- What transformative experiences can I share that will help bring about systemic shifts?

Self-Discovery

- When do my Cultural Patterns help me?
- When do my Cultural Patterns hurt me?

- What Cultural Patterns do I have that give me a better understanding of my Protective Patterns?

- What beliefs do I hold that color the lenses through which I look at life?

- Is there a current situation in my life where my Cultural Patterns influence what isn't working? If so, what might be different if I uncover how my Cultural Patterns impact me?

> **"Our ability to reach unity in diversity will be the beauty and the test of our civilization."**
> ~ Mahatma Gandhi

Resilient Mindsets

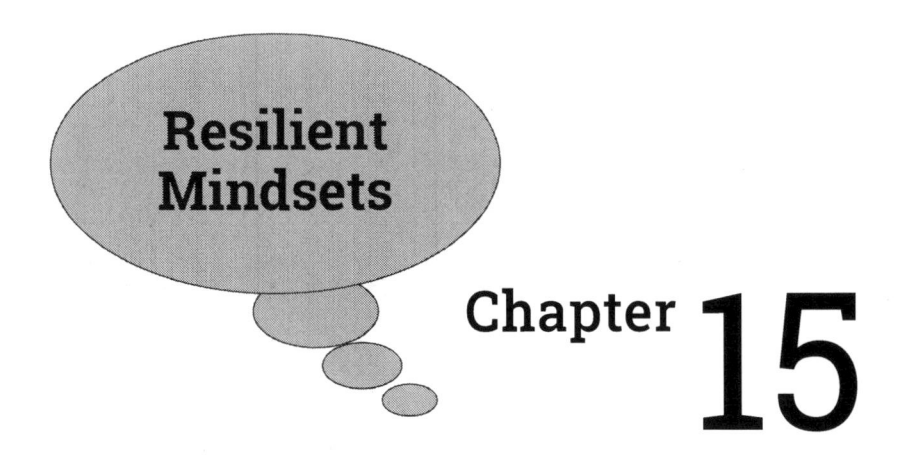

Chapter **15**

Resilient Mindsets
Opening Our Hearts & Minds

> "The greatest discovery ... is that human beings can alter their lives by altering their attitudes of mind."
> ~ William James, American psychologist

Last year, Noemi's best friend died suddenly. Noemi and Sabina had been best friends for most of their 28 years, even while Sabina battled addiction. Sabina had been clean for a while and talked regularly with Noemi. They were both hopeful about the future. Then Sabina experienced another trauma and to find relief, she bought a Xanax on the street. Unbeknownst to her, the Xanax was laced with fentanyl. She passed away in her sleep. When Noemi heard the news, she felt such a mix of sadness and fury. She wondered, "Why did this happen?" This significant life trauma devastated her.

In some ways, Noemi is more equipped to deal with this emotional devastation than many of us. She was first diagnosed with a mental illness early in elementary school, and now she has three different diagnoses. She has worked for two decades to gain Resilient Mindsets and Skills to address her mental health in real-life situations. All of us can use Noemi's tools: the Resilient Mindsets of Curiosity, Choice, and Courage.

Resilient Mindsets: What are They?

Resilient Mindsets are positive attitudes that help us approach life with a sense of possibility and confidence.

The mindsets of Curiosity, Choice, and Courage help us connect with what matters most. They are a frame of reference for how we think about ourselves and the situations we find ourselves in. Instead of being entrenched in unhelpful, habitual ways of thinking, we can use these Resilient Mindsets to create a life with more of what we want for ourselves and our world. They help us improve how we relate to ourselves and strengthen our relationships with others.

Using our Resilient Mindsets generates a "can do" attitude and energy.

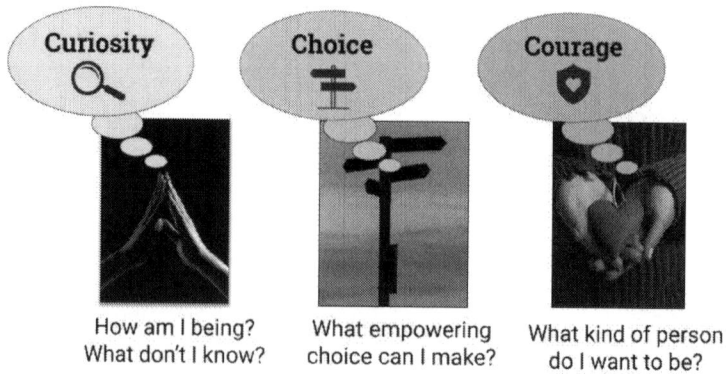

Resilient Mindsets

Curiosity	Choice	Courage
How am I being? What don't I know?	What empowering choice can I make?	What kind of person do I want to be?

How Resilient Mindsets Help

For Noemi, the Resilient Mindset of Curiosity transformed how she approaches life. Since she didn't want the "mental illness" label to dictate her decisions and her life, she spent a lot of time being Curious about herself to figure out more about her condition. As a child, she did art therapy to learn to express her feelings. That practice taught her to be self-reflective. To Noemi, it feels like her brain is divided into two—the part that wants to be like everyone else and the anxious part. The Resilient Mindset of Curiosity helps these parts communicate with each other in ways that work for her. Now, she can Notice and be Curious about her emotions and be self-compassionate rather than judgmental.

Because of her anxiety disorder, Noemi also practices the Resilient Mindsets of Choice and Courage. Since she hated the nickname her peers gave her—Worrywart—and wanted to be Courageous, she chose to do difficult things. As a child, her disorder made it difficult to go to school. By tapping into her Courage—she really wanted to go to school and be with friends—she could choose to go to school. In high school, she chose to go to Yosemite without her parents and do a solo six-mile hike to prove to herself that she could do it. Each time she used the Resilient Mindset of Choice to do something challenging, it built her confidence.

Noemi felt anxious going to restaurants because she didn't have control over the situation: she knew she couldn't leave at a moment's notice because paying the bill takes time. She overcame that challenge by continuing to listen to her Courage and making the Choice to go anyway. Now, Noemi sees restaurants as an opportunity to have fun with friends and explore new foods. When she learns of promising new chefs, she keeps a list of restaurants she wants to try.

By learning about her emotions at an early age, Noemi discovered she has a Choice in how she responds to each situation. She also understands how her response affects herself and others. When facing challenges like Sabina's death, she knows it would be easy to wallow in grief, sadness, and anxiety. Instead, Noemi uses the Resilient Mindset of Courage to think about the person she wants to be and what she needs to do to get there. While life has been challenging, and she sometimes falls into using her Protective Patterns, she often uses her *Centering Skills* instead. When she chooses to be happy, that energy flows into all aspects of her life. Her body works better and she thrives in her work.

As Noemi has learned, adopting a Resilient Mindset can transform us. When we shift from feeling stressed to feeling Curious about our emotions, we can quickly ease the burden of stress on our body—self-regulating helps us gain inner balance. Curiosity can transform reactivity into interest, which helps us engage with life and think more clearly.

Imagining Choices for ourselves opens up possibilities. When we realize we have options, we feel more in control of ourselves and the situations in our lives. When we recognize we have the power to choose and decide to shift our attitude or behavior, we are taking control of ourselves in a situation and how we respond to a challenge.

Being Courageous is about getting into alignment with our values. Listening to our hearts lets us feel, see, and hear what we care about most. From there, we can take action to be the kind of person we most want to be.

The mindsets of Curiosity, Choice, and Courage are foundational to the We Are Resilient approach because they guide us in noticing our Patterns and using our Skills. They help us become aware of our Protective and Cultural Patterns to understand how they impact us. This allows us to see and make new choices that are more meaningful. Each of the Mindsets is essential to effectively using our Centering, Connecting, and Collaborating Skills.

The Mindsets often work together. When we are Curious about a situation, we see Choices we might not have seen before. Then, we can use our Courage to make the best choice possible.

Influence of Cultural Patterns

We all have had influences that make it easier or harder for us to use our Resilient Mindsets. Noemi's parents are adventurous and curious about the world, but their generation did not focus on self-development. When she was growing up, they did not model introspection and a Curious Mindset about themselves. That made it harder for her to learn to be Curious about herself, but she was grateful they supported her by making therapy available.

Chuck and Meri—Our respective journeys have opened our eyes to how Resilient Mindsets can be transformative. We each were influenced by living in various countries, experiencing how different cultures shape people and their reactions to the world. It has given us a deeper understanding of how Cultural Patterns can influence how we use Resilient Mindsets.

Chuck—My alcoholic family kept secrets, so being Curious in my family was taboo. On the other hand, my seminal years growing up in the Philippines and Peru gave me a lifelong Curiosity about people and what it means to be a human being. I became fascinated by the world, which fed my Curiosity. My Cultural Patterns limited my view of Choice. My ancestral lineage, which was dominated by white male privilege and military service, determined what I felt were appropriate Choices. My opening to Courage came through martial arts, rock climbing, and a keen interest in spiritual development.

Meri—My family encouraged Curiosity about others, but my parents did not model introspection or Curiosity about oneself and one's reactions. For Choice, my parents encouraged me to "be anything I wanted to be." Equally as important, when I was in middle school, I saw my mother emerge from a deep depression after her divorce and create a new life for herself. These two Cultural Patterns gave me an extraordinary sense of autonomy and authority over my life, so I see a range of possibilities and understand that I can choose my life's path. My social justice-oriented upbringing gave me the Courage to see my life through the values of love and gratitude.

How to use Resilient Mindsets

At the most fundamental level, our Resilient Mindsets can motivate and guide us using the We Are Resilient™ approach.

First, we get **Curious** about becoming more resilient. What could that be like for us? How would it feel if we could bounce back from difficulties more easily? What if we could recognize and meet our deepest needs? Maybe we could engage in our relationships to reveal more of our authentic selves. Maybe we could have difficult conversations more easily when we needed them. Maybe we would feel connection and joy more often.

Next, we decide to improve ourselves. Great people, the kind of people we all admire, make this **Choice**. It is a decision to help ourselves, our families, and our communities.

Trying to change how we react to situations and others, even in small ways, is not easy. That is why it helps to practice **Courage**. It means we listen to our heart and act from that wisdom. Our hearts know what we need to do. When we align our Choices with our values and take action, we are on the path to a meaningful life.

Our Resilient Mindsets can also guide us in specific situations. While we can use each Mindset independently, we often use them together. As a recent college graduate, Adam used the three Resilient Mindsets of Curiosity, Choice, and Courage during a job interview. He was part of a large group interview in which the candidates were requested to bring an object and talk about it to the interviewers for one minute. All the candidates were lined up outside the room, waiting for their turn, and everyone was somber and intense. Adam knew connecting with others would help with his anxiety, so he used the Resilient Mindset of Curiosity to ask other people about their objects and stories. Using Curiosity, he shifted his energy from worry to connection and met some cool people.

Adam, a very private person, also used the Resilient Mindset of Courage and Choice by selecting an object connected to a deeply personal story. It was the first time he talked to strangers about his mental health. He made the Choice not to "frame" it as a nice story. Instead, he was as authentic as he could be and openly shared his experience as a real human being.

This experience was cathartic for Adam. He did not receive any feedback then, but the next day at the airport, he ran into one of the interviewers, who said Adam's story touched him. The Resilient Mindsets helped Adam navigate a difficult situation and probably contributed to his getting the position.

The next three chapters will examine each mindset in more detail, including how they work, how we can use them in daily life, and what practices we can use to strengthen them.

Resilient Mindsets

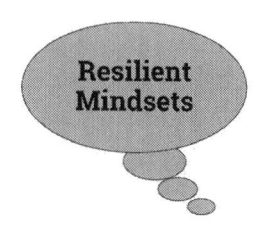

Chapter 16

Curiosity *Curiosity*

"Curiosity creates possibility."
~ Dr. Gina Johnson, pediatrician

Meri—I was often tense before meetings with one colleague in a previous job. The room felt like it was littered with hidden mines. What would I say that would set him off? The wrong words and woosh—here we go again! A rant or the same stories we had heard a million times before. It wasn't dangerous, but it felt like a waste of time. And yet, I had to work with him every day. He had power and control in the organization. It made it difficult for me to be in a meeting with him.

The Resilient Mindset of Curiosity helped me uncover a new way of thinking about these meetings. Instead of going in with an "I've seen this movie before" attitude, I began to think:

- "What might happen today?"
- "What if I have a different response? What can I try? Can I change the trajectory?"
- "What can I learn here?"

Moving into Curiosity wasn't easy. I had to stop my habitual judgmental thinking and tell myself, "I am curious." Just saying it helped me turn in a new direction. Putting on my Resilient Mindset of Curiosity helped me generate a "can-do" attitude and energy.

When we are judgmental, as I was in those meetings with my colleague, it can block our connection. Curiosity slows us down. It helps us not rush to assumptions and decisions before having enough information. Curiosity can open us up and deepen our understanding and connection with others.

Curiosity can also help us learn new information about others, which enhances our relationship with them and makes conversations more productive. As a professional development specialist in nursing, Stella trains nearly 200 nurses annually. She finds Curiosity essential to her work because it prevents her from reacting to trainees in ways that would shut down their learning. When she sees some of the choices made by nurse trainees, she immediately thinks, "OMG! Were you asleep on the job? What were you thinking?" Instead of voicing these beliefs, the Resilient Mindset of Curiosity helps her say, "Can you tell me about your thinking process?" It helps her identify whether the problem is a communication gap, knowledge gap, or both.

Stella used her Curiosity with a nurse who correctly documented that a patient was in respiratory distress but failed to provide the patient with a nebulizer. The nurse replied that the doctor stubbornly insisted that no nebulizer was necessary. Stella helped the nurse recognize first that, as a resident, the doctor was still learning. Also, in those situations, she should use her Curiosity to collaborate with the charge nurse to ensure the patient gets the best care.

Through the two decades she has practiced medicine, Dr. Samuelson has experienced the need for Curiosity with many patients. It is particularly true for patients who come in for minor complaints or repeatedly show up for issues that seem to be resolving, like nonexistent rashes or runny noses. Early in her career, she would get frustrated that people with "minor" problems were taking time and resources away from those with more significant medical concerns. Over time, she realized that often those people had something else going on. She needed to use her Curiosity to investigate if there was a root issue with which the patient and family needed help. She remembers a mom who kept bringing her one-year-old to the office for nonexistent problems. After several visits, Dr. Samuelson asked the mom, "Is there anything else you want to tell me?" Her Curiosity opened the door for her to learn that this mom was in an abusive relationship with the baby's father. He had threatened to take the mom's immigration papers away and told her she would be deported and lose her children forever. By using Curiosity, Dr. Samuelson learned she was the only safe person this mom could turn to for help.

Curiosity: What is it?

Curiosity is an inquisitive desire to want to understand something better. It is an impulse to know more.

Curiosity is noticing something of interest (like we feel anxious or someone's behavior impacts us or others). It opens us to learning. There is so much we don't know, and wondering about it helps us discover what's really going on.

When we are curious, we come with interest and openness. We intentionally pause our judgments because predetermined opinions block our ability to learn. Then, we notice a feeling, behavior, or situation. We wonder what we might learn that we didn't know. We wonder—what the heck is happening here (in me, another person, or in any situation)? It's about asking questions of ourselves and others, so we have more information about what is happening.

The Resilient Mindset of Curiosity is powerful because it can pause our Protective Patterns and help us see beyond our Cultural Patterns. It can break down our barriers with others because we learn important information about them—their thoughts, beliefs, and feelings.

We can use the Resilient Mindset of Curiosity to go inward to ask ourselves questions about our feelings and behavior or to focus outward and think about or inquire about others' feelings or behaviors.

Being Curious About Myself

How am I being?

Chuck—This morning, Sandy asked me a simple question, "Are you taking two water bottles on our camping trip?" Unfortunately, my Defending Protective Pattern kicked in. My first reaction was, "I'm not taking your nice new one!" (with an attitude). Immediately, I caught myself. I was acting like a jerk. Too often, I tend to think she is accusing me of something, and I try to prove that I'm either right or, at a more fundamental level, that I'm simply okay. Most of the time, she is asking for information. I immediately apologized, got Curious, and thought, "What's going on with me?" I realized my stress was catching up to me.

The two of us were about to go on a big trip—a 17-day river adventure down the Grand Canyon through the biggest rapids in North America. I had a ton on my mind as we prepared and packed. "Do I have the right gear, river clothing, etc.?" I'd had underlying stress for weeks about completing my work before I left while preparing for the trip. When I defend myself with Sandy, it's always because I feel bad about myself. In this case, I felt bad that I hadn't met a writing deadline and didn't want to leave Meri in the lurch. My stress came out with Sandy. Curiosity helped me recognize my Protective Pattern and make a different choice.

Using Curiosity can help us reduce our anxiety. In rural California, Zelma uses Curiosity when she wakes in the middle of the night with absolute terror, fearful that she has done something bad and that she is unsafe. That fear is a remnant from her childhood when her mother would lash out at her, and Zelma spent all her energy trying to keep herself and her little brothers safe. Now, when she wakes, Zelma uses the *Centering Skill of Breathing Mindfully* to calm herself and then moves into Curiosity. "Why am I scared?" she thinks, "Am I safe now? Will I be hurt?" As she recognizes that she is safe and won't be hurt, she can let go of her Protective Pattern. Curiosity helps her realize that her body's tension is from worry—not fear—and that she can worry tomorrow. Being Curious about her feelings allows her to process and release them and calms her nervous system down. She can then go back to sleep.

After Halima took the We Are Resilient training, she intentionally used Curiosity with herself and those around her. She was surprised at how it impacted her day. "Curiosity allowed me to stay calm," she explained, "I could avoid or anticipate problems and disagreements. My internal heart rate was lower."

Imani, inspired by her favorite superhero, agreed. "Curiosity helped me to listen to my family and colleagues better. I was able to watch my reactions."

Sometimes, we learn the most about ourselves when we fail to use Curiosity. Many years ago, Dr. Samuelson worked with a 13-year-old girl with anemia. Her treatment was not succeeding, so she kept coming back. Finally, the girl's mom spoke up and said that her daughter hadn't had her period in a while and perhaps was pregnant. Dr. Samuelson was shocked and embarrassed that she missed that possibility. Her Cultural Pattern made her assume the girl was too young, and she hadn't been curious enough to get past that. She asked herself, "How did I miss this?" The answer became apparent as she became Curious about herself and what was going on for her. Being overworked and tired narrowed her thinking, so she focused on the most common solution rather than being curious about other possible causes.

Like Chuck, Zelma, Halima, Imani, and Dr. Samuelson, Curiosity can help us learn more about ourselves. We can be curious about our own feelings and behavior. We can ask ourselves:

- How am I being?
- What do I notice about myself?
- I wonder why I...

- How do I really feel? What might be causing me to feel this way?
- Why did I react that way? Is this helping me?

Being Curious about ourselves is the heart of the We Are Resilient approach. By being Curious about ourselves, we begin practicing the *Centering Skill of Noticing Myself* (see Chapter 20). We can notice how we feel, if we need something to eat, sleep, or a good hug. When we get Curious about something that is bothering us, we can consider whether to use our *Centering Skill of Letting Go* (see Chapter 22) or if we want to take action. When we get curious about our reactions, we might notice our Protective Patterns (see Chapter 4) and discern whether they are helping or not helping. Curiosity also allows us to see the influence of our Cultural Patterns (see Chapter 12) and whether they might be creating a mind gap that is getting in our way.

Being Curious About Others

What don't I know? What might I learn about this?

Edwin, the CEO of the company Hugh worked for, sent Hugh a text in all CAPS. Since Hugh's Cultural Pattern was to save CAPS for high-stakes situations, Hugh's emotional system accelerated into the red zone, and his Protective Pattern of Attacking kicked in. He thought, "What's this guy doing? He can't talk to me that way." Hugh was about to react in kind. Then his Curiosity Mindset kicked into gear, and he thought, "Something must be up." He immediately phoned Edwin to inquire and caught Edwin on a plane just before take-off. Hugh's boss had been running between gates and had no idea his phone was stuck in all caps. Hugh's Curiosity prevented him from lashing out.

Curiosity helps us step outside of ourselves. Like Hugh, we can disrupt a spiral of negative assumptions when we ask why or how something is happening. Genuine Curiosity can make all the difference.

Nurse trainer Stella used Curiosity to prevent a conflict with her adult son, Reuben. While discussing a related topic, Reuben mentioned that his daughter Yashvi would never see the inside of a church. Stella could feel her Protective Patterns arising. She wanted to say, "You can't do that to her! Your daughter needs spirituality." Instead, Stella moved into Curiosity. She asked Reuben about what he wanted for Yashvi. Reuben shared that he wants Yashvi to be connected to a higher power/God, and he feels that connection in nature and with other people. He explained that his beef was specifically with the church because he sees it as hypocritical. His explanation helped Stella, as she realized Reuben did want to give Yashvi a sense of spirituality, just one different from church teachings. By being Curious, Stella changed her relationship with Reuben, which too often had become confrontational in their past. Now, she knows using Curiosity can give her a sense of connection and peace instead.

As a team leader for her company, Cora knows the tremendous value of the Resilient Mindset of Curiosity. One of Cora's values is "we are all in it together," so if a team member she supervises hurts another, Cora gets triggered. At one point, team member Gayle used strong, demeaning language in her email to another team member. Cora was livid, and her Attacking Protective Pattern emerged. She felt Gayle was intentionally undermining the team. Her immediate thought was, "I'm gonna pull her in here and tell her exactly what I think."

In the next moment, she remembered the Resilient Mindset of Curiosity. She asked Gayle to come in to talk, but instead of criticizing her, she asked questions with an open mind. Gayle explained that she wasn't trying to hurt her colleague but focused on creating customer success for the high-value client. Gayle's Cultural Pattern meant the client's needs came first. Because the stakes were so high with this client, Gayle felt she should write a strong direct email to her colleague. By using the Mindset of Curiosity in her coaching, Cora got to the core issue without alienating Gayle. They had a good conversation, and Gayle recognized that she could talk directly with her colleague next time rather than sending that type of email.

Meri—Steve and I were catching up with an old friend, Jolene, when a tender place emerged in the conversation. Many years ago, Jolene had a falling out with another mutual friend, and we wanted to facilitate a reconciliation. Steve asked a probing question, and Jolene jumped into a Defending Protective Pattern. "Why do you always bring this up? I try to avoid it, but you insist on talking about it."

We were surprised at the depth of Jolene's reaction. I moved into Curiosity. "Can you tell us more about your perspective?" My truly Curious question opened the door for conversation. She explained the depth of her sadness and frustration at the rupture with our mutual friend. Ultimately, our Cultural Patterns meant we still had separate viewpoints, but we held them with empathy for each other.

As it did for Hugh and Cora, Curiosity can interrupt our Protective Patterns and make room to learn about other people's emotions, reactions, and behaviors. As it did for Meri, being curious about others deepens our relationships. We become open to learning about who someone really is, what their Cultural Patterns might be, and what's happened to them that makes them the way they are. Curiosity starts with asking ourselves, **"What might I learn about this?"**

It can lead us to helpful questions to ask others:

- I am curious about...
- How did you feel when...?
- May I ask a clarifying question?

Even when we are in a situation where we can't actually ask someone else about their behavior, being Curious can help us be more compassionate. Giovanni found himself in that position when a colleague lost their temper in a meeting. Though they didn't say anything personally harmful, the situation escalated to Human Resources, which called a meeting to debrief the team. While some of Giovanni's other colleagues were quick to judge the angry team member, Giovanni recognized that this person was otherwise professional and just had a bad moment. Giovanni moved into Curiosity—what could have been happening to them that caused them to lose it? He recognized that sometimes the hazards of life are overwhelming, and he didn't want to write his colleague off because of one instance when their Protective Pattern of Attacking emerged.

Even though he didn't learn the underlying reasons why the person lost their temper, Curiosity led him to have empathy and compassion.

Influence of Cultural Patterns

> "'Curiosity killed the cat' was a cautionary cultural expression meant to... [suggest] it is best to mind one's own business. All civilizations built, at some point, walls around certain types of knowledge."
>
> ~ Mario Livio, PhD, *Psychology Today*

Curiosity has often been discouraged by those in authority as a way of maintaining that authority. The less others knew, the more submissive they would remain. Nafuna's community shut down anyone asking questions, suggesting that people who asked questions were stupid. She learned to keep her questions to herself.

Giovanni's dad never seemed Curious, as if his constant, proclaimed judgments would make him be seen as authoritative and wise. Giovanni, a thirty-something man, thinks his dad's behavior helped him see the costs of being judgmental. Giovanni is grateful he grew up in a diverse area with many people who taught him the value of Curiosity. His Cultural Patterns about Curiosity came from all these different people—his teachers, doctors, friends, and those he was dating. Since they had varied beliefs, he recognized that he could learn a lot about the world and others if he was Curious and asked questions. He also realized he didn't have to see eye to eye with people to like them.

Giovanni also sees how many of his peers seem to be judgmental for sport. They throw people under the bus almost like entertainment. "Maybe it is easier to be down on someone. Maybe it is fun to gossip." But Giovanni has experienced the other side and knows how hurtful people's judgments can be. He has not always been perfect himself, and he is grateful to those who were Curious about what was going on for him and gave him the benefit of the doubt.

Chuck—Growing up in my family, there was a Cultural Pattern that some knowledge was off-limits. It wasn't okay to talk about my dad's drinking or to inquire about his work. It wasn't until high school that I found out that he was in the clandestine services of the CIA. During the Bay of Pigs crisis, we were living in Miami, Florida. One night, I woke up and heard him drive away from the house with a screech of tires from his Ford Mustang. The next morning, I asked my mom what was going on with Dad, and she said, in her perky voice, "Oh, he had to go on a quick business trip." He was gone for two weeks, and nobody talked about it.

As most children are, I was curious about everything, but I learned to keep my Curiosity to myself. I wanted to know so many things—about my dad, why he and his brother didn't speak, and why my granddad had left my grandmother. My family's message was, "Don't ask." I still now sometimes hold back from asking certain personal questions.

Meri—When I was growing up, Curiosity about ideas, other people, and the world was rewarded. My siblings and I were encouraged to read, learn, and try to make sense of the world. My parents shared a lot about their lives at the dinner table, and we could ask questions. Most stories about other people had a backstory to learn the context that might be shaping their behavior. We had endless discussions and debates at home as we tried out our ideas, and even questioning my parents was okay if we did it with logic. My teachers also rewarded Curiosity if I was respectful and on topic.

Challenges With Curiosity

If Curiosity is taboo as a Cultural Pattern, it can be challenging to cultivate. For some people, being Curious is outside their comfort zone. "I know what I know" is how Rhoda remembers her mother talking about it, implying that anything she didn't already know was not worth knowing.

Being Curious can make us feel vulnerable. Like it did for Giovanni's dad, our assumptions and judgments can make us feel powerful, like we know more than others. Being Curious would force us to admit that we may not understand something, and we may feel we are demonstrating less knowledge than we wish to project.

Being Curious can make us feel like we are prying. Florita's brother and sister complain if someone asks too many questions that are not "their business." For all of us, if the spirit of the questioning is too aggressive, and it seems like the person is just digging to get information for their own purpose or to gossip, it can feel invasive. We need to respect healthy boundaries. The Resilient Mindset of Curiosity is about learning something to support others, know ourselves better, or strengthen our relationships.

Sometimes, we say, "I'm really curious to know…." and then proceed to ask a leading question or assert something that is a judgment—our view of a situation disguised as a curious question. Pausing and ensuring that we are in an open frame of mind, with wondering, can prevent this.

How to use This Mindset

> "I have a certain curiosity for life that drives me and propels me forward."
> ~ Rachel McAdams, actress

As humans, when we don't have information, we create stories in our heads, stories that may or may not be accurate from all perspectives. We also become trapped in mental models—beliefs, attitudes, assumptions—about "the way things are" or "the way they should be." As discussed in Chapter 12, we call these **Cultural Patterns**, and they can block our individual and organizational growth. The Mindset of Curiosity, on the other hand, opens our minds and helps us consider many perspectives. We pause, notice our feelings and judgments, and wonder what might be going on.

Resilient Mindset: Curiosity

1. **Pausing**
   ⇩
2. **Noticing**
   ⇩
3. **Wondering**

What am I curious about?

Pausing

To use Curiosity, we first have to **pause our judgments**. We start the process by stopping our mental chatter that has already made up its mind about something:

- Meri had decided her colleague was annoying
- Dr. Samuelson had decided that her patients with minor complaints were wasting her time
- Stella had decided that her nurse trainee was incompetent
- Chuck had decided that Sandy was blaming him
- Hugh had decided that his CEO Edwin was upset with him
- Cora had decided that her team member Gayle was attacking her colleague
- Steve had decided that forcing Jolene to dig into a situation would change her mind

Curiosity helps us pause our judgments so we can challenge our assumptions. It allows us to be open to a different story. Curiosity can prevent us from acting impulsively. Not every action deserves a reaction.

It can also help us stop trying to solve problems for others—we can be present to them, and their story—like Meri and Steve were for Jolene.

Only when we realize our preconceived judgment might be wrong and stop that mental path, can we move to the following two steps of Curiosity: **Noticing** and **Wondering**.

Noticing

Meri noticed she brought lots of negative mental energy into meetings with her colleague that hurt their work together. Dr. Samuelson noticed patients making appointments for minor ailments that didn't need treatment. Stella noticed her nurse trainee did not follow through with the recommended treatment. Cora noticed her team member Gayle wrote a harsh email. Meri noticed Jolene had deep feelings about the rupture with the mutual friend.

Curiosity helps us Notice. We notice things with genuine interest—without being attached to them a certain way. We pay attention to how things might be different from our preconceived ideas. When we notice and observe without judgment, we are open to learning something we didn't know.

When Brenda's husband Damon suggested they throw a Super Bowl party on the day they were arriving home after a long trip, noticing helped her feel her resistance. She paid attention to her feelings and realized she wouldn't have the energy to host a party.

Wondering

After Damon suggested they host the party, Brenda used her Resilient Mindset of Curiosity to stop her Protective Pattern of Attacking. She wondered what Damon had in mind for the party. She asked him, "Tell me what that Super Bowl Party looks like to you." When he said, "Have two couples over and ask everyone to bring snacks," it was totally different from what she had imagined. She had conjured up, "I'll have to prepare a lot of food and decorate for a house full of people." Brenda realized Damon's suggestion was okay and could be fun.

Wondering can free us from our preconceived ideas and open our hearts. As we engage our Curiosity and wonder, we can look at an idea, situation, or new skill the same way we might look at a new flower—full of awe and not knowing how it will unfold. When we wonder about a feeling or another person with that kind of Curiosity, it can make a world of difference.

What might come next…what is now possible?

When we are in true wonder, we can shift from our heads to our hearts. We are curious about what will emerge in our learning and knowing. We can ask questions in the most helpful way. This is what Albert Einstein did all the time. He "discovered" what was possible without constraining the outcome. Part of this wondering is embracing uncertainty. We embrace that we don't know everything and that there is always more to learn. Curiosity thrives when we are willing to be uncertain and explore.

Meri, Dr. Samuelson, Stella, Giovanni, Cora, and Brenda all wondered what new information might come up if they asked the right open-ended questions with genuine Curiosity. Rather than assuming they knew beforehand, Curiosity helped take their relationships in a new direction. Wondering can break through our Cultural Patterns and open up unforeseen possibilities.

Strategies for When we Have Trouble Being Curious

- Our judgments of others or a situation can block genuine Curiosity. If we notice we are rushing to judgment, we can be empathetic with ourselves for wanting to protect ourselves from vulnerability. This can create some space from our judgmental mind, which is often in the way of Curiosity.

- Sometimes, we simply don't know how to express our genuine Curiosity. We might think being Curious will be viewed as nosy. Our tendency to move to judgment can be helped with a ready phrase:

   "Tell me more about that." Or, it can be as playful as, "Wow, I've never thought about it that way. What made you think that?" Or, "Paint me a picture of what happened/what you want."

- Our Cultural Patterns may mean we are uncomfortable being inquisitive with genuine wonder. We can ask someone first if they are okay with us wanting to know. Asking permission can break the ice and unite us in our shared curiosity.

Deeper Insights

Meri—In elementary school, I was a little shy and more curious about books than my classmates. I didn't fit in very well with my peers, so I spent recess and lunchtime devouring books. I fit in better with my peers in my larger junior high school. As I felt safer socially, I discovered that the wide world opened to me through books could also be opened to me through people if I was brave enough to ask them questions. I learned how curiosity about others can lead to deep connections, and I created lasting friendships. My close friends and I spent a lot of time curious about and wondering about other people (mostly boys!) and their feelings and behavior. I learned that curiosity about others could create community and a rich and rewarding life.

In high school, college, and graduate school, the Resilient Mindset of Curiosity helped me thrive. I used it to learn through books and projects and to understand the world and the people around me. I had been raised to think Curiosity is a good thing, and it rewarded me with a world rich with learning and friendships. However, I was not taught to be Curious about myself, my emotions, and my feelings. While somewhat self-reflective, I didn't understand how powerful being Curious about myself could be. I remember, as a young mother, going to a workshop and learning that my emotions could set the tone for the household. I had never thought about self-regulation, let alone be Curious to try it. When I realized that MY feelings and behavior would significantly impact my children and my ability to parent them, I became more motivated to learn how to regulate my emotions.

Noticing Myself is still a *Centering Skill* that requires intention for me. While I can quickly intuit what might be happening for someone else that causes them to feel and behave in a certain way, it is more challenging to turn my Curiosity lens on myself. When I am off, or when one of my Protective Patterns has emerged, I must intentionally focus on being Curious about myself. I am working on moving beyond labeling my emotions as "Sad, Mad, or Happy" and being more granular in thinking about them.

I am still very curious about other people, and I love learning about their lives, what is important to them, and how they feel. My children used to be embarrassed when they brought friends home because I would ask their friends so many questions. Only later, after high school, did they realize that their friends loved the attention and that I clearly cared about them and was genuinely Curious about their lives.

Practices to Strengthen Curiosity

Curiosity is practiced by asking these kinds of questions:

To yourself:

- What's going on in me that I'm acting this way?
- What am I feeling?
- Is my current response helpful? What might I do differently?
- What don't I know about this? Do I understand this correctly?
- What story am I telling myself, and what other story might be more helpful?
- What might help me broaden my perspective and access my compassion?

To others:

- I am curious about...
- Tell me more about that.
- Can I ask a clarifying question?
- What were you feeling when...?
- What was it like for you...?
- What is important to you about this?
- Is there anything more about this you would like to share?

> **How am I being? What don't I know?**

Resilient Mindsets

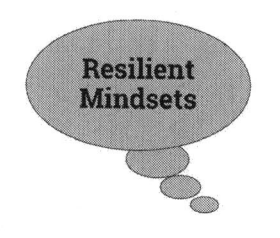

Chapter 17

Choice

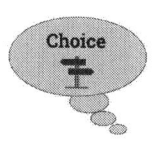

**"Life is a matter of choices,
and every choice you make makes you."**

~ John C. Maxwell, author

Meri—"I am sorry. I am calling to tell you that your MRI is being canceled," said the nurse. I was walking with a friend, having squeezed in the walk before leaving for the hospital. I almost didn't pick up, but I thought it might be my husband who would be driving me to the appointment. As she spoke, I could feel myself moving into the split-second "pause" that we can create between a stressor and its impact on us. *It was the third time they canceled my MRI within the last month. I could be very frustrated at the constant rescheduling. But was this such a bad thing?*

"There is an emergency, and we need to handle it," the nurse continued. There it was—she handed it to me on a silver platter. I knew my best response. "Well, I am glad they are using the resources for an emergency," I said. "If I had an emergency, I would be glad to know they would change the schedule for me."

"Me, too," said the nurse, pleasantly surprised that I hadn't berated her about the repeated, last-minute rescheduling. "As for rescheduling…"

"I won't be rescheduling," I interrupted her. "I am going to wait to see if my problem comes again. You have given me the gift of time and money," I said.

"Well, that might be a wise decision," she said. "As long as you are sure." She seemed quite taken aback by my cheerfulness. After we finished the call, my friend added, "I bet she rarely gets that reaction when she has to cancel appointments. I'm sure it was a breath of fresh air for her."

That is why I decided to make that choice. I could see the situation wasn't going to change. Someone at the hospital had already changed the schedule. But by choosing my response to be upbeat and kind, I made her day and mine a little better.

Eve had a more difficult choice to make. Five years earlier, her husband Jack had unsuccessful back surgery, and the resulting nerve damage in his spine gave him weakness and neuropathy in his left foot. Then, a year ago, Jack was diagnosed with metastasized, stage 4 prostate cancer. Jack's physical condition was even more challenging because it forced him to face a massive identity shift. He had been a runner for over forty years, and now he couldn't walk without his walker.

Eve was his primary caregiver, but she also wanted to relate to him as his wife and friend. Since she felt Jack's safety depended on her, any issues where he might be unsafe tended to trigger her. Eve worked hard on using her Resilient Mindsets and Skills as much as possible to avoid reacting from her Protective Patterns of Hypervigilance or Hyper-Caretaking and letting her Protective Patterns dominate their relationship.

Every night, Jack ran the bathwater for Eve because arthritis makes it difficult for her. One evening, his elbow knocked the faucet, and he turned the water on full force without realizing it. He then went into his man cave to watch TV. First, the bathroom flooded, and then water moved into the bedroom, soaking the rug.

When Eve discovered the flooding, she became so angry she couldn't talk. She used the Resilient Mindset of Choice to see her options and decided to leave Jack alone while she silently cleaned up the mess by herself. She couldn't trust what she would say to Jack, so giving herself space and not interacting with him then was the best choice for her.

As a theater costume designer, Brenda uses the Resilient Mindset of Choice to deal with stress. For one show, she needed some advice. Brenda tried to talk with the director, but she didn't respond to her texts or calls. Her colleague's lack of response compounded Brenda's stress, and she started to feel rejected. Rather than let her Protective Patterns emerge, Brenda made a different Choice. She used the *Centering Skill of Breathing Mindfully* and then moved into the *Connecting Skill of Empathizing*. She thought, "There is probably something going on with the director that I don't know about." So she sent a Curious text: "How are you doing?" The director immediately called and shared some personal problems that had nothing to do with the show. Brenda was grateful that she chose to move into Curiosity rather than remain hurt and angry.

Since her dad passed away last year, community college professor Kendra has felt a heavy burden trying to help her mom. Though she has three siblings, she feels like she's the one to ensure her mom is okay because she's living closest. Kendra knows her mom is lonely and overwhelmed by finances and the difficult situation. Kendra loves her mom and wants the best for her, but she knows she can only handle so much. When the phone rings and Kendra sees it is her mom, she feels her stress rising and a heaviness in her chest. She worries she can't deal with her mom. One way of caring for herself is using the Resilient Mindset of Choice. Sometimes, she lets her mom leave a message, and other times, she chooses to deal with what her mom needs at that moment.

Choice: What is it?

Choice is seeing possibilities and deciding which is best.

In much of our lives, we follow a routine and do what we have always done automatically. We would get stuck if we had to stop and think about every potential decision. Yet, understanding that we do have Choice in many situations, especially in our response to others, can make all the difference. Meri, Eve, Brenda, and Kendra understood they could choose their response. Meri could have become cranky with the nurse. Eve could have chided Jack for his poor decision-making, which forced her to clean up water for two hours, aggravating her bad back and arthritis and exhausting her. Brenda could have been angry and hurt at the director's silence. Kendra understood that sometimes not answering her mom's call would preserve her energy for when it was truly needed.

Improving our resilience requires us to make these kinds of choices—decisions that will improve our wellbeing, strengthen our relationships, or enhance group resilience. It means that we understand we have many choices we can make—that our response to life is not beyond our control. When we know that we have the power and ability to make decisions that matter, we can be intentional in our choices.

Choice is seeing that we have possibilities, assessing those options, and then deciding which is best. It is about being flexible and adaptable and making different choices—pivoting—when we get new information. Choice is fundamental to our resilience because we can make decisions that impact us—and the trajectory of our lives—every day. Meri chose to be kind to the nurse as well as not reschedule her MRI. Eve chose the *Centering Skill of Breathing Mindfully* and gave herself space to calm down while she cleaned up her husband's mistake. Brenda chose to be Curious about a colleague's silence rather than hurt by it. Kendra chose not to answer her mom's call when she wasn't ready to take it.

Each evaluated what would work best for them and chose accordingly. Meri and Brenda chose a *Centering Skill*, while Eve and Kendra chose the Protective Pattern of Avoiding. We practice the Resilient Mindset of Choice when we notice our Protective Patterns, assess whether they are helpful, and consider our options. The Resilient Mindset of Choice is an extraordinary superpower.

As Meri, Eve, Brenda, and Kendra recognized, our power to choose a response changes how a stressor impacts us. The event itself is less important than our response to it.

Influence of Cultural Patterns

Our Cultural Patterns can make it difficult to see our power of Choice. Sometimes, we get stuck thinking, "This is how life is," or "I am sorry I reacted that way, but that is the person I am." Knowing we have the agency and autonomy to select between two or more options is not always clear, yet it is fundamental to our ability to use the Mindset. To make a Choice, we must believe in our personal agency, that we can shape our own lives with our Choices, and feel empowered enough to make those decisions.

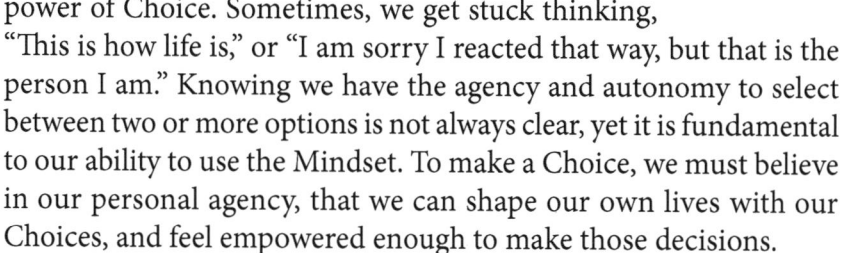

Music lover Adam had always been an over-achieving person, but that developed into an eating disorder during college to cope with stress. Adam was used to being active and having many things on his schedule, but that tipped into unhealthy behaviors tied to his self-worth. He thought, "I must always be very busy and productive." He felt he had no Choice and was obligated to do everything on his list, especially going to the gym or exercising. His Protective Pattern of Avoiding helped him ignore his feelings.

With help from therapy, Adam is slowly understanding that he actually has a Choice and that most of his ideas about living are self-imposed rules that he can let go of. They are Cultural Patterns that he can choose to modify. Once Adam recognized that he has autonomy in his life, he shifted into using the *Centering Skill of Letting Go* of his negative internal "should" voice. Now, he is trying to live into the idea that he doesn't actually "have" to do anything. Of course, Adam has obligations, but as a single twenty-something with no children, he doesn't have many. He now feels more comfortable not doing so much and allowing himself to "be."

Meri—My husband, Steve, a white male from a privileged background, was raised to believe he had all the choices in the world: if he worked hard at something, he could achieve it. This ability to see most of life under his control has benefited our relationship. When something's off, or we are not communicating well, Steve puts extra effort into communicating with me. He knows he has a choice in how he talks to me and that those choices impact me. He tends to our relationship and is caring, compassionate, and careful. When he makes a mistake, he is quick to apologize.

However, he also experiences the downside of this Cultural Pattern. By believing his choices control his world, when he gets outside his comfort zone, he beats himself up for making choices that put him in challenging situations. He has trouble living with ambiguity and "not knowing." When he is in unpredictable situations, he feels his life would be secure if he made different choices. He feels entirely responsible for his life, and thus situations outside his control make him feel like he's done something wrong.

Irish American Maeve, on the other hand, was part of a very large family with an alcoholic mother and a largely absent dad. She experienced lots of trauma growing up and was raised to believe that little of life was under her control. When she was in an abusive relationship and reduced to lying on her couch in a fetal position, it took her months to escape and move into the home of a welcoming friend. Even when her situation was destroying her, she had difficulty making choices to improve it.

Maeve is using the Resilient Mindset of Courage to work on healing herself. Her courage helped her seek out therapy, a 12-step program, and several personal growth courses. She became financially self-sufficient and purchased a home. Still, career and relationship setbacks throw her for a loop, and her trauma-influenced default perspective is to see "what life will bring" rather than focus on how her current choices can shape her future.

Giovanni was strongly shielded when he was young. He developed Cultural Patterns with such a fixed perspective on Choice that that he had difficulty as a young adult. His parents and friends gave him clear paths, which was helpful then, but now he realizes that too much was figured out for him. Giovanni didn't have practice making his own Choices for his life.

Challenges With Choice

Thinking about Choice can be triggering for some people because there are so many things about life in which we have little or no choice:

- We had no choice in the family or circumstances in which we were born or how we were raised.

- Our choices may be limited by our economic reality, educational opportunities, physical places, and other family obligations.

- Our choices are often a result of privilege—i.e., the more privilege we have, the more choices we have for our economic reality, educational opportunities, physical place, and other family obligations. Inequity inherently means those with less privilege have fewer choices and less control in many situations.

For all these reasons and more, we don't always have a choice in the situation we find ourselves in. Understanding where and how we can choose and act is fundamental. We always have a choice in how we respond.

Secondly, there are situations in which we might feel like we don't have Choice, but we actually do. In these situations, the Resilient Mindset of Curiosity can help us see possibilities for our own agency. Irish American Maeve had been divorced for ten years, and most of that time she has talked about wanting to be in a serious relationship with someone new. She created an online dating profile for a while and went on several dates but gave it up as too difficult. She continued to talk about what she wanted, but she didn't make many choices to increase her chances of meeting the right person. She acted like the right person would come into her life if it was "meant to be" rather than actively pursuing it. The Resilient Mindset of Curiosity might help her understand what might be happening in herself that blocks her from pursuing a relationship, as well as give her new perspectives about how she could pursue a relationship in a more life-giving way.

Choice is sometimes presented as shorthand for "make the right choice," with an expected positive outcome. We can get stuck when we make what we consider the wrong choice. When Giovanni made his first career decision out of college, he accepted a job in a profession that turned out to be unsatisfying. Though he then applied to different types of jobs, he didn't get any offers, and every rejection compounded his feeling of being permanently stuck. His first choice forced him into such a debilitating spiral that he let his job determine his confidence and his happiness. He beat himself up for making that one decision and felt that everything wrong in his life was because he had messed up.

"I spent so much time beating myself up and feeling sorry for myself," Giovanni recalls. "The stressors of not letting go of this choice left me with much less positive space in my head, and it hurt me and those closest to me." Giovanni was so demoralized by one bad choice that he felt unqualified to make good choices moving forward.

However, the Resilient Mindset of Choice is actually about making the best choice with the information we have at the time. Once Giovanni understood and believed that, he gave himself compassion and let his self-judgment about the lousy choice go. He used the Resilient Mindset of Curiosity to pause his negative self-judgment and instead wondered about a different future. Giovanni saw new possibilities for himself. He put his energy into learning new skills, practicing interviewing, networking, career fairs, and talking to people in the role he was interviewing for. Those choices helped him land a job that he is now enjoying.

Finally, not consciously making a choice is deciding by default. College student Levi learned that lesson the hard way. His university selected him for the honors program, so he needed to choose an advisor. Levi talked to several professors that spring, who said his ideas sounded interesting. However, during the summer, he let time slip away while he focused on his internship and time with friends. When fall arrived, Levi tried to recover his options, but his potential advisors were booked, and he couldn't get into the program. He realized that his Protective Pattern of Avoiding had arisen because he wasn't sure he wanted to do the honors program. By not making a conscious choice, he had walked the middle ground until the choice was made for him.

Choosing Resilience Skills

Using a *Centering Skill* can be one of our most powerful choices. When we make this choice, we modify our emotional reactive pattern and "flatten our emotional curve." We return to our Center more quickly and with less energy depletion.

Brenda chooses *Centering Skills* when she needs them. As a theater costume designer, she has some work flexibility. She has learned she needs to exercise regularly even when she has a lot of sewing to do. Though she might want to continue working on a project, Brenda knows that when she gives up her exercise, she isn't as productive and is often in a terrible mood by the end of the day. By choosing the *Centering Skill of Nurturing Myself* every day for her exercise, she maintains her positive spirit.

Runner Audrey kept waking up in the middle of the night, worried about a potential lawsuit threatened against her adult son and his wife. She knew her son was frustrated with his wife for some actions that triggered the lawsuit. Audrey understood how easy it was to make mistakes with significant consequences, so she empathized with both of them. With all her heart, she wanted to swoop in to fix it. She made the Choice to use the *Centering Skill of Breathing Mindfully*. She realized that her impulse to try to fix things for her kids was not helpful for them. She reminded herself, "None of us grow unless we struggle." That helped her Choose the *Centering Skill of Letting Go*.

We can also choose a *Connecting Skill* to strengthen our relationship with another person. *Connecting Skills* help us improve our Relational Resilience. We can choose a *Collaborating Skill* for similar reasons—we want our group to achieve its purpose in the most effective and generative way, and we want to maintain good relationships with others in the group. This is a decision to improve our Group Resilience.

We also have a choice in how we perceive the world—the internal "story" we have about ourselves, our situations, other people, and life in general. When Noemi went away to college, she was grocery shopping, and she had an encounter that changed her life. A fellow shopper asked Noemi to model for a celebrity runway show. Noemi's first inclination was to turn the offer down flat. As someone with mental health challenges, the Choice to be up in front of all those people felt alien. The recruiter's vision for her didn't match the story Noemi had told herself about who she could be. She thought about it a moment more. What if it *could* be her? She used the Resilient Mindset of Courage to say yes. Making that Choice was not easy—but it led to a three-year career in modeling, built her confidence, and opened new doors for her.

> **"It is our choices, Harry, that show what we truly are, far more than our abilities."**
>
> ~ J.K. Rowling, *Harry Potter and the Chamber of Secrets*

Celeste used the Resilient Mindset of Choice to create better boundaries with family. Celeste has many roles in her family: daughter, sister to six siblings, niece, cousin, goddaughter, and godmother. Her Cultural Patterns taught her to be responsible for others and adopt the Protective Pattern of Hyper-Caretaking. While she enjoyed being this person everyone depended on, she realized she was not "watering her own plant." She felt she had no room to use the *Centering Skills of Noticing* or *Nurturing*. She didn't see any other choice but to be bound by her self-imposed obligations.

Her Resilient Mindsets helped her recognize that she needed to set boundaries in her relationships. She used Curiosity to examine her Cultural Pattern which said she must do all these things for others. Now, when situations arise with her family, she uses Curiosity before jumping to solve everything. How can she honor others' capabilities? Will this nurture her? She won't stop Hyper-Caretaking completely, but now she recognizes that she has a Choice in how she interacts with her family.

How to use This Mindset

Our beliefs and attitudes impact how we perceive everything. While it can feel like we have to react in a familiar way to a particular situation, that "pre-programmed reaction" is a product of our Cultural and Protective Patterns. We can choose to change our response.

First, we need to understand that we have choices and control over many aspects of our lives, particularly how we respond to challenging situations. This gives us agency—the ability to decide and to act.

We then have to see possibilities and assess the impact of our options. Finally, we can decide on a specific action, intent, or thought pattern and act to fulfill it.

Resilient Mindset: Choice

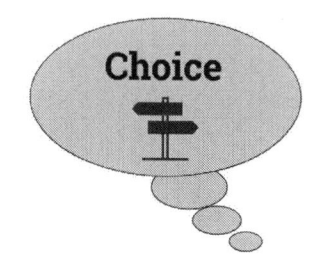

1. **Seeing Possibilities**

   ⇩

2. **Assessing**

   ⇩

3. **Deciding**

What empowering choice can I make?

Seeing Possibilities

A few months ago, an internal recruiter reached out to mystery-novel lover Meredith with an opportunity to take on a new role. At first, this new possibility was very exciting. Being chosen for this new role stoked her ego. Meredith appreciated dreaming of a new future for herself.

For Meredith, like the rest of us, the first step in using the Mindset of Choice is recognizing we have possibilities. We don't have to do what we have always done. We can choose a new way. The Resilient Mindset of Curiosity can help us see these possibilities, and then we can choose to pivot if that helps us.

When a stressor occurs, there is a "space in-between" in which we can choose our attitude and response. When we take advantage of that space, we can see the possibilities open to us. We may need to pause to be in the space to choose. (See Figure 8)

"Between stimulus and response, there is a space.
In that space is our power to choose our response.
In our response lies our growth and our freedom."

~ Attributed to Thomas Walton Galloway (1917)

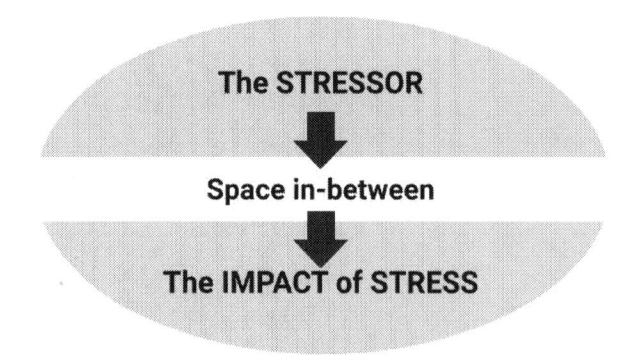

```
The STRESSOR
    ⬇
Space in-between
    ⬇
The IMPACT of STRESS
```

Figure 8

Music lover Adam had to see that the duties he felt were crushing him were stories he told himself, and he could replace them with a new narrative. Irish American Maeve had to see another way of living that didn't include abuse from her ex-husband. Giovanni had to see that while his first job may have limited his possibilities, he still had many others.

Assessing

When faced with a Choice, we start processing and evaluating in new ways. Looking beyond the familiar shows us new opportunities that we need to assess. A conscious decision demands we think about what determines our decision. It is helpful to be mindful—to Pause and Notice.

Why would we make one choice versus another? We assess possibilities based on our values, needs, desires, or another set of criteria. Sometimes, it is a question of safety—do we feel safe enough (emotionally, physically, socially) to try something new? Are we willing to be vulnerable? Sometimes, it is a question of practice—have we practiced a *Centering Skill* enough to use it when we want to?

We make choices either by default, or we choose to live by our values, meaning, and purpose. The Resilient Mindset of Courage can help us pay attention to our inner voice and ensure our choices help us. In any situation, it can be useful to think: **What empowering choice can I make?**

Meredith knew she could choose to follow her new job opportunity or stay with her current one. She evaluated the pros and cons of the new role. She knew her current job was just an okay fit for her. Earlier in her career, she had positions she felt were the best job in the world, but that wasn't true now. On the other hand, she appreciated that her current leadership was fantastic. Meredith assessed her choices. "At this point in my life, do I want to take on something new? Higher stress? What would the work/life balance be in this new role? Where do I want to focus my energy?"

Meredith realized that being recruited for a position didn't mean it suited her. She knew it would take six months to get up to speed, but she wanted to retire by then. She was looking forward to spending time with her husband, family, and friends, doing photography, traveling, and creating workshops.

Deciding

After we assess our options, we are at a crossroads. We must decide on a specific intent, thought pattern (internal story), or action to help us. Sometimes, as we gain new information, the best choice keeps shifting, and we might need to pivot again to make better choices.

Ultimately, Meredith decided that her most empowering choice was to pass on the new job. Making this Choice was a powerful moment for Meredith because she used the Resilient Mindset of Courage and claimed what was essential to her. She had some guilt because she didn't like to let someone down, and she wouldn't have turned it down in the past. Previously, she had craved these types of jobs—highly visible and focused on strategic opportunities. She realized she was a different person now, who was in the process of creating a new life for herself, running workshops on topics she loved.

Chuck—I had a trusted relationship with my former next-door neighbors, but they moved. Now, we are in the delicate process of creating a relationship with new neighbors. My wife and I appreciate the beauty around our home, and it was comforting to see our new neighbors care for their property by fixing things up and improving their landscaping. However, soon after moving in, they placed a messy pile of firewood on a fence that abuts our front driveway, which we could see right out our kitchen window.

I was faced with a Choice. I was tempted to choose my Protective Pattern of Avoiding until I eventually got used to the woodpile, but I knew that Choice would upset me because I really care about the aesthetics around our home. Another choice would be to use my *Connecting Skill of Speaking Authentically* and tell them how we felt through a kind, caring conversation. Using the Resilient Mindset of Courage, I chose to talk to my neighbor. My Choice helped establish a new friendship.

Chuck's situation is common. A situation triggers us, and one or more of our Protective Patterns might arise. Will we let our Protective Pattern determine our reaction? Though we will eventually calm down and return to center, it may deplete us or harm our relationships. Often, it is better to choose a Resilience Skill to find the best way through.

Strategies for When we Have Trouble With Choice

- Using the Resilient Mindset of Choice can be difficult. This is normal. We have used our Protective Patterns for many years, and our Cultural Patterns can limit our vision of our possible choices. Self-compassion and self-forgiveness help as we move from our usual reactions to something different. Identifying the Protective and Cultural Patterns affecting our decision-making helps to free us.

- Making a choice when uncertain about the impact is one of the most challenging aspects of choice. It is easy to be afraid of making the wrong choice. We may have gotten burned in the past by choices or critical messages from family or friends. It takes Courage to make choices when we don't have all the necessary information to understand their impact fully, yet it's common for most important choices. Being thoughtful by writing down the pros and cons can be helpful. It is also beneficial to remember we will have more choices ahead that we can't see yet.

- Sometimes, making choices that align with our values and preferences is difficult because we feel pressure from others. It takes Courage to make choices that go against the opinions of those we care about. The Resilient Mindset of Courage helps us listen to what our hearts are telling us.

- Pausing in the moment to choose a response can feel awkward and vulnerable. Taking the time we need to see possibilities, assess them, and make decisions is also a choice. It might sound like, "I need a few minutes here. I want to respond, but I need some time first."

- Learning how to Choose may take practice over time. Even with practice, we are not going to make the best choice for ourselves all the time. That is part of being human.

Deeper Insights

> "Everything can be taken from a man but one thing;
> the last of the human freedoms—to choose one's attitude in
> any given set of circumstances, to choose one's own way."
>
> ~ Viktor Frankl, *Man's Search for Meaning* (1946)

As an Austrian psychiatrist imprisoned for three years in the concentration camps of World War II, Viktor Frankl has a depth of understanding about the power of choice few of us know. Though most of his family was killed, and he survived the most horrendous trauma, he discovered that personal freedom in how we respond is always available within us. He also learned that hope helps us believe in possibilities. When we have hope, it strengthens our ability to have Choices.

Meri—I remember the day the Berlin Wall came down so clearly. I studied International Relations at university in the early 1980s, and the fact that the world was divided between the Soviet bloc and the American bloc (with a few countries trying to create a third bloc) was a foundational premise of my courses. That was how it was, and our efforts should be to improve our world within that fixed set of parameters.

Until it wasn't fixed anymore. Brave people pushed the system until the Berlin Wall came down, and suddenly, all the boundaries that had been so fixed became fluid. At that moment, I realized that we could dream beyond the limits that others had set for us. Everything is impossible until it isn't.

That hope still fuels me today. Viktor Frankl revealed the power of hope to open up choices in our lives. More significantly, hope and choice reinforce each other in a virtuous cycle. Sometimes, I am overwhelmed by the challenges and despair in the world. I get difficult images swirling in my head: All the children who go to bed hungry, frightened, or abused. The politicians and corporate titans who manipulate us for their own benefit and profit. Natural disasters accelerated by climate change that claim thousands of lives and millions of homes.

My best way through this morass is to choose hope. I choose to believe that we can make a difference. My hope is fueled by the millions of people who are working on these challenges. There is no certainty that we will solve or even make them better, but there is no certainty that we won't. My optimism is a choice, a choice that feels better than pessimism, and a choice that fuels my efforts to be a force for good. It fueled my drive to create the We Are Resilient approach with my colleagues during the pandemic, even when finances were precarious. I could have been wrong, but I chose to believe in hope.

Practices to Strengthen Choice

Every time we make a choice, we are choosing to be the kind of person we want to be (i.e., kind vs judgmental, thoughtful vs reactive, or caring vs rude).

Choice often requires Courage. By listening to our hearts and getting clear on our highest values, we can choose to do difficult things that are important to us.

- Use Curiosity to ask what possibilities we have. Are there options we may not have considered? What might we do differently?

- Create a continuum of the full spectrum of all the possibilities in a situation, from doing the least (nothing) to the most drastic action. This often opens up our perspective.

- Journal to uncover our honest feelings and values.

- Use Relational Resilience to talk with a trusted friend about possible options.

- Look deeply at our Cultural Patterns to decide which help us and which don't. Do we have more options than we have been telling ourselves?

- Be Curious about our Protective Patterns. Can we choose different responses when our Protective Patterns are not working for us?

> **What empowering choice can I make?**

Resilient Mindsets

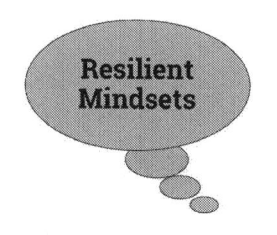

Chapter 18

Courage

Courage

> "Let yourself be silently drawn by the strange pull of love.
> It will not lead you astray."
>
> ~ Rumi, 13th-century Persian poet

Chuck—As I meditated one morning, I felt I was "off." I noticed I was sad but also grateful. A dear friend has an alcohol addiction, and he compulsively uses alcohol to cope, which is sad. I also feel grateful because he is an amazing person—a lifelong friend, caring nurse, intuitive healer, and generous, warm-hearted person. I enjoy being with him.

I have used alcohol from time to time throughout my life, and drinking definitely numbs my emotions. Even that first sip can shift me from tense to relaxed. My friend also clearly drinks to numb himself. He has had a lifetime of pain—physical, emotional, and spiritual—as well as loss. His dad died of cancer, he is twice divorced, he has a problematic relationship with his kids, and is addicted to oxycodone due to years of pain management. Despite all of that, he is a positive, good-natured person.

I love my friend deeply. I empathize with and understand him, care deeply about him, and have compassion for him (and his family). When I saw him recently, I wanted to have an honest conversation about his addiction. I was afraid he would get mad, push me away, and it would hurt our relationship. But the Resilient Mindset of Courage brought me the emotional strength to follow my heart, even when I knew it might be difficult. My fear melted away when I opened myself to my love for him, and I was free to be open, kind, and authentic with him. Courage helped me choose the *Connecting Skill of Speaking Authentically*, so what I imagined would be difficult became a conversation of caring and healing. He heard my concerns without being defensive, and we are closer because of my sharing.

Courage is something I rely on every day when my Protective Patterns emerge. It helps me lean into my heart-centered values: honesty, trust, respect, forgiveness, and acceptance. As a black belt in Aikido, the peaceful martial art, I am taught over and over how extending love toward my opponent is the only way to true power. When someone attacks me on the mat, I have to connect to love in myself and equanimity toward my partner. Then, I can receive their attack and remain balanced, centered, and connected with my partner.

Walter, a retired bank manager, used the Resilient Mindset of Courage to evaluate a long relationship. Throughout his career, Walter worked closely with Anton in several Latin American, Asian, and European countries. They spent great years with each other's family, and Walter chose Anton to be the best man at his second wedding. He came to think of Anton as his best friend. But others often asked him, "How can you get along with that guy? He's a total jerk." At first, Walter blew off their comments, but he recognized the truth over time. Anton was using Walter to get what he wanted. After Anton made it big with a successful investment opportunity, he started snubbing Walter. Walter was incredibly hurt. "I had to use my Courage to stop my self-deception about this relationship. When I listened to my inner voice, I knew I had to end it." For Walter, terminating this relationship with Anton felt as bad as divorce.

Courage: What is it?

Courage is the emotional strength to do something difficult when it matters.

Courage comes from the Latin "cor," meaning heart, so when we use Courage, we follow our hearts. Brave is about being bold, and people are brave for various reasons. Sometimes, it is for an adrenaline rush, like when they dive or bungee jump off of a high place, or they drive or ski fast. On the other hand, the Courage Mindset is doing something difficult for a purpose. It requires knowing our values and being guided by them. Chuck used Courage to talk with his friend because he cared about him. Walter used Courage to end his old friendship because he realized that person had different values.

For 16-year-old Jacinda, the Resilient Mindset of Courage opened up new possibilities while helping her let go of what was holding her back. In a happy coincidence, Jacinda learned about the power of the Mindset of Courage when she auditioned for the part of Cowardly Lion in *The Wizard of Oz*. She had performed with this children's theater company for seven years but never had a leading role. The same children seemed to get the leads every show, so Jacinda felt it was a long shot. Since she really wanted this role, she asked for advice from a mentor. The mentor told her not to hold back and even to embarrass herself during the audition. Jacinda summoned courage and let go of all her worries during the audition. She went outside her comfort zone, sang a ridiculous acapella song, and felt she made a fool of herself. Being freely herself worked, and she won the role. When Jacinda got the news, she cried with joy, and her self-confidence soared. Courage can help us be the person we most want to be.

Sometimes, we need the Resilient Mindset of Courage to support our loved ones. Donna's husband Chester needed jaw surgery to repair it from damage caused by cancer treatment. The surgery and its recovery were enormous challenges for both of them. They expected help from home health care and nurses and didn't realize the help was about training Donna so she could care for Chester. Wound care for his jaw was complicated as they had transplanted the tibia from his leg to replace the mandible in his face. Donna felt the wound care was way beyond her skill set, but she had to use her Resilient Mindset of Courage and do it because Chester needed her. Several times a day, she had to suit and glove up, put a headlamp on, and use forceps. If things didn't look right, she sent photos to the doctor for advice. She was emotionally exhausted, but she did it anyway.

As Chester recovered, things became even more challenging, because Chester became the "expert" and wanted to direct every step of every activity. Every day of the three-month recovery felt long. Donna used the *Centering Skills of Breathing Mindfully* and *Positive Reframing* to gain perspective. But even using the *Centering Skills of Noticing Myself* and acknowledging her anger about the situation didn't eliminate all her frustration and anxiety. She needed Courage to forge ahead and do what her heart knew was right.

Influence of Cultural Patterns

Our Cultural Patterns inform and influence our values. For some, our Cultural Patterns make it easier to tap into our Courage.

Meri—Growing up, my Cultural Patterns taught me to use Courage to lean into my values and help others. At our Catholic church, our priest preached about social justice. More importantly, he modeled it by marching with Cesar Chavez on behalf of farmworkers, spilling his blood on the Trident missiles to protest the war-industrial complex, and supporting refugees in our community. My mother actively campaigned for candidates and helped organize school bond measures and other initiatives for a better community. A beloved biology teacher, Mr. Fisher, organized us students to volunteer for the environment. These influences taught me how to use my values to ground my decisions.

Martha also grew up in a family and community that used their Courage to support those in need. Martha's church met in a motel that housed many military vets and others who were subsistence living.

Many church members, like Donald, were trying to get their lives together. As a single father, Donald cared for his young daughter, Kelly, solo because Kelly's mother had a substance use disorder and other unhealthy behaviors. When Donald had a relapse, Kelly had no one to care for her. Kelly's situation was not unique. When no community member stepped up, children were sent to other placements, which made them very vulnerable. These fears prevented parents from taking essential steps like entering rehab to improve their lives.

While the church community tried to sort it out, Martha realized that if she became officially certified as a foster parent, she could care for children while their parents got their lives back together. In the end, Kelly's stepmom was located, and she cared for Kelly. While Kelly's story turned out well, Martha knew it was a signal for her. Even though her plate felt full, as a pediatrician in a low-resource area and running marathons in her spare time, Martha used her Courage to become certified as a foster parent. Using the Resilient Mindset of Courage helped her align with her values and be available to families who needed her.

But when we decide the values of our family or community don't work for us, we need the Resilient Mindset of Courage to face and change them. Nurse Stella was raised in a strict Catholic family who taught her not to question authority. Her Cultural Patterns, from her parents, teachers, and other adults, told her to have blind trust and faith. Stella used her Courage to move past this Cultural Pattern and chose Curiosity instead. She quietly questioned what she was told and chose to explore her spiritual self independently. When she found a faith community that fit her—Unitarian Universalist—she used her Courage and the *Connecting Skill of Speaking Authentically* to talk with her parents. They reacted as she expected, which was that Stella was going to hell and she needed mental help. Stella knew her Courage had helped her come through that storm stronger. Her mom now lives with her and has dementia, and often tells Stella, "You are going to Hell!" While Stella can ignore the words, she hates that her mom's belief that Stella's soul is in eternal jeopardy causes her such pain.

As a 16-year-old gay Latina, Jacinda uses the Resilient Mindset of Courage to try to remain grounded in her identity without letting others define her. In her experience, Latino culture is rife with homophobia, and the "perfect Mexican family" has no room for homosexuals. After she sang a beautiful solo at a wedding, some extended family put her on a pedestal as if she were a child prodigy or an angel. A judgmental aunt and a homophobic uncle would smash that image if they learned she was gay, and they would influence others in the family. She knows her grandma and one aunt support her, but it is challenging to be at family events. When celebrating her Quinceanera with her extended family, she was terrified her secret would emerge. She tries to understand her family through the perspective of Cultural Patterns, but she feels pain from the homophobia in her family.

Challenges With Courage

> **"Courage is not the absence of fear, but rather the assessment that something else is more important than fear."**
> ~ Franklin D. Roosevelt

Courage does NOT mean we are not afraid. Instead, it is taking a step even though we are scared. Since our Protective Patterns often surface when we are vulnerable, choosing to act differently can take a lot of courage. Using our Resilient Mindset of Courage can be especially difficult if we have low self-confidence, are afraid of failure, lack support from friends and family, or have had traumatic experiences. Thirty-something Giovanni had trouble using Courage to make new career choices because his confidence was damaged when his first job was unsatisfying. He had to build up his confidence before leaning into Courage and trying a new job search.

For Alice, she needed to overcome a fear of failure to make a career pivot. Alice's skills as a human resources officer led her to the top of the ladder as Chief People Officer in a successful information technology company. She helped build the company from 100 to 1,100 people over five years but gradually became increasingly disengaged and unsatisfied. When the company was getting ready to go public, and thus a lot of money was at stake for her, Alice realized she didn't want to help it grow bigger. Alice is an introvert who craves intimacy. "The problem was I didn't know what I wanted to do instead. It scared the crap out of me."

Alice overcame her fears through coaching and personal work, including walking in the woods and listening to Led Zeppelin. Her Resilient Mindset of Courage strengthened until one day, "A beam came through me, and I knew what I wanted." She wanted to become an executive coach for women in human resources. Using her Courage, she asked her company to fund a new position for her as an executive coach. That way, she could launch her new career while mentoring her replacement within the company. Listening to her heart gave Alice the Courage to leap.

It was difficult for 16-year-old Jacinda to use the Resilient Mindset of Courage because it meant cutting herself off from girls she had viewed as her support. Though Jacinda had put a lot of time into these friendships—hanging out with the girls, helping them with homework and through relationship breakups, and inviting them to great parties—at one point, she realized that the girls were not there for her when she needed them. One of the girls took a mistake that Jacinda had made four years earlier and used it to launch a cyberbullying campaign. For three weeks, the girls sent threats to Jacinda, posted mean things online, and even texted lies to her mom. Jacinda was terrified to go to school because she knew they had connections that could hurt her. She was afraid of getting jumped when she walked alone on campus. Her English teacher suggested a restraining order, but Jacinda declined because she feared it might escalate the problem. Jacinda used her Resilient Mindset of Courage to walk alone until she could find new friends. Eventually, the other girls moved on, and she did too. She is proud of herself for moving on from a toxic friend group and creating new friendships.

Practicing the Resilient Mindset of Courage often means facing our fears, as Giovanni and Alice did with their job changes and Jacinda did with her former friends. We must step outside our comfort zone to become the people we want to be.

How to use This Mindset

Using the Resilient Mindset of Courage means feeling our emotions fully, listening to our bodies' wisdom, and taking actions that align with our values.

Resilient Mindset: Courage

1. **Feeling**
   ⇩
2. **Listening-In**
   ⇩
3. **Taking Action**

What kind of person do I want to be?

Feeling

Using the Resilient Mindset of Courage starts with feeling our emotions fully. When we *Notice Ourselves*, the sensations in our body, and what we feel emotionally, we can learn from our body's wisdom. What are my emotions trying to communicate to me? Am I upset or anxious about something? Am I excited about something? Am I afraid to say or do something?

Carla's children attended an inner-city, under-resourced school. As much as she wanted to support the community by having her children in the neighborhood school, the staff's high turnover and constant funding struggles concerned her. Carla's unease increased when her teacher-coach job at another district school was eliminated, and the principal at her children's school suggested she apply there. The potential job change forced her to deal with her anxiety about the school. "I woke up one night, and my gut was wrenched, and I felt so confused. Can my kids thrive in this school? Should I take this position or not?" As she wrestled with her feelings of discomfort and unease, she recognized her fear was part of other big life decisions. Acknowledging these familiar feelings helped her draw on her Courage to pursue the job opportunity with an open heart. A conversation with the principal led to a job offer, and she chose to take the job. She believed that by being a part of the school, she could help propel its growth to support her kids and all the students to learn and thrive.

Meri—The first year I was dating my now-husband Steve was pretty tumultuous. I spent a lot of time arguing with him. My Protective Pattern of Attacking quickly rose because I had used it growing up and in a previous relationship. I thought I needed to Attack to keep myself emotionally safe and preserve my boundaries. Fortunately for me, Steve never took my bait and rarely got defensive when I attacked him. He stayed calm and reasonable throughout our discussions. One day, I realized I felt safe and relaxed with him. Steve would be there for me, and I didn't need to use my Protective Pattern with him. By paying attention to my feelings, I could use the Resilient Mindsets of Courage and Choice and create a different type of relationship with him.

Listening-In

> **"The heart has reasons that reason does not understand."**
> ~ Jacques-Bénigne Bossuet, 17th-century theologian

Listening to our hearts helps us discover what our bodies are telling us. When we listen to our hearts and pay attention to what our feelings are communicating, we let our inner wisdom guide us. We can hear our inner truth, understand our strongest values, and align with our authentic selves. Great people, the kind of people we all admire, have learned to cultivate their inner wisdom. Listening to the heart helps us, our families, and our community.

Listening to our hearts can be called intuition, which is different from rational thinking in the head. Intuition comes from experience and inner knowledge, not the logic of what our thinking brain might conclude.

Chuck—As a 15-year-old, I took a course at the North Carolina Outward Bound School, and the program captured my imagination and changed my life. I learned I could be much more than my Cultural Patterns had told me.

Because wilderness adventure made me feel so alive and I loved helping people, I wanted a career as an adventure education professional. In my early twenties, I became an Outward Bound Instructor and then a Course Director. In my early thirties, after I earned my Master's in counseling, a permanent staff position opened up at North Carolina Outward Bound School as Director of Mental Health. It seemed perfect. I was enthralled about following my life's plan as I went through the interviews. However, during the final round of interviews, I realized something was off. My head had put a lot of energy into getting this job and concluded it was the right career move, but my heart knew something was wrong. I listened deeply to my heart. To manage mental health instruction in the field, I would have to be away from my family for ten days or more at a time. I had two daughters in elementary school, and putting my family first was essential. Though I had wanted this dream job for years, my heart knew it was wrong for me. I used my Courage to trust that I would have other choices and withdrew as a candidate.

My heart again led the way in my career when I lost a job in my fifties in the 2008 downturn. It was a complete shock. I was directing a new cross-addiction recovery program when, one day, I got a call that the stock-market crash had wiped out our start-up funding. The paychecks for my 20 staff would bounce, and I had to find new recovery program beds for our 12 long-term clients. Every staff member followed their heart and worked for two weeks knowing they had no pay coming. Once I managed the crisis, I faced the fact that I had recently moved across the country for a job I had just lost and needed an income. I went into a deeply meditative period, including long silent meditations, and felt a deep inner peace. Then, equally unexpectedly, I was offered a founding director position at Dovetail Learning. Though no money was available to pay me, my Resilient Mindset of Courage was strong. My heart knew to take the job even though it made no rational sense. I have been overjoyed to work at Dovetail for the past 15 years.

Meri—I built my "failure muscle" when I lived in Beijing for a year. Since I didn't speak the language, I spent much time doing things poorly and being okay with that. The best example was my yoga class. Not only did I not understand the instructions, but I was 20 years older than the other students. I was the worst student in the class and could not keep up with what was happening. Still, I showed up twice a week. I spent a lot of time listening to myself and my inner wisdom. I realized I was doing it for me, and what anyone else thought didn't matter. Learning to embrace failure and continue to do it anyway was good practice for using the Resilient Mindset of Courage.

Sometimes, we feel our head is saying one thing, and our heart and gut—our intuition—are telling us something different, as they did for Chuck and Meri. Courage is trusting our intuition and not letting the rational mind overpower it. By being willing to live outside of our comfort zone, our hearts can guide us based on deep inner values, and through that, we build confidence in our ability to handle difficult situations.

Taking Action

Once we pay attention to our feelings and listen to our inner wisdom, we can create the life we want. Courage helps us to make the changes to be the person we most want to be. That may mean leaning into creating a new life for ourselves, having hard conversations, or working toward healing. It might be telling a friend that they have hurt us or speaking up for others in ways that can be uncomfortable. When we show up authentically, for ourselves or others, we align with the truth in our hearts.

Noemi needed to use the Resilient Mindset of Courage to choose the type of person she wanted to be. After living with her partner for four years and adopting a dog together, her partner initiated a breakup.

Noemi knew she could choose her response to this devastation. On the one hand, she could let her emotions run amok and deal with her pain by using a Protective Pattern to be malicious or slander her former boyfriend. Noemi knew she could wallow in sadness, eat ice cream, and only talk about relationships. Some friends suggested she reach out to her former partner to fix it. Courage helped Noemi see that none of these choices were right for her. Instead, she used the Resilient Mindset of Courage to envision a new life. Her Courage helped her choose the *Centering Skill of Letting Go* of her old dreams and former partner. Courage enabled her to see new possibilities—a new career, travel, new friends, and new cities—and take action to make them real.

Any time we take action against discrimination, racism, or any wrong, we use our Resilient Mindset of Courage to stand up for our beliefs. When Paxton was 11 years old, he led his Boy Scout patrol. At one meeting, one of the other boys started making remarks disparaging gays. Paxton took the boy aside and told him he was inappropriate and hurtful and not to use that language again. Paxton's Resilient Mindset of Courage allowed him to speak up even when his peers might judge him for it.

Meri—Two decades ago, I worked for a small organization with a very hierarchical management structure. The man in charge made all the critical decisions and did not like to be challenged, especially in a public setting. Because many of my colleagues needed their salaries and lacked transferable skills, they felt vulnerable to his bullying. My salary was pitifully low, which I was not happy about, but I knew the low salary gave me a certain amount of freedom. I could "afford to be fired" because it would not significantly impact my family. At one particular meeting, the boss gave an older colleague a dressing down. As I could feel my ire build, suddenly I said, "Stop it! You need to listen to each other." Everyone was shocked that I had intervened, but it stopped the bullying. Listening to my values, I knew I had a responsibility to speak up.

Sometimes, our most courageous actions look like "non-actions," like when Chuck used his Courage to NOT take his dream job with Outward Bound. Using our Resilient Mindset of Courage might mean using our Protective Pattern of Avoiding, at least for a while, like when Chuck Avoided a frantic job search after the 2008 market crash. We might not make that phone call or not send that email that we have carefully crafted because we know it is the wrong choice. Our "non-action" might include waiting to see how things develop or how people change before deciding to intervene. Sometimes, it is walking away from situations or people, like Noemi did with her boyfriend.

Last year, when Eve's husband was diagnosed with stage 4 prostate cancer that had metastasized, she used the Resilient Mindset of Courage to see this new stage of their relationship as an opportunity for personal growth. Though she wants to protect her husband's health, her highest priority is assuring his dignity—though precisely what that looks like changes many times in a day as his needs and her energy wax and wane. Then, while they were dealing with his health crisis, the costs of their condo jumped significantly, and their income and assets couldn't keep pace. They made the difficult decision to sell the condo and move to a mobile home. Eve is using her Courage Mindset to lean into surrender. She is using the *Centering Skill of Letting Go* for many aspects of her former life and is looking for possibilities in her new reality. Leaning into surrender is a courageous "non-action."

Strategies for When we Have Trouble Using Courage

Sometimes, we have difficulty using Courage because we are afraid to fail. For many of us, our Cultural Patterns tell us we must be "successful," and our fear of failure blocks our ability to listen to our wisdom within. When we step into life and simply notice the feedback (i.e., whether a job works for us), we can keep learning, be guided by our values, and make new decisions.

> **"There is no failure. Only feedback."**
> ~ Bandler and Grinder, founders of Neurolinguistic Programming

- If we have a history of trauma, it can be triggering to try to listen to our body and our needs. If we try to use our Courage and get stuck in negative reactive patterns, we may need help. Trusted friends can support us in using our Courage and following our hearts. We might need a mental health professional to help us for a time as we learn to become comfortable listening to ourselves.

- We may need practice if we don't spend much time listening to our heart's inner wisdom. Practicing Courage means setting aside time and space to contemplate what is in our hearts. Quieting the thoughts in our heads and feeling what is in our hearts is an enormous gift to ourselves. A meditation practice can help.

Deeper Insights

> **"It is only with the heart that one can see rightly; what is essential is invisible to the eye."**
>
> ~ Antoine de Saint Exupéry, *The Little Prince*

Chuck—My heart attack was an enormous gift. My broken heart broke me open to my whole self and let me see how I had lost myself. My Courage helped me listen to my heart, act on my highest values, and integrate what I was teaching to others. Through the intricate interdependence of body, mind, and spirit, I gained a self-compassion I never had before. I can be gentle with myself, knowing that my trauma—and my Cultural and Protective Patterns—have given me challenges but also vital strengths for resilience and wellbeing I didn't know were possible.

The power of listening to our hearts is embedded in our literature, philosophy, and sacred traditions.

The heart's inner knowing in the language we use

When I listened to my heart ...

My heart told me so.

What is the heart of the matter?

From the great philosophers

Bossuet – "The heart has reasons that reason does not understand."

Goethe – "What is uttered from the heart alone, will win the hearts of others to your own."

Gandhi – "In prayer, it is better to have a heart without words than words without a heart."

Rochefoucauld – "The heart is forever making the head its fool."

Sentiments from the sacred traditions

Christianity – The Kingdom of Heaven is within.

Buddhism – Look within, you are the Buddha.

Islam – Those who know themselves know their Lord.

Judaism – He is in all and all is in him.

Confucianism – By exhaustively examining one's own heart, one can know heaven.

Practices to Strengthen Courage

> "Courage is the most important of the virtues because, without it, no other virtue can be practiced consistently."
> ~ Maya Angelou

Changing ingrained habits and stepping outside our comfort zone is difficult. That is why we need the Resilient Mindset of Courage. Like most things, it can become easier when we have more practice using it. Spending time listening to our inner voice regularly can help.

- Spend time feeling our emotions. Sometimes, that means opening ourselves to the vulnerability of a good cry.

- Quiet our minds so we can listen to our hearts. We can do this by walking, spending time in nature, talking with a friend, journaling about what we value, or meditating.

- Pay attention to our values. What is important to us? What is worth fighting for? What kind of person do we want to be? What do we want for ourselves and our world? What are we willing to do to get there?

- Be intentional about moving outside of our comfort zones. Do one thing that scares us each day. Remember that courage is not the absence of fear but rather the ability to act in the face of fear. By setting small, achievable goals that push us outside our comfort zone, we gradually work up to more challenging tasks. Through these intentional steps to build our courage, we can develop the confidence and resilience we need to face bigger challenges.

- Embrace failure. We are not listening to our inner wisdom if we never fail or change course. Failure is often the best way for us to learn and grow. When we fail, we learn we can get up again. Sometimes, deliberately doing things we don't care if we succeed, like taking up a hobby, can help us feel stronger and more confident and open us up to listening to our values.

> "I've failed over and over and over again in my life. And that is why I succeed."
> ~ Michael Jordan, professional basketball player

- Surround ourselves with supportive people. A strong support network of friends and family who encourage and believe in us can help us feel more confident and capable. Seek relationships with people who inspire and challenge us to be our best selves.

What kind of person do I want to be?

Centering Skills

Chapter 19

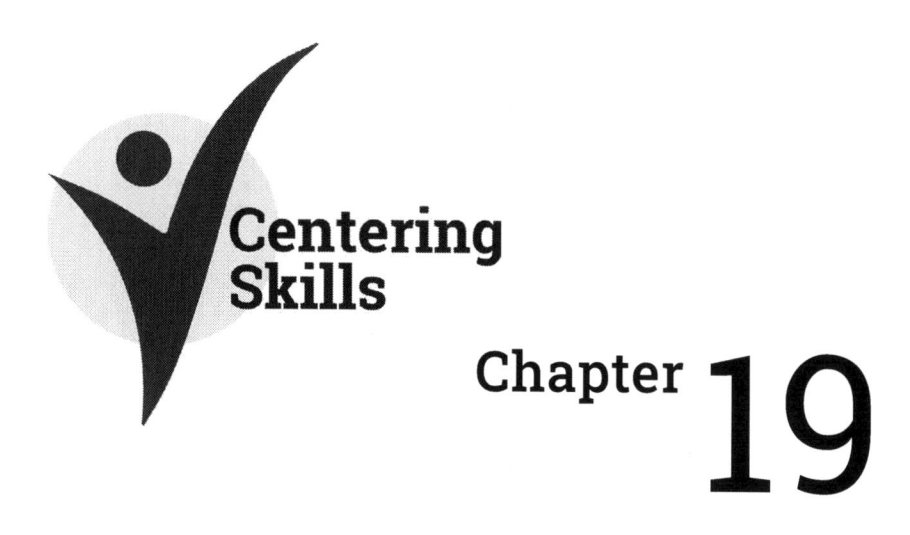

Centering Skills

> "Centering is not about being perfectly centered at all times, but rather having the ability to quickly return to that centered state when you become off-balanced."
>
> ~ Richard Strozzi-Heckler, *The Leadership Dojo*

Chuck —As I plunged through Crystal Rapid—one of the largest rapids in North America at the bottom of the Grand Canyon—I was amazed by the calm I felt in my body. Enormous waves crashed over the top of me and engulfed the boat. My breathing flowed powerfully while my arms pushed hard against the bow to keep the boat from flipping. My heart was singing with gratitude as I relished the movement of the water, the brilliant sky above, and the light of the burning sun on thousands of feet of ancient rock. It was an incredible experience of Centering! I was in love with it all amidst one of the most tumultuous experiences of my life.

I feel like I have come home to myself when I am Centered. I let go of judgments, expectations, and fears and am fully in my body—peaceful and present. I have robust Personal Resilience and am living a joyful life.

In day-to-day life, it is not so easy. Too often, when my wife gets upset with me, I have an emotional reaction that throws me off-center, and my childhood trauma surfaces quickly, like a crashing wave. Centering Skills help me regain my sense of balance. These skills allow me to drop into my body, self-regulate, and feel safe. I can choose my reactions.

Centering Skills helped Ramona navigate her stressful work environment. As a juvenile probation officer in an urban community with a high level of racial inequity, Ramona felt overworked and underappreciated. Her supervisors used intimidation as their management style, making Ramona and her colleagues feel psychologically unsafe. Even when she took on extra projects, she was overlooked for recognition. Her coworkers and managers had often previously experienced trauma, but they were not really interested in learning resilience skills. In fact, they did not seem interested in working through any of their issues at all. She was getting frustrated and wanted to throw in the towel.

But Ramona sought a different story for herself. She loved her work and felt a great connection to serving her community. Through the We Are Resilient training, she learned Centering Skills that helped her remain calm and reconnected her to her purpose. Ramona used the *Centering Skill of Letting Go* for all the things she could not control and instead focused on what she could change.

When she noticed her colleagues' Protective Patterns—mainly Attacking and Hyper-Caretaking—Ramona learned not to take their behavior personally. Through the *Centering Skill of Positive Reframing*, she was reminded that while hurt people hurt others, she had an opportunity to make a difference. With the high rate of police brutality in her community, Ramona could be a voice for change. Ramona also focused on using her Resilience skills to engage parents. She Centers herself first because she knows her modeling is most important. She reminds parents how resilient they are already and how they have the inner strength and skills to do what is best for their family. She teaches them how to use the *Centering Skill of Noticing Myself* and their Protective Patterns and *Notice Others,* like how their behavior impacts their children. These skills support parents on their journey to become their most resilient selves.

Centering Skills: What are They?

Centering Skills are the skills we use to ground ourselves. They are strategies to bring us back into balance, helping us recover from a Protective Pattern or avoid using one completely. Chuck and Ramona have learned to use their Centering Skills to calm themselves in stressful situations, for both everyday annoyances and difficult life events.

Centering Skills help us regulate our emotions and open our minds. When we are calm, we think more clearly and make better decisions. Centering also helps us connect with others and strengthen our relationships. We can listen more deeply and speak more authentically.

***Personal Resilience** is the inner ability to adapt and strengthen oneself to meet challenges. Strong Personal Resilience creates balance, wellbeing, and a sense of safety.*

Just as it supported Chuck and Ramona, Personal Resilience helps us get through the ups and downs of life. Centering Skills reinforce our Personal Resilience, giving us inner strength for a more joyful life. They help us be more of the person we most want to be.

The six Centering Skills that we explore in this approach are:

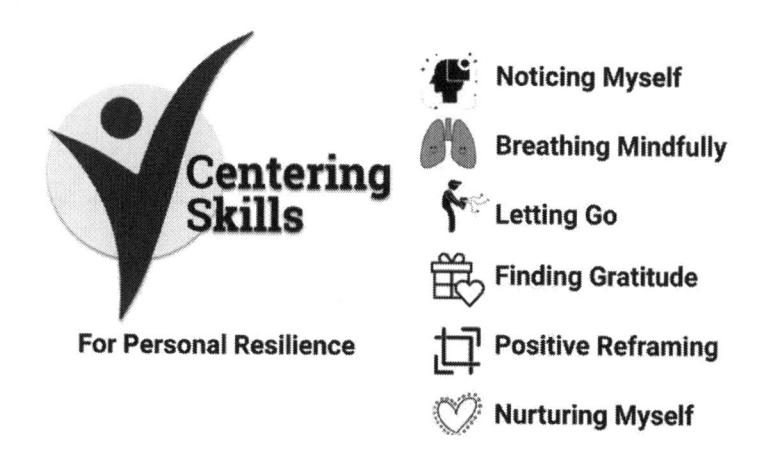

Centering Skills
For Personal Resilience

- Noticing Myself
- Breathing Mindfully
- Letting Go
- Finding Gratitude
- Positive Reframing
- Nurturing Myself

Meri—Two years ago, I was particularly grateful for having strengthened my Centering Skills. At 96 years old, my stepfather Vic had been declining for some time. It was difficult to judge if he would recover because he had rallied so many times that my friends joked he had nine lives, like a cat. Then Vic landed in the hospital again, and after three days, he was moved to a rehab facility. With three siblings and three stepsisters and their families involved, I found it challenging to balance my needs with those of my mom, siblings, children, and other family members. So many questions left me anxious:

- How much longer did Vic have to live?
- Could we get family members on the same page for hospice care?
- How would my mom react to Vic's decline? Would it make her Alzheimer's worse?
- Could we navigate planning a funeral with the conflicting needs and opinions of the family without erupting in acrimony?
- What would I do if Vic passed during the three weeks my siblings were out of the country for long-delayed vacations already postponed by COVID?

All these questions and more left me continually reaching for my Centering Skills. As Vic moved from rehab back to the hospital and finally home on hospice, I Noticed Myself and listened to my internal cues. Was I getting worked up? Was there tension in my tummy? Just Noticing my emotions and tension and naming them helped. Centering Skills that helped include *Breathing Mindfully*, especially if I had trouble sleeping. *Letting Go* helped me accept what was true—Vic was dying, and I needed to *Let Go* of what I could not control (everything but my response and my behavior). I was able to *Find Gratitude* in the small things—a few moments of coherence and joy with my mom, some good conversations with my siblings, and the support of my husband. I made sure to *Nurture Myself* through long walks with friends and time spent just chilling. Having a set of Centering Skills that I knew well and had practiced before this difficult period helped me get through it more gracefully.

When the call finally came in early August that Vic had passed, I continued to use my Centering Skills—and my Connecting and Collaborating Skills— to plan for the funeral with my mom, siblings, stepsiblings, and other relatives. When differences of opinion became flashpoints, I stepped outside, away from the heat of the moment, and *Nurtured Myself* for a few moments. When family members requested things that I felt were too difficult to do, I could lean in with the *Connecting Skill of Heartfelt Listening* to hear their underlying concerns. Every night, I would spend time *Noticing Myself*—what was my stress level? Was I paying attention to my own needs in the middle of trying to meet everyone else's? I had a pattern of "powering through" crises, not taking time off, and answering work emails on the side. Even though I wasn't sure I needed it (because my Protective Pattern of Hyper-Caretaking argued against it), I decided to take several days of bereavement leave to be aligned with the spirit of *Nurturing Myself.*

I know all these practices make a huge difference. When we are Centered, we can Connect and Collaborate with others more easily. Even in this sad time, I could work with my family effectively to bring all the pieces together. In the end, almost all the family was pleased with the arrangements, and my mother actually enjoyed the funeral and having the whole family together to commemorate my stepfather.

How Centering Skills Help

Centering Skills restore our inner balance through mindful strategies focusing on the present. Awareness of the present—mindfulness—places our attention in the here and now, reducing negative thoughts that can cause anxiety and stress. Chuck needed Centering Skills to both navigate the whitewater rapids skillfully and manage his emotions. Ramona needed Centering Skills to give herself and her colleagues compassion and grace when dealing with traumatic events and to help community parents become the parents they want to be. Meri needed Centering Skills to deal with the passing of her stepfather and prevent family drama.

Centering Skills can help when we face a big change. Jerome, a former chief operating officer, spent 25 years building his organization's brand. After it was sold, he landed at another company and hoped to parlay his expertise to boost it as well. However, six months into his tenure, he was called in for an early morning strategy meeting, where he was dismissed. He felt blindsided. Jerome needed to use his Centering Skills to regain his balance. Through *Noticing Myself*, he recognized he felt angry and hurt. He had put together a long list of safety issues to be addressed, and the CEO responded by firing him.

After calling his wife, Jerome settled in a coffee shop to reflect. He had to *Let Go* of his focus on the former company. He admitted this had been a "rebound job," which he needed to do, but not for too long. The company was not an excellent fit because it had different standards and a culture that failed to align with his personal integrity. Since he had practiced *Positive Reframing*, Jerome could quickly see this as an opportunity for a new vision of himself. As he moved into his job hunt, circling back to previous leads, his commitment to *Nurturing himself* through exercise supported his mental and physical health. In addition, Jerome spent time *Finding Gratitude* for his old company, which he had served for so long. That company gave him the resources to innovate and provide excellent customer service. He and his colleagues created a fun, learning, and supportive culture, and he appreciated that his career included such a highlight.

Centering Skills can also help us during emergencies. Kaori's family was backpacking in the middle of nowhere when her sister-in-law fell and twisted her ankle badly. Though it was not life-threatening, it was stressful. Kaori used her Centering Skills to stay calm and see the problem clearly. She then led her injured sister-in-law and the rest of the family in practicing Centering Skills. They started by *Breathing Mindfully* together and then *Finding Gratitude* for how they handled things. They *Let Go* of the expectations for their planned trip. Her sister-in-law was safely helicoptered out and the rest of the family hiked out, satisfied they handled it well.

As Chuck, Ramona, Meri, Jerome, and Kaori discovered, Centering helps us:

1. **Feel** better. We are calmer, more balanced, more free, and more at home in our bodies. We have self-control over our emotions.

2. **Think** better. We can be intentional and focused. We get clarity on reality and the bigger picture and can see options. We can better prioritize and choose our direction. We are empowered and have more confidence.

3. **Connect** better. We can be more authentic in our relationships when we feel grounded and see more clearly. Centering is a "gateway skill" for Resilience because when we are centered, we can connect and collaborate with others more easily.

Beatrix described it well: Centering Skills "take us on a little vacation."

Centering is not just a "nice to have." The flip side of Centering—when we are unintentionally reacting and out of balance—can cause real physical, mental, and emotional harm to us and negatively impact our relationships. The field of psychoneuroimmunology demonstrates that emotions are the glue that holds our body and mind together and are a key to healthy immune function. Some physicians attribute up to 90% of illness to stress and anxiety. Common physical effects of stress include headaches, fatigue, upset stomach, overeating, skin problems, sleep problems, and many more. Effects on mood and energy include irritability, lack of focus, anxiety, and depression. Body symptoms and mood affect our ability to connect in relationships and collaborate in groups.

Gizela, a senior business leader at a Fortune 200 Tech Company, uses Centering Skills personally and professionally. "Knowing how to evaluate quickly and Center myself applies to my personal and professional relationships. I have seen how my ability to center myself in high-energy or high-stress times makes me a more effective leader for my team. I believe every business should invest in strengthening the resilience skills of their teams to help build a healthy, collaborative organization."

Influence of Cultural Patterns

Ramona had never been taught the Centering Skills growing up, and she didn't have anyone in her family or circle of friends who modeled them for her. With a high level of intergenerational trauma, Ramona learned how to react to keep herself safe. However, when her Protective Patterns didn't serve her, she didn't know other ways to respond intentionally.

Chuck—I learned Centering Skills in a variety of ways. While my dad spent too much time using his Protective Pattern of Avoiding through drinking alcohol, he also did a lot of Nurturing Myself in nature. He was a lifelong birder, loved fishing and canoeing, and was the one who taught me the most about the joy and renewal of *Nurturing Myself* in the out-of-doors. He was also an expert marksman, as had been my grandfather. Shooting included training in *Breathing Mindfully*. My mom used *Finding Gratitude* and *Letting Go* to a fault. She never let anything bother her, and I became an optimist from her modeling. Most importantly, I took martial arts classes starting at age six, which taught Centering as a core skill. To this day, my practice of Aikido aids me in *Noticing Myself*.

Meri—My family modeled some Centering Skills for me. My mother was pretty good at pivoting using *Positive Reframing* and *Nurturing Myself* for her health and resilience. My faith tradition helped me with *Finding Gratitude*. Other skills were new. I had little experience with *Noticing Myself* and *Breathing Mindfully* as practices, and I didn't know I could practice Centering Skills to be able to access them when needed. I didn't know I could be intentional and thus remain Centered when I wanted to be.

How to use Centering Skills

A semi-retired accountant, Carol finds the Centering Skills helpful when thrown off-balance. She loves to wake up slowly and quietly. One day, when she was sipping coffee to prepare for the day, the loud noise of lawnmowers, edgers, and weed whackers interrupted her peace. The lawnmowing company was mowing her lawn early. Her frustration surged. "I *Noticed Myself* feeling quite irritated. Why can't I just have a quiet morning?" she wondered. "Why are they here so early?" Then Carol tried *Positive Reframing*. She remembered it would be 90° in the afternoon and realized, "They need to start early because it will be too hot to do my yard later." Carol also Let Go of her attachment to having a quiet, peaceful morning. She unloaded the dishwasher and did other chores she wouldn't have done at that time. She pivoted to *Finding Gratitude* for the people mowing the lawn and having the resources to hire them. Carol appreciated having a range of skills to choose from and often finds it helpful to use several Centering Skills together.

How do we center? Like Carol, we choose one of the six Centering Skills that might help us in the moment. As individuals, we all have different preferences for Centering. Many of us already use one or more of these skills. Some people have more familiarity and comfort in one skill and less in another. Each person has a different place they start from and a different place they will end up. We can use any Centering Skill in any order and modify it for ourselves. We can use any combination of skills. Only we can judge which one is best for us at any time.

Learning a new set of skills includes a process of discovering them, trying them out in different situations, and practicing them until, ultimately, we become better at them. Our Resilient Mindsets—Curiosity, Choice, and Courage—can help us through the process. When off-balance, we can use Curiosity: *Which Centering Skill might help?* We can then Choose a skill to try. And, like Meri, Jerome, Kaori, and Carol, we might need several at once.

The Resilient Mindset of Courage can help us when we encounter challenges. To learn and practice these skills, we might need to unlearn our old ways of being and behaving. The unlearning is often the most difficult part. We may need to remind ourselves that we usually can't change the situation, but we can change how we react. By changing how we respond, we step into becoming the kind of person we want to be.

It is also important to recognize the power of **intention.** We know how easy it is to say, "Oh, I've got this! I have done this skill all my life! I don't need to think about it anymore." Whether one is comfortable using a skill or it is brand new, we strengthen it when we practice intentionally. The more we take the time to learn about it and practice it, the more it impacts us. It is also helpful to practice centering when not activated so we can use the skills when stressed.

In the following six chapters, we explore six Centering Skills and describe how practicing them can make us more resilient:

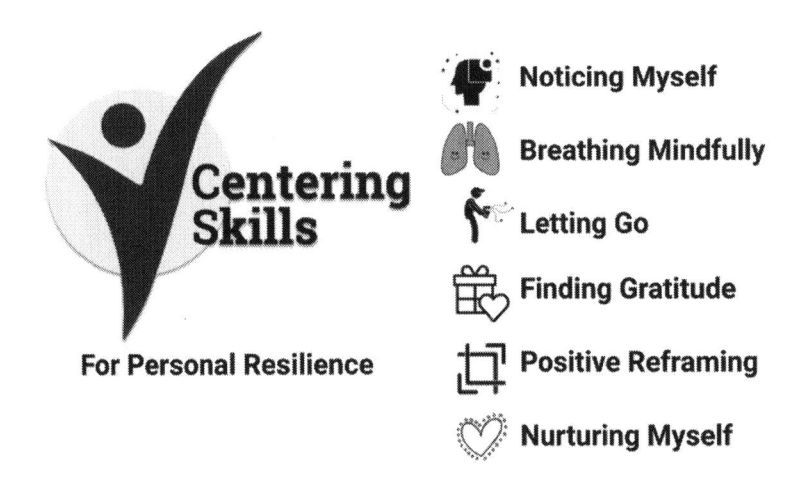

Centering Skills For Personal Resilience

- Noticing Myself
- Breathing Mindfully
- Letting Go
- Finding Gratitude
- Positive Reframing
- Nurturing Myself

These skills include noticing ourselves and listening to our internal cues, breathing mindfully, accepting what is true and letting go of what is harming us, finding gratitude, finding a positive way forward, and being kind to ourselves. All of these skills have robust research supporting their power for Centering us and their physiological benefits. Some of this research is cited in our Resource books, which can be found on our website dovetaillearning.org.

Centering Skills

Chapter **20**

Noticing Myself

> "Without understanding how our feelings, thoughts, and behaviors work together, it's almost impossible to find our way back to ourselves and each other."
>
> ~ Brené Brown, *Atlas of the Heart*

Meri—I had just returned from a long vacation. I had seen old friends, attended a much-anticipated family wedding, and finished up with adventure travel. I thought I would be able to jump back in, refreshed and eager to complete tasks I had left undone after my crazy summer. Instead, I could barely put one foot in front of the other. And then, at a routine morning work meeting, a colleague admitted he needed to thoroughly shake up our work plan. It just wasn't working for him, and he wanted something different.

So here I was. Completely depleted. I realized I needed to Notice Myself at a deeper level. *"Pause, what's the cause?"* What was going on? As I sat there thinking for a while, a realization emerged. My depletion was not just physical. It was also emotional. I realized I was feeling sad. I wasn't sure of all the reasons, but I knew I needed time to work through it. Deep sadness needs time and space. I moved some of my commitments and gave myself time to process and Notice Myself.

I didn't do anything special that week other than move slowly and pay more attention to my feelings. Sometimes, I just sat and gave myself room to feel. During my daily swim, I let my mind roam to all the things I felt sad about. I realized I had a deep need for grieving:

- My stepfather Vic had died only three weeks before. After his death, I moved right into *"planning the funeral mode"* and then into *"planning vacation mode."* Though I had known it was coming, I needed space to grieve this big loss.

- I also needed space to grieve the changes in my family. Vic and my mother had been the center of our extended family for 40+ years. Now, with Vic gone and my mother at diminished capacity, we would have to create new traditions and ways of connecting.

- My work had changed significantly over the past year. I lost a dream when we didn't get a grant we hoped for and were forced to downsize our organization. While my beloved colleagues were fortunate (and talented!) to get new jobs quickly, I missed their presence in my life.

- I had spent two decades creating a wonderful circle of friends in my town as we raised our children together. In the last few years, after their kids launched, quite a few friends had moved. My social group was smaller.

I knew these transitions were normal with aging. But transitions can be painful, and I had not given myself space to grieve them. By Noticing Myself and giving myself time to feel the pain, I was able to work through a lot of it. By the next week, when it was time for my colleague and me to discuss a new future, I felt more Centered. I had room once again to be creative.

Noticing Myself can help us with our mind-body connection. Esther, a 70-year-old artist, finds Noticing Myself critical to her physical well-being. "I get so focused on what I'm doing I forget about my body. When I work in the garden, I might completely ignore that my arm is aching from the repetitive stress of using clippers. I can even forget to eat when I'm too involved in something and eventually feel a stomach ache from lack of food."

Noticing Myself can help us in the small moments. Tatiana, a therapist, was driving to work after dropping her daughter off at preschool. By Noticing Myself, she realized she was anxious. Then, she identified several reasons why she might be worried. It did not change her anxiety, but she felt a little better about it. By Noticing Myself—naming her emotions and identifying potential triggers—Tatiana felt a little more in control.

Noticing Myself can help us point our lives in the direction we want. Beatrix, an avid cook and a forty-something communications professional, doesn't have the best track record with New Year's resolutions. Her journal intentions, exercise routines, and book-reading pledges have all been victim of her New Year's goals turning sideways. Sound familiar?

Last year, rather than throwing personal growth out the window, Beatrix changed her approach. Instead of adding external things like journals, books, or gyms, she chose to focus on Noticing Myself and pay attention to what brought her joy and what did not. Beatrix took a walk one brisk, sunny winter day. Experiencing the cool breeze, the warm sun on her face, and the sweet sounds of a toddler giggling as she and her dog walked by was joyful. This memory then helped Beatrix Center herself whenever she was not feeling her most resilient self.

Noticing Myself: What is it?

Noticing Myself is paying attention to our behavior and the signals from our bodies, feeling our emotions, and learning from those feelings.

Our Centering Skills are strategies to bring us back into balance, helping us recover from a Protective Pattern or avoid using one completely. Noticing Myself helps us be aware of when we are out of balance, feel our feelings, and identify underlying causes. As Meri, Esther, Tatiana, and Beatrix discovered, Noticing Myself makes us mindfully aware of what is happening for us at that moment.

Noticing Myself is the practice of being curious and asking ourselves:

- What am I noticing/sensing/feeling?
- What emotions am I feeling?
- Are my Protective Patterns being triggered?
- What is happening in and around me?
- Is there something stopping me from being able to notice?

Noticing Myself includes pausing long enough to pay attention to the intelligence of our senses, body, emotions, mind, and intuition. Some may first notice the physical body (tension, fatigue, upset stomach, or relaxed and calm), and then feel emotions. Others key in on their emotions first. When we feel angry, upset, happy, or peaceful, we can pause and turn toward Noticing Myself, asking ourselves, "What is happening in my body and around me?" so we can respond skillfully.

Once we notice our bodies and emotions, we can dig a little deeper. We can think, *"Pause, what's the cause?"* We can consider what might be impacting our emotions. When Meri paused, she noticed she was depleted. After exploring what might be causing that feeling, she recognized she was grieving. Esther noticed she was not in touch with her physical aches and pains. Tatiana noticed her anxiety and identified why she might be anxious. Beatrix noticed her joy while walking her dog, giving her a Centering memory to access when needed. Each of them spent time Noticing themselves and thus felt more grounded in the process.

When facing difficulty, being honest with ourselves about the root cause can be challenging. We can better tend to our inner needs using our Resilient Mindset of Curiosity and the greater awareness that comes with Noticing Myself.

Influence of Cultural Patterns

Families and communities pass on habits and behaviors about Noticing Myself that impact how, when, and where we can use this skill. Many people's Cultural Patterns make Noticing Myself feel self-centered or inappropriate.

Chuck—In my family culture, talking about anger, sadness, or disappointment wasn't safe. My mom pretended everything was fine when it wasn't. By the time I was a teen, I had locked much of my inner life away. I also absorbed a Cultural Pattern from my family and American society: "Boys don't cry." It was so ingrained that I never cried until I started therapy in my thirties, and I relearned how to Notice Myself. The process opened a huge door for me, and I realized how much of my early life I had repressed.

Darius had a similar Cultural Pattern growing up—with a twist. He was taught, "Black men don't cry." Since certain emotions and behaviors help with survival, and survival rates for Black men are disproportionally lower, many Black families don't feel like they can encourage their boys to have a range of emotions. As a young Black boy, he was taught that he had to be the best, better than everyone else, to have a chance for success.

Noticing Myself is viewed as selfish by some families. "Your role is to help others—the family and the community—not to think about yourself." Mei remembers her Chinese mother's prohibition from talking about any bad things. If Mei was frustrated, her only permissible outlet was screaming into a pillow. She was told to "suck it up" and hide her emotions so she could focus on the needs of her family and community. As an adult, Mei is working on Noticing Myself and talking about all her feelings, even the "bad" ones. When her husband gave her a "dammit doll" to encourage her to express her feelings, it almost felt counterproductive. Taking her feelings out on a doll felt like a return to her mother's restrictive Cultural Pattern. Instead, Mei wants to Notice Myself more and talk about her feelings with others.

Meri—In my family, we shared our feelings loudly and openly. That worked well when we were celebrating and having fun together. Others enjoyed our lively celebrations. But we were also quick to express annoyance or anger with loud voices. When I am upset, I get it off my chest. It works for me because my feelings are communicated immediately so they don't fester. When I am done, I am done. I am shocked when someone brings me a grudge and shares the emotions they carry from a past event. I carry few grudges linked to my past emotions because they are long gone.

My sharing of emotions can be off-putting to those with different Cultural Patterns. I remember being angry early in my marriage during a Christmas visit with my husband's family. They were taken aback to see so much anger at something that was probably relatively small. When I realized this mismatch in our Cultural Patterns, I initially felt like I couldn't be myself. Over time, my husband and I have come to appreciate each other's ways of being and have influenced each other to meet more in the middle, so we both Notice ourselves for a range of emotions but are sensitive to how expressing those emotions might impact those around us.

In other families, Noticing Myself might be communicated more implicitly. Some families use music to Notice and express emotions. For Alina, a young Native and Latina woman, her family knew to give her mom space when she played a specific song because it meant she was unhappy. When a dance song was played, it was a signal to dance and play together, and a happy rhythm was restored. The music at family gatherings signaled the mood of the family.

When Noticing Myself is Difficult

When we are having difficulty using a Centering Skill, we can start by shifting into our Curiosity Mindset and ask ourselves the following questions:

Am I using a Protective Pattern? *Chuck*—I've been upset with my older brother for as long as I can remember. Growing up in our alcoholic family, we became hurt kids with no idea what to do with our feelings. We often fought. Because I wanted his love and affection, I'd tease him mercilessly. My teasing would spur him to chase me so he could pound me with his fists. Most of the time, I outran him. Once in a while, it would go the other way.

My primary coping skill was my Protective Pattern of Avoiding my feelings. To not feel pain, I distanced myself from him—which became a kind of impasse for both of us over the years. Though I love him dearly and know he loves me, we don't see each other much. We rarely talk. When we get together in person, I feel something is missing.

We know our Avoiding Protective Pattern can be helpful and keep us safe. However, like it had become for Chuck, Avoiding Noticing Myself can limit our ability to feel emotions. It is normal to want to avoid painful emotions. We may have created a habit where Noticing Myself generates negative self-talk, and we don't want to hear it. We might be afraid of feeling sad, angry, overwhelmed, or depleted, especially if we don't have the skills to handle the emotion. We may just not want to feel what we are feeling!

Exploring our Protective Patterns to see what lies underneath helps us strengthen our skill of Noticing Myself. Then we can make time later when it is safe to practice Noticing Myself.

Do I have a habit that no longer serves me? *Meri*—I've realized I need to practice Noticing Myself. Too often, I am so busy with my "doing" that I am not really paying attention to my "being" or emotions. How can I? I have things I have to get done! Noticing Myself seems very inconvenient. Most of us have long to-do lists, whether for projects, meetings, emails, or other tasks—not to mention the ever-shrinking personal time for family and household duties, seeing friends, taking care of ourselves, and having fun!

Many of us think, "Paying attention to my emotions will not help. I simply don't have the time!" However, I've learned that Noticing Myself is like the "check engine light" for my emotional self. I may think I don't have time to attend to it now (especially when a crisis erupts), but I cannot operate smoothly if I don't listen to my emotions regularly. My emotions, through my body signals, send me essential information. And if I don't listen, I miss what's important:

- *I feel tired.* Am I working too hard, or am I grieving a loss?
- *My stomach is tense.* Am I anxious? Have I prepared for that meeting?
- *I feel relaxed and happy.* My time with friends is something I need more of in my life!

Learning to Notice Myself has helped me work from a more Centered place. By listening to my emotions, I can complete *more* of my to-do list.

Do I have a more meaningful value that might help me Notice Myself? *Meri*—Two years ago, my daughter got engaged to a wonderful man. He had invited our family to witness the proposal (from a respectful distance!) and celebrate with his family afterward. It was truly a joyous moment, and I couldn't have been happier. Except I wasn't. Throughout the event, while I enjoyed meeting his family and friends, I felt a little numb.

I did not want to remain numb at such a happy time. Later that night, when I was trying to sleep, I finally took time to Notice Myself. I recognized that I had used my Protective Pattern of Avoiding to ignore bad news about work that had come in earlier that day. I needed to let the news in so I could move past it.

I cried for an hour when I really let in the work stress that had been building for months. Feeling my sad feelings wasn't what I preferred to do. But I wanted to feel true joy from my daughter's engagement, and I couldn't do that unless I stopped using my Protective Pattern of Avoiding and started Noticed Myself. I had to notice ALL my emotions to feel joy. After processing my grief, I could feel the joy of my daughter's engagement.

Marc Bracket, Founding Director of the Yale Center for Emotional Intelligence, writes,

> "The irony is that when we ignore our feelings, or suppress them, they only become stronger. The really powerful emotions build up inside us, like a dark force that poisons everything we do, whether we like it or not. Hurt feelings don't vanish on their own. They don't heal themselves. If we don't express our emotions, they pile up like a debt that will eventually come due."
>
> ~ Marc Bracket, *Permission to Feel*

Does trauma affect my ability to Notice Myself? *Chuck*—At three years old, I felt ashamed when my dad yelled at me. At six years old, I felt ashamed when I didn't do my homework and was sent to the office. At 12 years old, I felt ashamed about being sexually molested. I felt the pain, the uncomfortable feelings in my body, and the awkward awareness that something was wrong. However, this was my life, and it was all that I knew. The trauma impacted me deeply but stuffed my feelings inside so I wouldn't have to feel them.

If we have experienced trauma, we may not be capable of Noticing our bodies or emotions. It can be too challenging to pay attention to our feelings when they are so painful. We bury our shame because it feels so awful. As a teen, Chuck avoided his sadness, grief, and rejection by misusing alcohol, drugs, food, and other distractions. Avoiding Noticing Myself may be the most useful strategy in trauma—for a while. However, Avoiding too long can block us from moving toward healing. If we are brave and choose to feel our feelings, they can guide us on how to live more fully. We may need help from a friend, a family member, or a mental health professional to understand our difficult feelings. It is good to ask for help when we need it.

When to not Notice Myself

Sometimes, Avoiding our feelings is essential. Avoiding our feelings may help us complete tasks we need to finish. As a nurse practitioner in a busy women's clinic, Elsie knew that very well. One moment, she was in an examining room, helping a patient suffering from intimate partner violence. The next moment, she was called to help a woman having a miscarriage. Elsie's professional duties don't leave her time for Noticing Myself during her workday. The challenge for Elsie is ensuring she spends some quality time Noticing Myself regularly to process her emotions enough to avoid burnout.

Meri—Sometimes crises erupt that preclude me from Noticing Myself. One day, the babysitter across the street rushed over, carrying a small screaming boy who had cut off the tip of his finger. I calmly put little Cayden in my car, buckled the car seat, and drove him to the emergency room. While the ER staff worked on him, I focused on keeping him calm. Only later, after I got him home, did I process my feelings of distress and fear. I was afraid and upset for Cayden and his parents. How could this little boy go through life without the tip of his finger? I was also agitated because I hated blood, injuries, and hospitals. I was glad I had Avoided feeling my feelings until after the event to stay calm for Cayden.

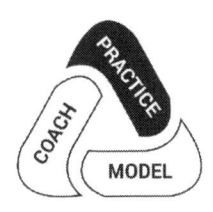

Practicing Noticing Myself

Use This Skill When…

- I'm upset or cranky, but I'm not exactly sure why.
- I'm stressed and taking my frustration out on others.
- I'm feeling numb or alone.
- I feel happy and want to recognize what is making me happy.
- I need to take a break and check in with myself.

Three Aspects of Noticing Myself

> "We are not thinking machines that feel,
> we are feeling machines that think."
> ~ António R. Damásio, professor of Psychology

Noticing Myself involves three aspects: noticing my body, listening to my feelings, and exploring what might be causing those feelings. We may do these aspects simultaneously or in any order. We may need to pause to pay attention to each aspect.

Noticing my Body

All day long, our bodies send us signals about how we are doing, but we may need practice to listen to them. After Nariko's mom had surgery, Nariko spent a lot of time caring for her mom and other family members. Through Noticing Myself, she realized her shoulders were tense, and she felt utterly exhausted. These signals from her body alerted Nariko that she was anxious and worn out. She realized that she had been Hyper-Caretaking her family to avoid her anxiety about her mother. Once she recognized Hyper-Caretaking was neither good for her nor honored the capacities of other family members, she told them, "We can all help." She gave herself room to process her feelings and attend to herself and her family from a more centered perspective.

Mystery-novel lover Meredith tries to pay attention to her body's signals. She uses Noticing Myself when her body becomes tight with stress. Then she pauses and then uses a simple meditation, focusing on relaxing her hands or feet. Meredith imagines her feet on a beautiful grassy knoll or putting her hands in a lake, ocean, or warm hand bath. That type of mindful Noticing Myself calms her down.

Chuck—Sometimes, our body sends us very loud signals, like my heart attack. It was my body's way of stopping me in my tracks and getting my attention—fully! I was sitting on my couch on a beautiful Sunday evening when suddenly I felt something wrong in my body. My stomach was churning, and my chest felt like someone was sitting on it. I was confused. Was my stomach upset from dinner? Was I getting ill? Within minutes, my wife called 911. Soon, four large firefighters lifted me on a blanket and carried me to a waiting ambulance. EMTs transported me to the hospital, where an emergency stent was placed in my right coronary artery. It saved my life. Four months later, I had triple bypass surgery to restore full blood flow to my whole heart.

I had no idea I had heart disease. Over the past two decades, I ran and meditated most mornings, had a regular Aikido practice, and ate healthy food. I realized my early bad habits contributed to the deterioration of my heart. But I also learned that heart attacks are often precipitated by emotional distress as much as physical heart disease. I had spent years trying not to Notice Myself, repressing my feelings about crucial men who had broken my heart, and listening to a harsh inner critic that judged many of my emotions as bad. All those emotions finally broke through in this heart attack wake-up. As I recovered from this health crisis and the resulting surgery, I focused on Noticing Myself and listening to my emotions better.

Identifying the Wisdom of Emotions

The powerful felt-sense of "feelings" we call emotions are complex neurological and biological signals our bodies produce. We need to listen to our feelings because each emotion is a signal to pay attention. Feeling our feelings lets us know how life is working for us. Sometimes, we feel the joy of love and friendship, and if we are listening, we know we want to continue what we are doing so we can feel that emotion again. When things aren't going so well, our emotions tell us what is off. Nariko listened to the wisdom of her fatigue and anxiety and asked for her family's help. Meredith listened to her body's anxiety and meditated to calm herself. Chuck's heart attack woke him up to emotions he had repressed.

It can be difficult to listen to the wisdom of our emotions because we might have to feel some "challenging" emotions to get there.

Chuck—Recently, I felt down and immediately thought, "Haven't I learned enough to stop feeling bad?" Noticing my critique gave me an essential insight into my Protective Patterns of Avoiding. I was judging my emotions as bad and trying to stop the feeling. Only when I set aside my mental chatter and dropped into my body sensations to actually "feel" them could I hear the message of my emotions. In this case, I was feeling sad. Though I didn't want to feel sad, I needed to feel it and I had a good cry. Feeling allowed me to process my emotions and get the message from them. I realized I was sad that I had limited myself so much of my life. Noticing the emotion, feeling it, and understanding its message cleared my body's held-in energy, releasing its grip on me.

When we are present and aware of our emotions and stay with them long enough to Notice them:

1. Our emotions have essential information for us.
2. When we feel the emotion, it moves through us, and we become more integrated and whole—which transforms us.

Dr. Ellen Langer, a renowned Harvard psychologist who researches mindfulness, writes that we live more authentically when we notice our emotions and accept what we notice. When we are more authentic, we feel better about ourselves.

Emotional intelligence is often defined as the ability to manage both our own emotions and understand the emotions of people around us. We can't manage our emotions if we don't get in touch with them first. Emotions actually have an intelligence within them. They signal our consciousness with important information. When we are grateful, our bodies flood us with positive chemicals that bring us joy. When we are astonished, we are noting the surprise of something amazing. We can have many different emotions in rapid succession or even at the same time.

When we listen to our emotions, even the most difficult hold vital information:

Anger signals that an important value has been violated.

Regret lets us know we have done something we don't want to repeat.

Frustration signals that we may need to change our expectations or actions.

Hopelessness signals we may need to change the expected outcome or positively reframe how or when it might occur.

Guilt lets us know we have violated our own standards and need to do something to ensure we don't violate them again.

Modified from *The Emotional Hostage* (1986), Cameron-Bandler and Lebeau

Pause, What's the Cause?

When we pause and give ourselves time to process both the signals from our feelings and what might be causing those signals, we can learn so much about ourselves and what we want and need.

Emilia was getting really annoyed with her boyfriend because he was slow to respond to her texts. She thought maybe something was wrong. First, she paused and realized her annoyance was worry. She noticed her spiraling negative thoughts and asked herself, "Why am I worried about this?" In her heart, she knew he was swamped, and his speed at responding was nothing about her. Then she took out her phone journal and thought about the cause behind her worry. Emilia pondered the more profound question, "Why am I feeling like this?" She remembered feeling unwanted by her peers as a child. In her efforts to connect and make friends, too often, she had done whatever other kids had wanted. She didn't want to be that girl in her present relationship—she wanted more agency. Looking at the writing of her younger self helped her understand where her Protective and Cultural Patterns developed and connected her feelings between her past and present.

Arjun, a software engineer, was devastated after his first big breakup. He felt that he did something uniquely wrong and was a personal failure with an irreparable flaw. He felt miserable, and processing those feelings took him a while. Talking with friends and family helped Arjun realize that breakups are a shared experience that almost everyone goes through. Part of his processing was to figure out the cause behind his misery. He realized his Protective Pattern of Avoiding had emerged, and he didn't talk with his girlfriend about their misalignment in their views of the future. Now Arjun realizes that using Noticing Myself and sharing his feelings is essential, even when it feels scary.

When we think "*Pause, what's the cause?*" we can explore the context for our feelings or the feelings of others. Our emotional signals, plus the context and potential impetus for the feelings, give us powerful information to guide us in creating the life we want.

I can Practice This by...

- **Paying attention to my feelings**, senses, and intuition.

- Pausing and **thinking about what my body is telling me**. My emotions are signals from my body telling me to pay attention to something important. What are they telling me?

- **Noticing my self-talk** and whether I am using negative or positive words about myself and others.

- **Noticing how my reactions impact me** and others.

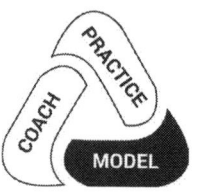

Modeling and Coaching This Skill for our Families

Meri—My children are now well-functioning adults, but like most parents, I have some regrets about my parenting. My children's big emotions—particularly their pain—were hard to hold. I felt that since I was older and wiser, it was my job to give them perspective and maybe some solutions to their problems.

I wanted to help them move on from their pain. I know now that I was also avoiding my pain in the process. I was not Noticing Myself or helping them Noticing themselves. It is difficult to just be with anyone who is really sad or struggling. If there was one parenting behavior I would do over, I would sit with my children when they were upset. Maybe I would help them name their emotions. But I would not try to "fix them." Even as the parent of adult children, I still need to work on this!

Chuck—I am so glad I went through years of training as a therapist because I broke the family Cultural Pattern and learned to *"be with"* my feelings so I could be with my daughters when they felt strong emotions. I learned that I didn't need to fix their feelings. They simply needed to be held in a space of acceptance and love—they needed permission to feel. They could discover that their emotions were okay, they were okay, and that it is normal, healthy, and healing to feel our emotions.

Practices to Model and Coach Noticing Myself:

- Saying out loud what feelings I Notice in myself and how I manage these feelings. "Hold on for a minute. I need to feel this."

- By sharing my feelings, I model how to talk about their emotions for my children. "I realize I am having a bad day. I'm not sure what I feel right now, but it's not about you. Give me a few moments to get in touch with my feelings."

Reflective Activity: Pause. What's the Cause?

When I have a conflict, large or small, I take a moment and ask myself, *"Pause. What's the Cause?"* I pause to feel it. What are my emotions and my body telling me? What am I actually feeling? After I name and feel my emotions, I ask myself for more information: What are the elements of the situation? Have my values been compromised? What is the story I am telling myself about the situation?

I can reflect on a past situation. How did it impact me? What was I feeling? I can think of my emotional response and give myself some time to go inside and feel it. Then, I can talk with a friend who listens well or write out what I think is the cause of my emotional response and why.

Activities to Strengthen Noticing Myself:

- **Noticing.** Pause to Notice what is true for me while waiting for coffee, at stoplights, filling up gas, in line, or on hold. Notice how my body feels. Frustrated? Anxious? Relaxed? What are my emotions telling me?

- **Reflective noticing.** After an off-centered moment, reflect on what happened. What can I notice in hindsight? Can I notice my emotional triggers? After a centered moment, also reflect on that situation. I learn more about what I want when I am more aware of how I feel and what it took to get there.

- **Notice how I treat myself.** Notice when I am using negative words about myself and others. Notice how that impacts me, makes my body feel, and affects my emotional state. Notice how using positive words about myself and others impacts me, makes my body feel, and affects my actions and energy levels.

Deeper Insights

Chuck—I sat alone in the high desert mountains on the Eastern side of the Sierra. I'd been fasting for three days, only drinking water while sleeping under the stars at night. In the early morning, just before sunrise, I communed with a bristle cone pine as I sat about ten feet away from her. She was majestic in her simplicity in the cold, clear, thin, still air. My awareness came from a different place, not in me but through me. I felt no separation between me, the pine, and this awareness of presencing the light of nature. Joy and love welled up within me, from the pine, from the light. I also felt lonely in this place, but I knew all was well. My sadness was perfect, as I was far from those I loved. Tears of joy and sadness flowed while my spirit soared, knowing life was a miracle.

When I drop into deeper consciousness, whether on the Aikido mat, sitting on a meditation cushion, communing with nature, or under the stars at 10,000 feet in the Sierra, I access another dimension of Noticing Myself. In these moments, I drop away from my little self and access my larger Self that experiences no boundary between the "I" that I usually identify with and a larger domain of presencing "what is" that I can only understand from a spiritual perspective.

Centering is a core part of many faith and wisdom traditions. A universal principle is "coming home" to oneself—Centering Myself—as a spiritual practice. Prayer, meditation, and walking in nature are all forms of Centering. As a transpersonal psychologist, I am familiar with the teachings from many wisdom traditions (Eastern, Western, and Indigenous), as well as modern research into nonordinary states of consciousness. We all can Notice a greater presence beyond the boundaries of our individual selves. It puts the mundane trivialities of life in perspective—life, death, meaning, and love.

The wisdom traditions tell us that accessing our inner Self is the path to wholeness. We simply need to get out of our own way to experience it. People do this through music, art, dance, and many other practices that take us beyond ourselves to notice our interconnection with the whole of life. Modern neuroscience shows that these higher states of consciousness are physiologically our most resilient states of Being. Here, our breath, thoughts, and biology synchronize in a state of flow that produces a robust immune response and extraordinary capacities of the body and mind.

Self-Discovery

- What is the underlying message behind my emotions—body feelings?

- What words (thoughts) do I say to myself? Do my inner stories support me as the author of my own life or cast me as a victim? What do my complaints tell me about myself?

- What brings me joy and happiness? Do I know how to improve my mood?

- How might noticing my emotions change my relationships?

Centering Skills

Chapter 21

Breathing Mindfully

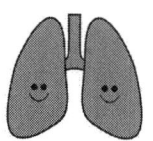

> "Breathing in, I calm my body and mind.
> Breathing out, I smile."
>
> ~ Thich Nhat Hanh, Vietnamese Buddhist monk

Meri —I finally said to myself, "Okay, I guess I will have to get up." Something—anxiety? Hormones? Full moon?—was giving me insomnia again, and I could not will myself back to sleep. Fortunately, I knew if I couldn't sleep after lying in bed for a while, I had a skill that could help: Breathing Mindfully.

So I sat on my floor and used a form of Breathing Mindfully I had learned in yoga. I raised my arms above my head and breathed in slowly. After holding it a bit, I slowly exhaled, even more slowly and fully, and lowered my arms. With round one finished, I repeated the cycle. After 20 more rounds, I was so relaxed from Breathing Mindfully that I could fall asleep quickly.

Breathing Mindfully can also help us interrupt a Protective Pattern. Ariana, a retired tech executive, asked her husband Jonah if he had gotten her mother's car cleaned, as they had discussed. Jonah responded, "No, I didn't get it cleaned. I watched the Patriots game."

The mention of football triggered Ariana because she hated football. Multiple concussions cause lifelong health problems for football players. Not only do football watchers support this unhealthy sport, but they also tie their mood to their team's performance.

Ariana wanted to shout, "You chose football instead of my mother!" Instead, when Ariana noticed her Attacking Protective Pattern emerging, she took three Mindful Breaths. As she became more Centered, she shifted into the Resilient Mindset of Curiosity. She calmly asked Jonah, "When do you think you can get the car cleaned?" Breathing Mindfully made all the difference for her.

This simple skill can work even in traumatic situations. Dr. Thomas, a pediatrician, saw powerful results when she used Breathing Mindfully to calm Hùng, a teen battling asthma and childhood trauma as well as stress from the pandemic and nearby raging wildfires. After several trips to urgent care and the emergency room, he was admitted to the hospital with a respiration rate more than double the norm for his age. Hùng's heart rate and blood pressure were also sky-high. His lungs were crystal clear, and his oxygen was 100%, but his medications weren't helping his breathing difficulties. After learning his history and previous medical interventions, Dr. Thomas recognized that Hùng was having an anxiety attack. "Our minds are incredibly powerful. His mind had taken over, and he was very anxious about everything happening, which was understandable."

Dr. Thomas decided to try Breathing Mindfully with him and co-regulate their breath together. With nurses in the room watching the monitors, she closed the shades, dimmed the lights, and played calming ocean music. She also rested her hand on Hùng's hand so he would know he wasn't alone. They closed their eyes and together practiced Breathing Mindfully for 10 minutes. After a few minutes, they could see the heart rate dropping. His blood pressure and his respiratory rate also slowly dropped to normal.

When they finished Breathing Mindfully, Hùng opened his eyes. Dr. Thomas turned around and saw that the nurses had eyes as big as saucers and that their jaws had dropped. They were incredulous. "Wow!" one said. Dr. Thomas knew Breathing Mindfully was powerful because she practiced it herself. However, she had not done it before in a hospital after they had exhausted other medical interventions. Hùng was so happy to feel better. His relaxed state lasted more than three hours, and when he started feeling anxious again, they practiced Breathing Mindfully again. After the second time, Hùng recognized how he could practice Breathing Mindfully in the future when feeling anxious.

Breathing Mindfully: What is it?

Breathing Mindfully is the intentional practice of focusing on our breath and feeling the sensations of breathing in our body.

Our Centering Skills are strategies to bring us back into balance, helping us recover from a Protective Pattern or avoid using one completely. Breathing Mindfully uses our breathing to calm our bodies and minds, as it did for Meri when she couldn't sleep, Ariana when she was upset with Jonah, and Hùng when he was anxious.

Breathing Mindfully can start with the Resilient Mindset of Curiosity: *Where in my body do I feel my breath as I inhale and exhale?*

Meri—I learned a version of Breathing Mindfully almost two decades ago when I started yoga. Though it was helpful for me, I missed the real power of it. I focused so much on counting my breaths that I missed the essence: feeling my breath in my body. When we pay attention to the felt-sense experience of our breath inside us, we connect with our body and give our mind a rest. We calm ourselves.

A robust field of biological and neurological research supports Breathing Mindfully. The science—understanding the "how" and "why" behind the power of breath—gives us a deeper appreciation for why it is so helpful. The vagus nerve, one of the most important in our body, connects our brain, heart, and gut. This central pathway integrates our nervous, endocrine, and immune systems. Breathing Mindfully increases the activity of the vagus nerve, which helps to decrease blood pressure, relax muscles, and strengthen our immune system. It also calms our heart, which activates the frontal cortex of our brain so that we can think more clearly.

How cool is that? By Noticing the sensation of our breath, we have a calming superpower that we can use whenever we need it. It works, and no one else needs to know that we are doing it!

Breathing Mindfully is a common Centering practice across many disciplines. Hampton learned it in acting class. For Chuck, it was crucial to his rock climbing and martial arts training, Doris uses it as a singer, and Laila learned it as a softball player. Many others use Breathing Mindfully to enhance performance. It is a central skill taught in mindfulness practices, from medical Mindfulness-Based Stress Reduction to Mindful Schools, to the essence of Buddhist Vipassana meditation. Breathing Mindfully is also an essential part of many faith and wisdom traditions, and it is used in cultural practices worldwide (prayer, chanting, drumming, ceremonial dancing, etc.).

Influence of Cultural Patterns

Many of us did not learn Breathing Mindfully when we were young, so it can feel awkward. Even those who learned it in a specific context, like singing or public speaking, may feel uncomfortable using it in regular life.

Meri—When I first heard of Breathing Mindfully, it felt a little "woo-woo," like something people did who weren't practical and grounded. Learning about the neuroscience and biology behind Breathing Mindfully completely changed my perspective and helped me integrate it into my life.

Emilia was raised in an environment that supported Breathing Mindfully. Her mom is a doctor who recognized the value of Breathing Mindfully and brought it into her medical practice and home. Emilia was so glad she had the skill when she went to college. In this new, unfamiliar setting, without having the comfort of her parents nearby, sometimes Emilia woke up in the morning and felt anxious about nothing in particular. Breathing Mindfully calmed her and helped her slow down. It also helped her in the classroom, with all the people, the noise, and the chaos of college life. If she felt anxious or overwhelmed, she took a moment and Breathed Mindfully to settle and focus.

Chuck—In my early years as a school counselor, I worked in a middle school where the principal used faculty meetings to tell teachers what they needed to know or do. Since hardly any faculty wanted to be there, the Cultural Pattern was not to talk or ask questions to keep the meeting as brief as possible. The faculty also had a Cultural Pattern of complaining in the workroom. It was very uncomfortable.

With the support of the principal, I used Breathing Mindfully in these meetings to transform the school community's culture. We started by removing the rows of student desks and arranging chairs in a circle. I invited these educators to simply pause and notice their breath for a few minutes before we began the meeting. The first time, two senior faculty members got up and walked out. They were visibly upset and grumbled under their breath, "You're not going to get me to do this." It was too uncomfortable for them.

With the help of a few encouraging teachers, we transformed those meetings by starting with a few minutes of Breathing Mindfully, followed by the opportunity for teachers to speak honestly about their classrooms. Within a year, the two teachers who had walked out had become such converts that they didn't let us start the meeting without at least a moment of silence. The following year, one of them, a burly older man who had taught the students' favorite class—shop class—for 40 years, quietly cried in front of his peers while thanking them for saving his job at a school board meeting. Altering the Cultural Pattern from complaining to using Breathing Mindfully and the *Connecting Skill of Speaking Authentically* completely changed the teaching community in this school.

When Breathing Mindfully Is Difficult

When we are having difficulty using a Centering Skill, we can start by shifting into our Curiosity Mindset and ask ourselves the following questions:

Am I using a Protective Pattern? *Chuck*—Years later, I trained teachers about Breathing Mindfully in a high-needs district in Boston, Massachusetts. During the training, I asked, "Who found it difficult to focus on breathing?" A small scattering of teachers raised their hands, and one teacher admitted:

> *I don't like it. Breathing like that is my own business, and I usually only do it in church. It's just weird to do it here. We are here to teach kids, and they don't need me to be in a prayer vigil, they need me to maintain control of the classroom so they can learn!*

This teacher expressed resistance, which many people feel. Our Avoiding Protective Pattern can emerge because it can feel unnatural to pause in the midst of whatever we are doing to feel sensations in our body. Moreover, when we Breathe Mindfully, uncomfortable and unwanted thoughts and feelings may come up and interfere with what we need to pay attention to at the moment. It may take practice to get comfortable with Breathing Mindfully.

Do I have a habit that no longer serves me? When Beatrix was a child, she loved vegetables more than any other kid she knew. From kale to squash—she loved them all. But not onions. Now, at 40 years old, she has softened her opinion and admits that knowledgeable chefs are correct: onions enhance flavor. She sometimes even adds onions to her soups and sauces. Yet, when she cooks, reaching for them still feels out of place.

Much like onions, Beatrix had a tricky relationship with Breathing Mindfully. She experienced the benefit of using a breathing practice in her wellness routine. She read the science about how Breathing Mindfully impacts our nervous system. Beatrix even suggested pausing and Breathing Mindfully to her children when they were upset and needed to calm down. Yet—maybe because of her hyperactive brain—she rarely remembered to use it in the moment. She realized that perhaps she needed to practice it more. It is hard to change our patterns! Last year, Beatrix committed to focusing on Breathing Mindfully. She started her day by taking five slow, deep breaths. This simple practice took just a few minutes, and she discovered she could begin her day with a clearer mind.

Do I have a more meaningful value that might help me Breathe Mindfully? Esther, a grandmother and an artist, is emotionally sensitive. Though she loves being with people, social situations can bring out her anxiety. Recently, Esther was at a family memorial with family members she hadn't seen in years. She was anxious about it, but when she used the Resilient Mindset of Courage and asked herself, "Who do I want to be?" she knew she wanted to connect with these family members who were old friends. She used Breathing Mindfully to reduce her anxiety. "It helps me be calm, confident, and more relaxed when I center myself with my breath. Sometimes, Breathing Mindfully is a life-saver for me."

When to not Breathe Mindfully

Carla, a veteran third-grade teacher, has taught Breathing Mindfully to her classes for years. She works in inner-city Oakland, California, with kids who have had a lot of trauma. She finds that guiding kids in using Breathing Mindfully helps them enormously. "They can go from being wild and unruly to being Centered and calm within a minute of starting our breathing practice."

However, she has some kids who just can't Breathe Mindfully. "Emilio is one of my favorite students. He's like a jack-in-the-box—up and down out of his seat—moving around the classroom, cleaning erasers, and throwing stuff in the trash like a pro basketball player. He can be a bit disruptive. Academics are hard for him, and so is Breathing Mindfully. He just can't sit still, and when he does focus internally, it makes him more moody and disruptive. It makes so much sense, given his trauma history. He and I have an agreement that when the rest of the class is practicing Breathing Mindfully, Emilio gets to draw with his pencil. He's not a great artist, but moving the pencil is soothing and calms him down in a way that works for him."

Emilio is like many people who have experienced trauma. Sometimes, Breathing Mindfully is not helpful for them. Resting quietly might be triggering if thoughts, feelings, or experiences emerge that they are working hard to forget. Other types of self-regulation may be more helpful, or Breathing Mindfully may need to be guided externally by an app, a coach, or a therapist.

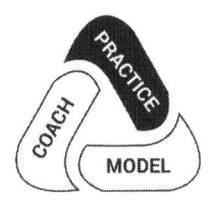

Practicing Breathing Mindfully

Breathe deeply. Feel it completely.

Meri—I sat there, frustrated and depleted. I just spent an hour dealing with the county assessor's office, trying to figure out their antediluvian system, which makes us fill out forms by hand to tell them information that we had already emailed them over a year ago. This is to dispute a charge that would keep reoccurring unless we spent valuable staff time on it. These issues made me hate "the system." As I put my hand over my face, my training kicked in. "Breathe deeply and feel it completely." So I started to breathe deeply in and out while feeling the sensations of breathing in my body. Wow! I could feel myself calming and my head clearing. My problem hadn't changed, but my ability to deal with it was much better. Because I had been practicing Breathing Mindfully, I could drop into my body-breath awareness with minimal effort. Definitely a win!

Use This Skill When…

- I want to savor the moment I'm in and become more present.
- I want to feel calm and relaxed.

- I want to be able to think more clearly.
- I'm stressed.
- I'm having difficulty sleeping.

I can Practice This by...

- **Pausing to focus** on 3-5 slow, complete breaths.
- **Feeling the sensation** in my body as my breath moves in and out.
- **Noticing the space** between my breaths.
- **Noticing how Breathing Mindfully improves my emotions.**

Sometimes, we might notice we are holding our breath. Are we engrossed in a situation where we stop breathing briefly? Do we feel tense? If so, a practice of Breathing Mindfully can help us let go of those habits.

Isabella loves to practice Breathing Mindfully on her way to and from work. As a new mom, it was challenging to transition back to the workplace. By Breathing Mindfully, she Centers herself as she leaves behind the morning's chaos and prepares herself for her workplace. Then, by Breathing Mindfully on the way home, Isabella leaves behind work stress to show up completely as the wife and mother she wants to be at home.

Choose some ways to structure a practice:

- **Set the tone for the day** by starting with Breathing Mindfully.
- **Breathe in transitions.** Practice Breathing Mindfully at the start of a meeting, before walking in the door to work, just before greeting a patient, family member, or colleague, before starting a new task, or before returning home.

- **Breathing for patience.** Practice Breathing Mindfully at stoplights, in a waiting room, in line, on hold, or while waiting for the computer to power on.

- **Breathing in challenging times.** Before a difficult conversation, when we hear difficult news, get frustrated, or have conflict around us. Notice when we are tense or holding our breath throughout the day and take a few mindful breaths.

- Pause amid a busy day by **stepping outside to Breathe Mindfully.** Breathing consciously while noticing nature—flowers and trees, the smell of the earth, feeling of the wind or sun, the openness of the sky—can be completely rejuvenating.

- **Breathing for sleep.** Take relaxed full breaths while counting in five and counting out eight. Feel the body relax while sinking into the comfort of bed.

Breathing Mindfully can be done in a moment or longer—anywhere in our daily routine. By practicing breathing when we are not in the middle of a reaction, it is more available when we are stressed.

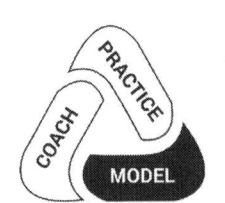

Modeling and Coaching This Skill for our Families

It is a funny thing about breathing—it happens without thinking, and we can control it. For Gideon, Breathing Mindfully became essential during the pandemic when he and his wife worked from home while his kids attended school on Zoom. It became critical to helping him work on not using his Protective Pattern of Attacking when he got upset.

"Practice makes better." That was so true for Gideon. Only after Gideon started practicing Breathing Mindfully while waiting for his morning coffee to brew could he stay calm using his breath in real-time stressful situations with his family.

Gideon's morning practice allowed him to Breathe Mindfully on the front lines of #DadLife. Gideon began to notice his breathing patterns, especially his tight, shallow breathing that directly preceded losing his patience. It usually happened the second time he asked his son to get off the computer—at the previously agreed "end of screen time." When these situations arose, sometimes Gideon felt like he turned into the Incredible Hulk yelling at his son. Breathing Mindfully, really breathing all the way down into his belly, instead kept Gideon grounded. It helped him *Speak Authentically*—clearly, kindly, and calmly—and remind his son that they had an agreement he needed to honor. Breathing Mindfully kept him out of power dynamics and preempted his deeper, louder voice. Breathing Mindfully helped Gideon become "a better version of himself." Moreover, by practicing in front of his son, Gideon modeled for him how Breathing Mindfully can be calming in stressful situations.

Practices to Model and Coach Breathing Mindfully:

- When I get upset at my kids, I can tell my family I need to take a moment to Breathe Mindfully. Afterwards, I can share how it impacts me. *"Okay, I feel calmer now. I'd like to talk about what just happened."*

- I can invite my kids to practice breathing with me. I can help them practice by creating a family breathing routine. We can do Breathing Mindfully together as we go through daily transitions or prepare for sleep.

Activity: Schedule Breathing Mindfully

"Practice makes perfect." Build a practice by setting the alarm twice daily to remind us to stop and take five mindful breaths, perhaps just before getting to work or arriving home at the end of the day. With practice, it becomes part of our routine, and we no longer need the alarm.

Structures help support our practice. Create a favorite spot to do Breathing Mindfully and stick with it, such as a specific chair in the living room, a bench in a garden, or a cushion on a favorite rug. It's also helpful to piggyback a new habit onto something we routinely do.

Challenge Activity: Asking for Guidance

Invite someone else to lead us through Breathing Mindfully if we feel unsure or resistant. Then, we can focus on breathing rather than on our thoughts and feelings. Take a yoga class. Many yoga teachers focus on movements and breathing and offer excellent training in Breathing Mindfully. Or, try out one of the many Breathing Apps, like the *Calm App* or *Stop, Breathe & Think App*, which have some wonderful guided meditations that make breathing easy.

Deeper Insights

Chuck—As a teenager, when training in karate, I learned about the power of my breath. I advanced quickly and was selected for special techniques, including breaking boards with my hands and feet. I was amazed at what was possible by focusing my mind and breath together. After years of serious training, at age 16, I broke a concrete block with my forehead (yup, I know, crazy, right?). With complete focus on the breath and total trust, it was as easy as cracking a dry twig over my knee.

Breathing Mindfully served me well when I switched to rock climbing. Rock climbing was both thrilling and sometimes terrifying. I loved pushing the envelope, so I'd stretch myself and climb difficult rock faces. I remember being hundreds of feet off the ground on the lead end of the rope, with my last point of protection way below my feet, and getting completely frozen with the fear of falling. My breath saved me. I'd breathe from deep inside my body, calm myself completely, and either move up through the difficulty or sometimes downclimb backward to a safer point to rest. I couldn't have done it without my breath.

Now, I love to practice Breathing Mindfully first thing in the morning in a meditative way. I sit on a chair, place my feet on the floor, and tune into my body. I align my spine and balance my head. I close my eyes and begin to notice my breath. With my mouth gently closed and my jaws relaxed, I feel the sensation of my breath moving in and out of my nostrils. Then I notice how my breath feels as my lungs rise and fall ... staying with the sensation of the movement of my chest expanding and releasing ... noticing the felt sense of air moving in and out of my lungs. I then feel the breath moving my belly as my diaphragm expands and contracts with each breath. By being aware of my breath, I also notice the sense of wellbeing it brings to my whole body, enjoying the inner peace that comes when I give time and space for it.

Breathing Mindfully can be an equalizer, a healer, a transformative agent of change, and a luminous experience of consciousness.

> **"When you arise in the morning think of what a precious privilege it is to be alive— to breathe, to think, to enjoy, to love."**
> ~ Octavius Winslow, 19th-century theologian

Research shows that respiration patterns directly affect our wellbeing. Breathing Mindfully shifts us from the sympathetic to the parasympathetic nervous system. This changes the heart's rhythm from a chaotic pattern to a synchronized pattern of the heart beating in harmony with itself (as measured by heart rate variability, HRV—the space between heartbeats). The link between vagus nerve activity and the high-frequency HRV component has been well established. Breathing Mindfully also changes our biology. Instead of releasing cortisol, we activate dehydroepiandrosterone (DHEA), sometimes known as the anti-stress hormone. By activating our voluntary parasympathetic nervous system, breathing soothes our sympathetic fight/flight nervous system (our Protective Patterns).

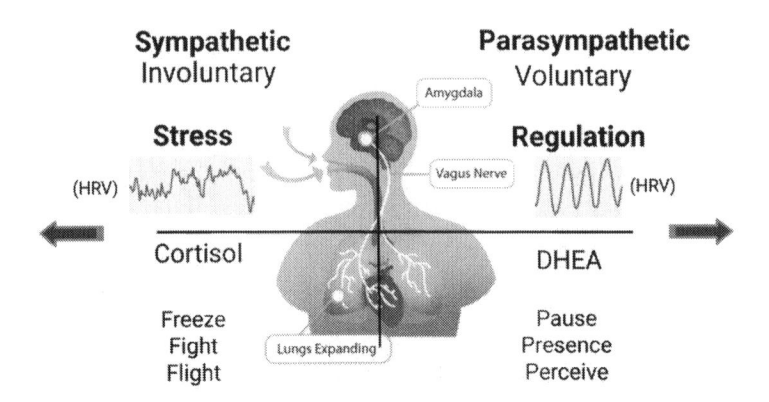

[Diagram: Sympathetic (Involuntary) – Stress, (HRV), Cortisol, Freeze/Fight/Flight | Parasympathetic (Voluntary) – Regulation, (HRV), DHEA, Pause/Presence/Perceive. Labels: Amygdala, Vagus Nerve, Lungs Expanding.]

Note: Neuroscience shows that in addition to our head brain (the one we're all familiar with, the "cephalic brain"), we also have a heart brain (the "cardiac brain") and a gut-brain (the "enteric brain"), all connected through the vagal nerves. Together, this triadic brain has immense intelligence and governs our holistic body and mind system.

Self-Discovery

- When do I feel stress? How might Breathing Mindfully help me relax and calm down?

- When during the day do I tend to hold my breath?

- Think of Breathing Mindfully as building a new "muscle." Can I commit myself to one week of practice? Start small. Notice how this impacts me.

- If it seems out of reach to "meditate," can I try reframing it into a simple breathing practice of being present to sensations in my body?

Centering Skills

Chapter 22

Letting Go

> *"You can't go back and change the beginning,
> but you can start where you are and change the ending."*
>
> ~ James Sherman, American playwright

Chuck—My friends Niles, Betsy, and I had planned a meeting, and then I had to cancel. I told Niles but not Betsy (thinking he would tell her), so she became upset with me. Though I apologized to her, my inner critic reared up, and I felt ashamed—an old pattern. My negative self-talk can be so harsh.

Then I thought about my Centering Skill of Letting Go, which reminds us, "Let go of what I can't control." I realized that if something happened yesterday, I couldn't change it. It seems so obvious, but it came to me as a significant personal shift. This concept helped me let go of my negative thinking and relax mentally and emotionally. I accepted my mistake, knowing I'm human, and forgave myself.

Letting Go is not always easy. Sometimes, we let go, only to pick up that concern, worry, or upset again later. It helps me to remember that the past is in the past—really, like, gone. My only option now is to attend to the impact of what happened and focus on changing the future. *Letting Go* releases me to be open to what's next.

Walter, a retired bank manager, let go of his worry about the winter storms impacting his home. It had rained hard for days, and the creek behind Walter's house was rising. Initially, he went out several times a day to look at it. Then he realized that his focus on the rising creek made him anxious. There was nothing he could do about it. Walter resolved to accept the conditions behind his house and let go of his anxiety. If the creek became dangerous, he would see it and hear it, and then he could take action.

An avid cook, Beatrix was working on *Letting Go* of trying to please others. Too often, Beatrix was that person who said yes, even when she felt like she couldn't possibly add one more thing to her plate. Too often, her Protective Pattern of Hyper-Caretaking emerged, and she said:

- *Yes, I can update the PTA website at the last minute.*
- *Sure, I can make homemade pasta for dinner on a Tuesday.*
- *Of course, I can juggle multiple work projects and not miss a deadline.*
- *Absolutely, I can help co-lead a new book club with friends and family.*

When she felt her anxiety growing and her resilience low, she knew she had taken on too much and needed to practice *Letting Go*. Beatrix learned to recognize two essential benefits of *Letting Go*. First, she realized it empowered her to let go even of those things she COULD control. When overwhelmed, Beatrix practiced responding to requests with boundaries. "*Instead of doing the website fix now, how about if I do it next weekend?*" Or "*I am happy to join a book club, but I don't have time to co-lead it.*" Second, she felt lighter when she accepted that she couldn't control how others reacted (i.e., how they felt about her not fixing the PTA website right now). Recognizing the empowering benefits of Letting Go helped Beatrix break her cycle of Hyper-Caretaking and anxiety.

Meri—I was twelve when my father left our family. I was furious. When we had a family counseling session to determine visiting times, I replied, "Never." I couldn't imagine spending time with my father ever again. Fortunately, over time, I used Letting Go to release my anger toward him. I began to recognize that life is complex, and he did his best in an overwhelming situation. He loved me. He was far from perfect, but so are the rest of us. Letting Go of my anger toward my father also helped me be okay when others—including myself—failed to achieve my high standards.

Letting Go: What is it?

Letting Go is releasing a worry, complaint, or attitude about an upsetting experience or a thought pattern or behavior that no longer serves us.

Our Centering Skills are strategies to bring us back into balance, helping us recover from a Protective Pattern or avoid using one completely. Letting Go keeps our focus on what is essential and releases what is not. Like Chuck, Walter, Beatrix, and Meri, we can use the Resilient Mindset of Curiosity and ask ourselves:

- What would be helpful to let go of?
- Do I need to let go of my expectations? Judgments? Attachment to an outcome?
- What situations are out of my control that would be helpful to release?
- What situations are in my control but would be beneficial to Let Go of to create healthy boundaries?
- Can a more meaningful value, goal, or perspective help me overcome this issue?

> **"Worry is like a rocking chair:　it gives you something to do but never gets you anywhere."**
>
> ~ Erma Bombeck, American humorist

As Walter discovered when he was concerned about storm damage, recognizing that our worry will not change an outcome can be a powerful motivator to let go. Brené Brown describes worry "as a chain of negative thoughts about bad things that might happen in the future." She reminds us that worry never helps. When we find ourselves in worry mode, we can ask, "Would it help?" Worry never helps because it does not change the outcome. Letting Go of worry helps us be more positive and creative in finding solutions.

Sometimes, we must let go of our expectations or attachment to a particular outcome. Liam is an executive vice-president for a global sales team. Early in his career, Liam's boss and colleagues expected him to go drinking with them every night after work. It was often more than a couple of drinks. Though Liam was uncomfortable, he felt he needed to go along to be successful in the business. One Friday night, after they had finished a huge business deal, Liam realized he had reached his limit. When his boss said, "Let's go to the bar," Liam said no. His boss was shocked. Sarcastically, he told Liam, "Don't worry about it. It is only your career." Though Liam knew he would no longer be on the inside track for promotion, he also knew his family was more important. He used his Resilient Mindset of Courage to stay true to his heart and stop the heavy drinking. By Letting Go of his aspirations for climbing that particular company ladder, he could create more of the life he wanted for himself and his family.

Even when the outcome we hope for seems positive and healthy, we might need to let it go. Jonah, who loves biking and hiking, found he was too caught up in tracking his activity. He felt he always needed to do better than he did before. One day, Jonah realized that the constant pressure to improve prevented him from enjoying his activity. He let go of his need to beat his exercise records, which helped him relax and have fun.

The desire to repair a relationship can also help us let go. Karlotta, a young Latina healthcare worker, realized a recent experience with her uncle was dragging her down. Her grandmother flew to California from Mexico to spend the holidays with her family but then got sick and was hospitalized. Karlotta, her parents, and her siblings focused on supporting her—visiting her in the hospital, calling her, and trying to lift her spirits to encourage her to get well. Karlotta's uncle and his family seemed to ignore the crisis and never even called her grandmother. Karlotta became very angry because her uncle's lack of attention violated her values and Cultural Patterns. After a few months, Karlotta saw that her grudge was not helping her, her grandmother, or her relationship with her uncle. She chose to let go of her resentment and work on forgiving her uncle.

Like Karlotta, many of us carry "emotional baggage" caused by upsetting words or behavior. We may hold onto old hurt feelings that don't serve us anymore. Unnoticed, unprocessed feelings weigh us down and may come up in unexpected and harmful ways. Sometimes, holding becomes a habit that we don't even notice. Naming the unhelpful baggage—seeing and acknowledging the burden—is often the first step. Letting Go helps us stop collecting negative stories we tell ourselves about ourselves or others.

Meri—When something bothers me, I usually talk with others and then can let it go. Those things I don't talk about, like the secret that my father left, are more likely to become my emotional baggage. Only when I could talk about my new family configuration with my friends, could I let it go. Eventually, I could use *Positive Reframing* to change the negative story—"I am from a 'broken home'"—to a positive one—"My family is flexible and inclusive."

The Resilient Mindset of Choice can help us Let Go, care for our needs, and regain our power. Rather than reacting to someone else's words or behavior, Letting Go stops us from letting the other person take up so much room in our heads or hearts. A single mom, Vivienne practiced Letting Go when she realized her Defending Protective Pattern emerged in reaction to her former husband's texts. Though he had a poor diet before their marriage, now he constantly texted her to check what the kids were eating. "Junior shouldn't have a milkshake before the game," and "What are your rules for Halloween candy?" Finally, Vivienne decided to stop reacting with snarky retorts. She realized she couldn't change him but could change her response. Vivienne practiced Letting Go rather than answering his texts. Ignoring and walking away from a situation can be an effective way of Letting Go and gaining our power back.

Cora also used the powerful Choice of Letting Go to care for herself. For Cora, one of the most challenging choices she faced in life was divorcing her first husband. While more than half of first marriages in the United States end in divorce, most people struggle with this decision and often feel alone, stuck, and scared.

Cora and her husband had a very connected and loving relationship for the first four years of their courtship. Shortly after they married, her husband got into a severe car accident, resulting in significant physical and mental health issues. Cora spent many years in her Hyper-Caretaking Protective Pattern, trying everything she could to "fix" him or at least make him feel better. However, her husband was stuck in a victim mindset, unwilling to leave the house or seek the help he needed. Cora became clinically depressed and felt like a failure. She truly loved her husband and felt caught between abandoning him or abandoning herself. Over time, she realized that she could not change him. Though her strong Cultural Patterns reinforced her feelings that divorce would mean she failed, she finally let go of her belief that she was ultimately responsible for her husband's happiness.

Influence of Cultural Patterns

"Real strength is not control.
It is knowing when to let go."
~ Christopher Barzak, author

Letting Go is NOT Gideon's jam. Gideon's difficulty in Letting Go is linked to his deeper Cultural Patterns—the messages he received about how a man should be in control, be persistent, and take care of everything. "I grew up being told I should NOT accept things as they are. I was heavily involved in sports, and my coaches pushed me to 'make things the way I want.' Never let go was the driving message." Gideon feels he doesn't want to "give up," "be a punk," or "take that." He also has a sense of justice and wants things to be fair. To him, Letting Go feels like a weakness, like giving up and letting the other person "get away with it."

Gideon has to use the Resilient Mindsets of Choice and Courage to help him let go. When he recognizes that letting go is better for his loved ones, he can lean into his values and make that choice. Letting Go also helps him feel unburdened, as if he has put down a weight that he was unaware he was carrying.

Fritz's father, Rodrigo, had a bad temper, and he blew up like a storm. Rodrigo's children knew not to approach him in the morning because he would stomp around and complain. Rodrigo scared others when he shouted, even into his nineties. Rodrigo could keep a grudge like nobody's business and became estranged from family members. Fritz saw the pain that holding a grudge creates, so he learned to let go. "I have tried to keep a grudge," Fritz admits, "But I can't stay mad at anyone. I am lucky if I stay mad for three days."

When Letting Go is Difficult

It is normal to have difficulty Letting Go and to hang onto things that bother us. The human brain evolved to notice problems so we would pay attention and deal with them. When we are having difficulty using a Centering Skill, we can start by shifting into our Curiosity Mindset and ask ourselves the following questions:

Am I using a Protective Pattern? We may fear being vulnerable or unsafe, which feels like rejection, failure, or losing control. We might hold on through our Protective Pattern of Hyper-Caretaking, when we solve a problem for someone else that is really theirs to solve. Esther recognized she was Hyper-Caretaking her 13-year-old daughter Harriet. "I wanted Harriet to understand I knew what was best for her. But she wanted to do things her own way." Ultimately, while Esther could provide guidance and guardrails, she had to let go. Harriet needed to make her own decisions. Noticing when our Protective Patterns are not helping our relationships helps us let go.

Am I afraid of losing something dear to me? Julia's dad needed a caregiver after his stroke. Julia's mom, Regina, kept asking Julia if she had received approval from the long-term care agency for this caregiver. "I told my mom that I would take care of the approval. I called the agency several times a day and followed up by email. My mom's nagging exasperated me, and I wanted her just to 'Let it Go!'" It felt to Julia that her mom didn't trust her to handle the problem. Then Julia realized that Regina was harping on the agency approval of the caregiver to deflect her natural fear of losing her husband. Regina could not let go of her relatively minor concern because then her big fears could surface.

Do I have a more meaningful value that might help me let go? Sometimes, we need to focus on a higher value that supersedes holding on. Our Resilient Mindset of Courage reminds us to consider, "What kind of person do I want to be?" Meri let go of her anger toward her dad because she wanted his presence. Karlotta let go of her grudge against her uncle because she valued her relationship with him. Liam let go of his career aspirations to spend time with his family. Cora let go of her fear of divorce to recover her emotional health. Gideon let go of his work frustrations to have a better relationship with his family.

Letting Go is NOT saying others' poor behavior is okay. It IS seeing what is happening and making the best choice for our values. It was not okay that Liam's boss and colleagues bullied him into drinking. It was not okay for Vivienne's former husband to use food complaints as a pretext to goad her. It was not okay for Cora's husband to give up on her for years and not try to connect with her. When we see things that are not okay, Letting Go reminds us that sometimes we need to

Let Go of our need to change other people's behavior. We can only control our own response.

Like Gideon, sometimes our Cultural Patterns stop us from Letting Go. Some confuse grit, toughing it out, or pulling oneself up by the bootstraps as "resilience." Resilience is NOT holding on to suffering or just trying to endure hardships. Sometimes, it IS saying no and holding firm boundaries. Some of our most resilient moments are when we choose not to fight what is happening or has already happened. Letting Go can help us feel relief, as it did for Beatrix, Meri, Karlotta, Liam, Cora, and Gideon. Releasing our internal pain or stress IS in our control, like letting go of a rope being pulled too fast out of our hands so it won't burn us.

When NOT to let go

Letting Go may not be helpful until we learn from a situation. When we don't want to Let Go of something, it may be because it is too important and we need to face upsetting or difficult things. Letting Go at the wrong point can potentially lead us to a harmful use of the Avoiding Protective Pattern.

Chuck—I have had a problematic relationship with my brother for much of my life, but I also love him dearly. My relationship with him is too important for me to let go of. And the things that have happened between us can't be ignored, so I keep them. My feelings let me know what is important!

Some issues or hurts really are too important to Let Go of.

- Instead, they might need to be faced:
    - There may be changes I need to make in me.
    - I may need to set boundaries that maintain my values or dignity.
    - I might need to change a situation so no one is hurt anymore.

- I might need to *Speak Authentically* to the person to get things right.
- I might need help and guidance from a mental health professional.

When we are not Letting Go of something, being Curious can help us distinguish whether we still have something to learn in going toward it or if the lessons have been learned and it's time to Let Go. The Resilient Mindset of Courage helps us address what may need to change or to accept what is.

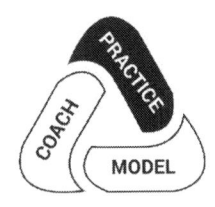

Practicing Letting Go

> "Accept what is, let go of what was, have faith in what will be."
> ~Sonia Ricotti, author

Use This Skill When…

- I find myself focusing on a worry.
- I can feel my Protective Patterns emerging and want to make a different choice.
- Something is out of my control, and I am bothered by it.
- I am carrying emotional baggage. I keep thinking about something hurtful.
- I want to be free from something that bothers me.

Four Steps of Letting Go

1. **Letting In**
   ⇩
2. **Letting Be**
   ⇩
3. **Letting Go**
   ⇩
4. **Letting Come**

1. **Letting In**—Identifying Our Truth

   The first step of Letting Go is Letting In, which is naming what is happening in our lives. It can be challenging to recognize what is happening. Sometimes, we don't want to see it and prefer avoiding the truth by pretending something isn't so.

   Randolph tried not to see what was happening in his family. When Randolph was a teenager, he spent his time enjoying himself, knowing his parents were taking care of things for him. Then, his mom was diagnosed with cancer. Randolph's dad was swamped, as he had to earn a living, take care of his ill wife, and care for the family. At first, Randolph tried not to see the massive shift in his family. Eventually, he had to Let In that his old family structure was gone.

   Costume designer Brenda also faced a change when she began working with a new director for the high-school play. He reduced the rehearsal schedule, eliminating Friday rehearsals and shortening tech week. Brenda was horrified. Could he really change the time-honored process that had worked for decades? She had to Let In the news that the procedures she had used for so long would be changed.

2. **Letting Be**—Accepting What Is

   After we identify what is happening, we are at a crossroads. Will we resist the change or let it be what it is?

   Randolph had to accept that he would no longer have his previous carefree life. He knew he couldn't help his dad much because he had never held a job or learned to do practical things. As he witnessed his dad's stress, he regretted that he had remained dependent on his parents for so long. Like Randolph, accepting a new reality may feel raw and painful for many of us, but feeling those emotions might be part of accepting.

   Brenda first tried talking with the new director. He very quickly responded that the new schedule was non-negotiable. His attitude set Brenda off. He wouldn't even allow a conversation! But she had to accept his stance. After calmly asking him a few things, she asked herself some hard questions. "Am I giving up too soon? Am I selling out?" But she saw no give on his part, so she accepted his stance. Like Brenda, Letting Be often involves seeing that any efforts to resist are futile or harmful. We will be better if we accept what is and move ahead.

   Accepting something—as it is—doesn't mean we don't want to change it. It means we face it wholeheartedly, as Randolph and Brenda did.

3. **Letting Go**—Forgiving and Releasing

   Once we have Let In and Let Be, we may be ready to Let Go. We can release what we have been holding. We can forgive ourselves or others.

   For Randolph, once he accepted his parents' new roles, he realized it was time to start Letting Go of his old ways and take responsibility. When Brenda saw the new director would not change his position, she accepted it. She Let Go of her attachment to how she had done it previously and chose to stay in the theater group. For Brenda, finding empathy for the other person without agreeing with that person's behavior, perspective, or experience was helpful.

Letting Go and forgiving the other person frees us from holding on to the pain. We can still hold boundaries and hold people accountable, but resentment no longer drags us down.

4. **Letting Come**—Making Room for New Possibilities

When we notice we are holding on to a disempowering or painful story, we have the power to let go of those lousy feelings and old stories. Letting Go helps us create room for Letting Come: creating new stories with new possibilities.

Once Randolph decided to become responsible, he pursued his course with full force. He studied hard and became a doctor. Moreover, like many of us, Randolph's experience as a teen shaped how he treated his own children. He was determined that his children would learn responsibility in a way he hadn't.

Though she was not happy about it, Brenda focused on doing her job and creating the best possible product within the constraints set by the director. Letting Go of her attachment to the old schedule allowed her to be more at peace and enjoy her role in the theater company.

For Randolph and Brenda, *Letting Go* made room for what was possible with others. That does not mean the past never happened, but it allowed for greater empathy, compassion, and forgiveness. Our most important relationships are ever-evolving when we face them fully, accept what was, let things be, Let Go of our hurts, and make room for something new.

I can Practice This by...

- **Letting Go of annoyances.** When I find myself getting wound up by irritants (being cut off in traffic, out of coffee, a slow internet), I notice that it is not in my control and practice just letting it go.

- **Letting Go of the hurt.** When someone says something hurtful, I ask myself: Is there a grain of truth in it? If so, I might look into it. Otherwise, their comment could be more about them (their needs, insecurities, etc.) than me. Let it go.

- **Letting Go of my judgments and expectations**—the "shoulds" I have for myself and others I carry around. I may also need to let go of attitudes, stories, or feelings weighing me down.

- **Letting Go of a Protective Pattern** when it's not serving me. Am I Hyper-Caretaking and not recognizing the capacity of others? Or Defending or Attacking in a harmful way?

- **Letting Go of stress and tension.** When winding down for the evening, review the day's events and ask—what negativity can I let go of? What body tension can I release for better sleep?

- **Letting Go of all the things not in my control,** like outcomes. A mantra, "this too shall pass," acknowledges the transience of things.

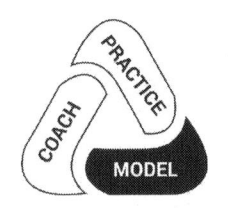

Modeling and Coaching This Skill for our Families

Beatrix's go-to Protective Pattern is Attacking. When she bought a new house (during the pandemic), many stressors popped up for her. On the last day of her big move, her youngest son desperately wanted to help move boxes like his big brother. While she knew she was lucky to have this problem, it created a sticky wicket for her. The box he so desperately wanted to carry was over-packed with her favorite, fragile, frequently-used kitchen items. Since it was the end of the move, everything left was thrown in. That extra-heavy, not-at-all-protected box was calling to her youngest son.

"At that moment, I was tired, hungry, sore, and about to snap." Beatrix felt it coming, and then she paused. She Noticed her Attacking Protective Pattern was chomping at the bit to be unleashed. Instead, she chose Letting Go. Nothing in that box couldn't be replaced.

By Noticing herself, Beatrix could see what mattered most. Her son needed to contribute to their family like his brother and be part of their new home. His needs were far more critical than any serving platter, and remembering that helped her Let Go. Beatrix's son could see and feel her Let Go of her angry reaction and shift to being kinder and gentler with him.

Practices to Model and Coach Letting Go:

- When I want to let go of something, I can explain why and how I let it go to my family.

- I can create a family practice of Letting Go. For example, I might ask my family to write down something they can let go. Then we can throw the papers away together and celebrate letting it all go.

Deeper Insights

Meri—We are selling my mother's house. She owned it for 57 years, first jointly with my father and then with my stepfather. A source of stability and joy in my childhood, the neighborhood kids often gathered there to play imaginative games in our large backyard, with its big playhouse, climbing bars, and abandoned plum orchard out our back gate. Yesterday, I spent a few minutes saying goodbye to each empty room, still filled with almost 60 years of memories.

Letting go of this house feels like letting go of a significant tangible part of my mom. As I stood in each room, the steps of Letting Go helped me process this loss.

1. Let In: The process helped me let in that we will no longer have this house in which to gather our big extended family for monthly celebrations like we have for decades. Over the last two months, we have disbursed into the world all the things that made those gatherings possible—from the pots

and plates to the tables and chairs. The house is empty and ready to be sold.

2. Let Be: Part of my heart wants to hold onto this house so badly (like I want to hold on to my mom), but I had to let it be that we are selling it. It is the right decision for so many reasons.

3. Let Go: Saying goodbye to the house helped me let it go. I appreciated all it gave us, and now I am releasing it.

4. Let Come: My Letting Go was fueled by my desire to be open to what is next. The house needs a new family to nurture. I will have other places that are meaningful to me and my family. My daughter reminded me that family gatherings will still happen, though they will take a different shape now, in different homes.

Letting Go of anything meaningful to us is never easy, but we don't change and grow without "shedding some skin." Like with my mom's house, sometimes letting go is painful. Knowing that it is necessary so that we can let come can help.

Activity: Inventory of Items That Weigh us Down

1. Take a moment to think of things that weigh me down. Are there things hurtful comments I hold on to? Am I upset with others in my life? Are there things I have done that I am beating myself up over? Write each one of these things on a separate small slip of paper.

2. Now, think about whether I have control over those things. Which would be helpful for me to let go of? Crumple up that paper and say why I no longer need it. Then, throw it away. Literally throwing the paper like a ball can give our bodies a sense of "getting rid of something."

Self-Discovery

- What do I constantly complain about? Which of those things would benefit most from working on *Letting Go*?

- What am I attached to that harms me or others (belief, attitude, behavior, person, substance, food)? How would *Letting Go* of these attachments impact me or others?

- What might I need to Let In and name accurately so I can accept it and begin the process of *Letting Go*?

Centering Skills

Chapter 23

Finding Gratitude

> *"Wear gratitude like a cloak and it will feed every corner of your life."*
> ~ Rumi, 13th-century Persian poet

Meri—Last Wednesday was challenging. I was excited to make a new vegetarian recipe, but it had lots of chopping. I decided to use a recent gift: a mandoline that slices very thinly. I had read that this tool was dangerous, so I was careful and used the holder to grip the fennel rather than my hand. And then... ouch! One slip and the tip of my right thumb was gone. I REALLY tried to avoid this, and I did it anyway. The whole experience was traumatic, including spending much of the day in urgent care. And it was painful.

I needed to escape my negative attitude and stop thinking about my pain. I turned for solace to my favorite Centering Skill—Finding Gratitude. When my doctor said it would take two weeks to heal, I was grateful it wasn't two months. I was grateful I could still type, though more slowly, and I kept missing the "n" and space bar. I was so very grateful for healthcare and how my providers put me back together. I was also grateful for my husband, who worked from home so he could tie my shoes... open jars... and do all the other things we need thumbs to do! Finding Gratitude gave me a more optimistic perspective. My injury was a bummer, AND I was grateful I could see so much good in my life, which strengthened my resilience.

Finding Gratitude can help with any significant challenge. When Ximena recently ended a long-term relationship, she chose to use Finding Gratitude rather than sit in bitterness. She was grateful for the time they had together and for experiencing healing after this breakup. She is thankful for what she learned and to be able to look forward to who would come into her life.

Even everyday annoyances can be helped through Finding Gratitude. When superhero fan Imani was stuck in traffic, she thought about how grateful she was to have a car. Finding Gratitude helped her Nurture herself. Instead of being annoyed by bumper-to-bumper traffic, Imani chose to call her friends and listen to music. When she completed her journey, she was grateful she got there safely.

We can also improve relationships with Finding Gratitude. Like many parents of teens, Halima is trying to change her parenting style to match her son's needs. "It is easy to become frustrated, so I remind myself why I am so grateful he is in my life. I also Find Gratitude in that he is open with his feelings and willing to question authority."

Finding Gratitude: What is it?

Finding Gratitude is intentionally looking for what we are thankful for.

Our Centering Skills are strategies to bring us back into balance, helping us recover from a Protective Pattern or avoid using one completely. Finding Gratitude gives us a larger perspective—our difficulties are not the whole story, and other parts of our story are good and maybe even amazing. Finding Gratitude opens our hearts so we can hold challenges AND appreciation simultaneously.

We can use the Resilient Mindset of Curiosity to seek and discover what IS working: What am I grateful for in this moment—in myself, others, or life?

Gratitude profoundly affects our sense of wellbeing. When we focus on gratitude, we strengthen our emotional resilience. In most situations, there is something we can find to be grateful for—though we might have to work a bit to see it. We all face life changes we have not chosen, but we may be able to Find Gratitude for some part of it. With a focus on intentionally Finding Gratitude, we often can turn a difficulty that seemed significant or insurmountable into a problem that can be solved, an understanding that things will change over time, or something we learn to appreciate.

Otis, a nonprofit executive director, was fired after a tumultuous year of declining revenue. Though demoralizing, he could Find Gratitude that the board of directors had forced the separation. Otis was anxious about losing his income and didn't know his next step, but the job stress had overwhelmed him, and he didn't know what to do about it. He could Find Gratitude for his relief.

Sometimes, it is others' suffering that reveals our gratitude. Ricardo, collector of Chicano art, has an occasionally rocky relationship with his parents. However, he could more easily Find Gratitude for them after visiting a friend's father who had cancer and was nearing the end of life. Seeing an imminent death up close made him feel very grateful for his parents' health.

Nursing supervisor Stella experiences Finding Gratitude more easily because she is familiar with other people's pain. "When I wake up, I am grateful that I can wiggle my fingers and toes. I know too many people who can't get out of bed."

Meri—When the stress of the pandemic eased, my spirits lifted beyond what I had thought possible. Finding Gratitude became even more important to me. I was grateful for so many things I had taken for granted—like grocery shopping without fear and walking down the street without a mask. I gained a newfound sense of awe and appreciation for the power of human connection. Even a simple in-person conversation filled me with gratitude, like when I was hiking around Pinecrest Lake in the Sierras, and all these strangers stopped to talk. When I spent time with family in person—with no masks—over the Fourth of July, it almost seemed magical, too good to be true.

Influence of Cultural Patterns

Our Cultural Patterns can make it challenging to Find Gratitude. Some of us were raised in families focused on solving problems or improving. For others, the focus might have been on worry, concern, or how the glass was half-empty.

Nettie, a single mom, came from a family that didn't model Finding Gratitude. Life had many challenges, and advice to Find Gratitude would upset her. Nettie struggled so much and felt others failed to recognize how hard she worked to improve life for herself and her son. She was angry anytime someone suggested that Finding Gratitude would help.

Chuck—In my family, my dad exhibited deep anxiety, while my mom professed over-the-top gratitude and optimism. I absorbed both their anxiety and optimism, but early on, I discovered that Finding Gratitude in nature could counteract my worry. In Lima, Peru, I was grateful for the comfort of our small garden behind high walls covered in bougainvillea. As I grew, I continued to be thankful for the natural world as an escape from my trauma. In Virginia, I loved paddling a canoe across a still pond, and in New Hampshire, I discovered the exhilaration of climbing mountains.

Meri—Finding Gratitude is integral to my faith tradition and has been part of my life for as long as I can remember. For me, prayer almost always has gratitude at the center. I feel rooted in the understanding that everything in my life is a gift of love. It is the reason my go-to Centering strategy is Finding Gratitude.

My appreciation for this skill deepened through living and working in developing countries. One job involved bringing water, sanitation, and tech training to a center in the slum of Kibera, Nairobi, and another involved agricultural training in West Africa. I also spent a year in India, working on a project combatting the lack of knowledge and stigma surrounding AIDS. Of course, I saw incredible heartache and challenges, but through all these experiences, I saw local people, even those living in entrenched poverty, finding joy and gratitude in their lives. I was repeatedly reminded that Finding Gratitude does not depend on being healthy or having a warm house, clean water, or healthy food.

When Finding Gratitude is Difficult

When we are having difficulty using a Centering Skill, we can start by shifting into our Curiosity Mindset and ask ourselves the following questions:

Am I using a Protective Pattern? Esther, a grandmother and artist, learned the Protective Pattern of Avoiding when she was young. "I grew up in an alcoholic family, which colored my life with difficulties. My father was in the Navy and would regularly be away on sea duty. When he was home, he tended to be emotionally unavailable. My mother worked full-time and had her hands full while my father was away."

Then, in Esther's late teens, her mom got breast cancer and died. Esther's family didn't discuss her mom's illness or her impending death at all. "Avoiding the truth threw my life for a loop. I loved my mom so much, and the pain of not talking about her dying was almost too great to bear. I struggled with depression for years before I found my way back to gratitude. As an older adult, I learned that my gratitude is stronger than the burdens in my life. When I am in nature or with my grandkids, Finding Gratitude uplifts me and helps me know, 'all is well.'"

Do I have a more meaningful value that might help me Find Gratitude? Gratitude can be hard to find when our emotional cup is empty. Because of her Cultural Patterns, Nettie felt that way. Still, so many others had suggested keeping a gratitude list that eventually, she decided it wouldn't hurt to try. Every day, Nettie wrote what she was grateful for. It helped her Let Go of her hoped-for outcomes and be thankful for other things along the way.

For Nettie, as a single mom, Finding Gratitude centered on her home, which gave her space for herself and her son to live peacefully. Every day, she felt grateful that her home kept her and her son safe and warm. Her Finding Gratitude practice also helped calm her son's anxieties. When he asked whether the doors were locked each night, Nettie modeled for him how to thank their home for keeping them safe.

One day, Nettie was putting away groceries when a spaghetti sauce jar slipped and shattered sauce all over her kitchen—the blinds, the walls, the furniture, and the floor. In the past, the thought of such a big clean-up job and the loss of the sauce might have pushed Nettie over the edge. However, Nettie's first thought was, "I am so glad I didn't cut myself." Her quick response of Finding Gratitude and its calming influence reinforced for Nettie the power of her simple practice.

Gloria's daughter Adriene discovered she had cancer two months into her pregnancy. Thankfully, it was removed quickly, and Adriene is now cancer-free. While it was difficult then, Gloria eventually found gratitude that her daughter went through that experience. What Adriene learned was more important than the initial fright of the cancer diagnosis. Her daughter now knows that some cancers can be detected and caught quickly, and survivors can lead a normal life. It has reduced the fear and stigma around cancer for her daughter.

Like for Nettie and Gloria, the values of becoming more of who we want to be and what we can learn can outweigh our difficulties in Finding Gratitude.

For principal and dad Gideon, gratitude seems far away when life is difficult. The word "Finding" is crucial because it reminds Gideon that his Resilient Mindset of Choice activates this skill. He has discovered he is happier when he flips what he says to himself—from "I have to pick up my kids from practice" to "I get to pick up my kids from practice." That simple shift, changing "I have to..." to "I get to..." unlocks the power of this skill. He relies on a quote: "Count your blessings before your burdens." Gideon doesn't want to deny the difficulties—he just wants to remember to focus on the blessings first.

When we Choose to search for gratitude, the very process of seeking and finding allows us to discover gratitude that may have been hiding. Once we make that choice, things get better. We feel more balanced when we simultaneously see what is difficult and what we appreciate.

When to NOT Find Gratitude

Finding Gratitude is not useful in every situation. First, some situations are worth staring in the face and saying, "This is awful." Second, if someone is harming or demeaning, we might need to leave the relationship or at least create firm boundaries that ensure we are not harmed. Finally, Finding Gratitude can be harmful if we use it to override emotions that are important to feel.

Chuck—Later in life, I discovered the healing power of feeling deep, difficult emotions. I learned that if my body needs to feel something, it's essential that I don't cover up the hurt feelings with Gratitude. First, I have to feel my feelings. Sometimes I curl up on the floor and cover myself with a blanket to go inside to feel. Getting in touch with the source of my emotions is always liberating. Often, feeling deeply includes a good cry, which can unburden me. If I go straight to Finding Gratitude, I may end up stuffing my feelings. If I do that too much, they can come back to haunt me, either as a physical symptom or by blocking other feelings. Though sometimes I might need to postpone feeling hurt, I don't want to sweep them under the rug for too long.

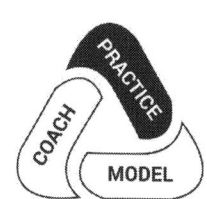

Practicing Finding Gratitude

Meri—For me, the Centering Skill of Finding Gratitude is like a tree in the center of my life. I have developed a practice, first learned through my faith tradition, of finding gratitude several times a day. Sometimes, I am grateful for the obvious things: My husband, my children, other friends and family, and for health. Sometimes, it is those things we take for granted—clean water, shelter, food, clothing. Often, especially now, it's for connection: a great conversation with a faraway friend, a shared joke while watching the Super Bowl.

Taking a few moments each day to focus on gratitude means I can find it more easily when I need to be centered, like when I am in the middle of a difficult conversation, expecting bad news, or when life throws me a curve ball. I find it most helpful when I am in an argument with my husband. If I can pause and remember all I am grateful for in him, I can shift the tenor of the conversation. I can reduce my Protective Patterns, and I am calmer. Giving my Gratitude Tree a little bit of water every day ensures that it is there in the middle of storms when I really need it.

Luz got frustrated when she received her landlord's letter warning of a rent increase. "What am I going to do now? That increase would kill our budget! How could he do this to us?" As she heard herself complaining to a coworker, she realized she needed a Centering Skill to feel more balanced and think more clearly. Finding Gratitude seemed like a good Choice, so Luz made a gratitude collage. She used a series of prompts like, "What food are you grateful for? Music? Someone who makes you laugh? Holiday tradition? What about your neighborhood? Your work or school?"

After completing her gratitude collage, Luz felt a shift in her body. She then could move into Positive Reframing. She now saw the landlord's letter as the push she and her husband needed to find a home to buy. Luz told her colleagues they would soon be invited to join her in celebrating a mortgage!

Use This Skill When…

- I simply want to feel the joy and beauty in my life.

- I want to balance a difficulty I am experiencing with something positive.

- I want to remember that I have a choice about how I see my life.
- I want to stop focusing on things or people that annoy me.
- I want to let go of my negative thinking.

Sanam, a pediatrician, started a gratitude practice after hearing about how helpful it can be. At first, she wrote down what she was grateful for every night. She gradually gave up the writing part because family, work, and life made it difficult to find time. Sanam's gratitude practice morphed into a mental list so that she internally noted what she was grateful for every day. She experienced a huge shift in her attitude. She had been struggling with negativity and burnout, and Finding Gratitude helped her become more positive and creative.

I can Practice This Skill by...

- **Asking myself** what I'm grateful for in myself, others, my situation, or life itself.
- **Writing** several things I am grateful for every day in a gratitude journal, or writing my strengths and talents and being grateful for what I offer to the world and those around me.
- **Pausing** for a moment in gratitude before eating.
- **At the beginning of meetings**, pause to be grateful for this opportunity, the people attending, and their gifts.
- **Identifying** three things from my day I am grateful for before I sleep.

Riya started her gratitude practice when she was raising teenagers. She felt a need to do something to keep herself strong and Centered with the turbulence parenting teenagers can bring. Every night, Riya jotted down a few things. On the more challenging days, it was simple: "My daughter is alive." or "She didn't just slam the door and escape to her room. She said goodnight first." Her gratitude practice has evolved but still includes many simple things, like "My coffee in the morning."

Jonah, a 60-year-old tech professional who loves to bike and hike, also started a gratitude journal. "It was being marketed to me on social media for months, but I ignored it. Then, one day, I decided to try it." He was surprised to recognize how it affected him. He has always loved to cook and to eat, but his gratitude has taken his appreciation to a whole new level. "Now I think, OMG, this is so good! I spend time being thankful for meals, and access to food, access to money to buy the food, and for living where I live." Jonah added, "I find more appreciation for everything. The other day, I was riding down Carmel Valley Road with the wind at my back. It was so picturesque, with the vineyards around me. I am so lucky to be here!" Finding Gratitude has made him aware of all the wonderful things he has in his life.

Modeling and Coaching This Skill for our Families

Avid cook Beatrix loves growing food for her family. She feels there is something magical about watching life and nourishment sprout from a tiny little seed. Last spring, as she moved her new spring crop from their seed starter home to larger pots, she noticed how tending to her seedlings is much like tending to her gratitude. When nurtured and loved daily, one tiny seed slowly begins to sprout and eventually, with continued tending and love, grows into a fully grown plant that showers her family with its fruits.

Beatrix added, "Focusing together with my family on even the smallest thing we are grateful for every day can grow our gratitude." But, like growing plants, it may not thrive if we don't tend to it. Choosing to practice the Centering Skill of Finding Gratitude every day shows her family what is important to her. It is as simple as watering new seedlings in the garden.

Practices to Model and Coach Finding Gratitude

- When I notice something to be grateful for, I share it with my family.

- At dinner or before bedtime, we share three gratitudes from our day.

- I help my kids list the things they are grateful for. Then, we can share our lists with each other and talk about how Finding Gratitude makes us feel.

- I attach a Gratitude whiteboard to the refrigerator so family members can randomly add their gratitude thoughts to it.

- Very young children might not understand gratitude, but they can relate to "What made me smile today?" Start a "What made me smile today?" tradition, sharing thoughts before dinner or bedtime.

Activity: Gratitude Inventory

- Make a list of 10 things I am grateful for in my life. Share this list with at least one person and notice how it makes me feel.

- Every day for a week, write down three things for which I am grateful. Write different things each day. Notice how this impacts me.

Challenge Activity: Gratitude in the Moment

- Take one minute to think about my day and a stressful situation. Think about one thing I am grateful for about that situation or person. How might finding gratitude during the moment change my stressful situations?

Digital Gratitude Activities

- **Create a group chat with friends or family members**: Whenever I complain, I text something I am grateful for. It helps me reframe my thoughts and feelings and helps us all stay connected.

- **Record my thoughts of the day**: Use my phone or another recording device to record my thoughts for the day. This practice combines "Noticing Myself" with "Finding Gratitude."

Deeper Insights

Meri—Though I learned about Finding Gratitude through my faith tradition as a child, my appreciation of its power grew through my twenties. Within four years, three of my friends contracted incurable cancer, and I journeyed with them through their decline. Though we all wondered, "Why them?" and were angry at the situation, their deaths also gave me a profound sense of the gift and sacredness of life. These friends didn't make it to age 30 and left behind loved ones who grieved them deeply. How could I not be grateful for the extra months, years, and decades I am living?

Around the same time, my husband's beloved Uncle Tom died suddenly at work of a heart attack, leaving behind his widow, Kate, with two young children. His sudden death—combined with the prevalence of heart issues in my husband's family—reminded me that my husband, too, might leave for work one day and never return. Tom's death imprinted on me a sense of the impermanence and unexpectedness of life and helped me find even more gratitude for my husband. Every evening when Steve returns from his job, I Find Gratitude that I have one more day with him. Even in the middle of an argument with him, I can pause and Find Gratitude, and it helps me halt my Protective Pattern and speak more authentically.

These deaths also reminded me of the moments we experience, the lives we touch, the love we share—that is true wealth, and I don't want to miss any of it. On our weekly walks for the past twenty years, my friends Maeve, Olive, and I call out "Beauty Alert!" so we can find gratitude in the new daffodils, the rising sun over the mountains, or the scurrying bunny crossing our path. We marvel at the enthusiasm and camaraderie of the families and friends walking their children to school. These walks provide us a safe space to voice concerns, feelings, worries, joy and to hear each other's wisdom and to offer our own. I have become so much richer by Finding Gratitude in these small moments.

Finding Gratitude also helps me feel a connection with other human beings. When I express gratitude before meals, I am reminded of all the people who contributed to the meal—my family who made it in our kitchen, but also the grocery store workers, the truck drivers and other transportation workers, the food packers, the farmers, and the farm workers. When I Find Gratitude for my health, I am also grateful for my doctors, nurses, pharmacists, lab techs, and radiologists. Everything we have is created and contributed to by so many others. This interconnected web of humanity supports me in thousands of ways I rarely think about. Finding Gratitude reminds me I am part of this world of kind, connected human beings.

Self-Discovery

- What am I grateful for in my life?
- How can I be more intentional about seeking my gratitude when I need it?
- What specific thoughts and images anchor me firmly to my gratitude? How can I use these anchors when upset and want to bring myself back to balance and Center?

Centering Skills

Chapter 24

Positive Reframing

> "Change your words, change your life!"
> ~ Joice Meyer, author

Meri—I was finished, completely out of ideas. As the executive director of a startup nonprofit in a Nairobi slum, I was charged with guiding it into financial sustainability. After several years of community engagement, staff training, and constructing an innovative water and sanitation building, as well as several months of providing service, we had few customers and little revenue, not to mention a host of technical problems. The vision had seemed meaningful, exciting, and workable. But it wasn't working.

As I lay in bed, feeling completely stuck and very sad at the end of the dream, I thought about the project's future. The building and the staff were still going to be there, even though the vision hadn't panned out. What would happen to them? It occurred to me that the board might bring in a "turnaround person" who could do something with our assets. And then I had another thought. Why couldn't I be the person to turn things around?

That epiphany began my understanding of the power of Positive Reframing. With much mentoring from industry partners, I worked with our team to develop a new vision and operational plan. It did not solve our problems overnight, but it set us on a path closer to sustainability. I learned that if I viewed a problem from a completely different perspective, new answers might appear.

Jerome, a fitness industry COO, also used Positive Reframing to change his perspective. He had been working with a new company for 18 months when his boss told him to fire a general manager and how to handle the termination. Jerome didn't want to fire the man, and he especially wanted to protect the employee's dignity. But he felt backed into a corner, so he followed the orders. Then, Jerome was forced to take his place and manage the organization while hiring a new general manager. By firing the popular boss, Jerome had given himself a crappy entrance. The whole experience could have been miserable—commuting an hour each way to do a job with angry people.

Instead, Jerome thought about how he could make this experience the least disheartening possible. He relied on Positive Reframing to see the possibilities. Since Jerome had not been the onsite manager for a fitness facility in many years, he relied on local staff to lead him through the procedures. He made sure the team was cared for and spent time building rapport. He cleaned up the basic operations and reduced workload by quickly filling other positions. Finally, because he believes "things happen for him, not to him," he framed the experience as an opportunity. By commuting on the train, he could study for his dream position, studying that would have been difficult if he had been working from home. He was uplifted by being able to do something positive and productive for himself.

Chicano art collector Ricardo recognized the power of Positive Reframing when he crashed his car during the pandemic. At first, he was really bummed, but he grew to see it as an opportunity. He had to walk to work, which took longer, but the walk took him past his favorite coffee shop so he could start his day with delicious coffee and a bagel. During that dark time, Ricardo could walk every day and enjoyed connecting with the barista. He began his day with positivity.

Positive Reframing: What is it?

Positive Reframing is intentionally shifting our thinking from seeing problems to seeing possibilities.

Our Centering Skills are strategies to bring us back into balance, helping us recover from a Protective Pattern or avoid using one completely. Positive Reframing looks at a situation from a more empowering perspective.

Our words shape our reality. We create the stories we tell ourselves about the world, ourselves, and others. Reframing means paying attention to our inner narrative. What story are we telling ourselves? Can we be curious and open to a different way of seeing things? Is there an alternative story that might be equally true and better? When we change the story, we change the meaning, and we change whether something is empowering or disempowering for us. These stories can be about work, family, or anything else in our lives. Meri, Jerome, and Ricardo all changed their inner stories during difficult situations and discovered more beneficial possibilities.

> "The words that come out of your mouth create the reality you inhabit."
> ~ Margie Warrell, author

Juana, a case manager, used Positive Reframing retroactively when reflecting on her forced job change. As a first-generation college student, she felt so proud of getting a job after college that required her degree. It was difficult when that job ended, and she entered the job search with trepidation. However, her new job turned out to be even better as it launched her into her chosen career. Juana realized that sometimes leaving a job, even involuntarily, can be the best thing that happens to us.

Superhero fan Imani uses Positive Reframing as her son moves into his teenage years. She changes the words she tells herself to more empowering ones. Rather than viewing this parenting phase as full of struggle, Imani wants to see it as an opportunity to have a new relationship with her son. She is working hard not to be extreme in her reactions to his behavior but instead to be grateful that he is changing and will continue to grow.

Reframing helps us create new meaning. We can reframe a problem as an opportunity, a perceived weakness as a strength, negativity as neutral, and unkindness as a lack of understanding. Sometimes, we must step back and gain perspective on what we are experiencing. We might then be able to find the positive intent behind someone's negative behavior.

Positive Reframing starts with Letting Go of our expectations and judgments. Once we are free of those, we can look at what is actually happening and see if we can craft something positive from it. When nursing supervisor Stella got frustrated about small things like a staff member who didn't listen to instructions, she shifted her perspective by using Positive Reframing. She knew feeling frustrated meant she needed to change her expectations. Stella realized her staff member might need better training, so she turned it into an opportunity to do valuable coaching. Her conversation with her nurse brought them closer and reminded Stella how lucky she was to work for a hospital that cares about a healthy work environment.

Meri—When I was in Nairobi, all I could see initially were the problems—few customers, no revenue, and many expenses. By switching my perspective, I focused on the assets, and the issue became—what can I do with the assets? A different perspective gave me hope and a lot of valuable answers.

When Drake's elderly parents were ailing, he retired earlier than expected to help them. Then COVID hit, and both parents passed away. Next, his mother-in-law moved in, his brother got Parkinson's disease, and Drake became the primary caregiver for both. At first, his wife Stella was frustrated that Drake was not pulling in a paycheck. She had expected his income would allow her to retire and give them financial ease in their later years. Positive Reframing helped Stella deal with her frustrations and let those dreams go. Stella let go of her judgment of Drake's housekeeping and instead celebrated Drake's fantastic care for her mom and his brother. She saw how Drake deepened his relationship with his brother and set an excellent example for their son, showing that caring for loved ones is most important.

Lightheartedness and humor can help us see the situation more positively. Jonah, a 60-year-old tech professional, shared humor with his team on a cancer fundraising bike tour last July. When the forecast predicted rain for all ten days of the tour, Jonah told his teammates, "At least we get to save money on sunscreen!" Jonah's positive attitude gave the team a laugh and lifted their spirits. Starting the ride with a sour attitude would have bummed everyone, and ultimately the ride was pleasantly cool with only two days of rain.

When life is at its most challenging, it is easy to let our Protective Patterns take over, but using Positive Reframing can help. In June 2021, avid cook Beatrix learned that her mother was diagnosed with a very aggressive cancer. Through the two weeks of her mother's illness and death, Beatrix found inner strength through Positive Reframing. This skill helped her appreciate her cousin, whom she had not seen in years due to very different political views. Instead of holding on to her grudge, Beatrix saw her cousin sitting at her mom's bedside with nothing but love in her heart. Beatrix also felt pride as her sister navigated all the moving parts of her mom's decline. Beatrix found a sliver of peace while talking with her mom about the end of her life and saw the beauty in her mom's acceptance. When we can find the positive, even in the worst times, it is easier to be Centered. When we are Centered, we can process the tough emotions and notice what we need more fully.

Influence of Cultural Patterns

Some families have rigid thinking. They believe there is only one perspective and focus all their attention on problems. Dranon, a forty-something single dad, had that view. His own parents had separated when he was young, and he didn't know his grandparents because they had been disowned or died early. Dranon's son, Marcus, who was in middle school, had lived with him since his divorce five years ago. Now Marcus wanted to live with his mom, and that choice hurt Dranon so much that he threatened to disown Marcus. Dranon's Cultural Patterns mired him in negative thinking so that he couldn't look beyond his own pain. Fortunately, counseling helped Dranon and Marcus each share how hurt and vulnerable they felt and how much they loved each other. Through hard work, Dranon learned to Positive Reframe his son's move to see benefits for both of them. It became a turning point in their complicated relationship.

Paxton's family, on the other hand, was good at rolling with punches. If something went wrong or they couldn't do something as planned, they pivoted quickly, which taught him how to Positive Reframe. Last winter, when Paxton was frustrated with his boss and job, he realized that his perspective was helping him. He had been viewing his job as if he should expect perfection. Once he adopted Positive Reframing, he recognized that no one gets everything they want all the time. Yes, work and life can be challenging, but they are also full of fantastic opportunities.

This change of perspective also helped Paxton appreciate how far he had come. Four years before, he was living with his grandmother, commuting two hours each way to a job at a company in crisis where his colleagues were resigning left and right. Those times were really tough. He dreamed of what he wanted—a nice place of his own, good friends, a better job, and a girlfriend. Positive Reframing helped him realize he had achieved all that.

Meri—Growing up as a Girl Scout, I camped with my troop every month for ten years. When we invariably ran into challenges, our troop leaders were masters of helping us use Positive Reframing. When the motorhome ran into mechanical trouble in the middle of nowhere, we used it as an opportunity to play games on the roadside while waiting for help. When the tube tent filled with condensation and got us wet, it was a chance to sleep under the stars. If we took the wrong trail on a hike, we got a few extra miles of exercise. I gained so much practice in Positive Reframing that I do it now almost reflexively. My experience of developing resilience through Scouting motivated me to lead my daughter's Girl Scout troop for 12 years.

When Positive Reframing is Difficult

Positive Reframing can be difficult if we have little experience seeing it modeled or are mired in a negative thinking pattern. When we are having difficulty using a Centering Skill, we can shift into our Curiosity Mindset and ask ourselves the following questions:

Am I using a Protective Pattern? Jonah wanted to get a part-time job doing Quickbooks. He thought he would get a job quickly. Someone would see he was qualified, and they would hire him. However, Jonah used his Protective Pattern of Avoiding when he never got responses to applications. He kept waiting. Even when his wife suggested getting certified, he put that idea off. Finally, Jonah Positively Reframed his situation. Rather than seeing his lack of work as an obstacle, it became his opportunity to plan a path toward certification. His plan included daily training classes, online live tutoring, and practice tests. When Jonah first took the certification test, he passed four of five sections. Rather than seeing that as a failure, he viewed it as an opportunity—he only needed to pass one more section! With his newly gained certification, he secured interviews with potential employers.

Do I have a more meaningful value that might help me Positive Reframe? Top administrators were scrutinizing Hampton's department, and he could feel it pull him off-center. "I was sure they didn't think I was doing a good enough job, and they were out to get me," said Hampton, a city employee. This thinking pulled Hampton down, and he knew it would not lead to a successful review. So, he used Positive Reframing to focus on the opportunity to showcase his outstanding colleagues. "We have the best team this organization has ever had. We communicate, are inclusive, and have each other's backs." With this new perspective, he felt more confident, and his presentation for the review was better.

Will exploring my options help me Positively Reframe? Like many high-school seniors, design enthusiast Emilia felt stressed by the college application process. Everyone in her family had gone to elite universities. Since she had worked hard at school, Emilia believed she would be able to attend whatever college she wanted. Then Emilia got rejected from the most elite ones on her list. She felt so disappointed and unwanted. Though she was admitted to a great university, because it had not been where she had envisioned her future, it suddenly felt like clothes that didn't fit.

That disappointed feeling colored her freshman year. She realized she didn't love her major in computer science and didn't want her job to be coding. Emilia considered transferring. However, writing her transfer application essays helped her Positively Reframe her college experience and allowed her to see new possibilities. As Emilia explored potential majors at other schools, she realized that she was intrigued by mechanical engineering and design, a major offered by her current college. Being excited about her major helped her see the other opportunities of her current school—including studying abroad and co-op work experiences—that she was drawn to in the first place. She became excited and happy to be at her university.

Can friends or family help me with the Positive Reframe? When Zainab moved across the country, away from her family, and changed her career, her previous anxieties surfaced again. Had she made a horrible mistake? She felt overwhelmed by the transitions, like she was in a giant spiral. One of her friends helped Zainab Positively Reframe her situation and create a more empowering story for herself. First, her friend helped her see that moving so far from her family and changing her career were significant life changes that might need time to process. Moreover, these moves were not a "pass/fail" situation. She could just "exist" with these changes for a while and see how they felt over time. With this shift in perspective, Zainab let go of her self-judgments and gave herself some grace.

When NOT to use Positive Reframing

Chuck—My mom had an over-the-top cheerful optimism. There was seemingly nothing that got under her skin. She automatically reframed everything as positive, which meant she denied my feelings and taught me to bury them. It took me years to unlearn and gain the essential skills of acknowledging and feeling my feelings. This type of "toxic positivity" is not Positive Reframing. Denying the difficult things in our lives and pretending everything is always fine undermines our emotional and physical health. "Feeling" our feelings and having a trusted person to talk to about them is critical for our wellbeing.

Positive Reframing is also not helpful when something serious has happened. Sometimes, we must stay present during a hardship or difficulty to focus entirely on what is needed. Like the other Centering Skills, Positive Reframing is only helpful in the right context. Only we can determine whether this Centering Skill benefits us in each situation.

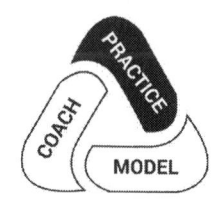

Practicing Positive Reframing

Like most skills, Positive Reframing comes more easily when we have practiced it. We can start small: "The coffee machine broke down" can become "It will be nice to stop at the coffee shop on the way to work." "A cranky patient yelling" can become "The patient is getting the care they really need."

Chuck—I vividly remember bushwhacking with a group of teens as a new Outward Bound instructor through steep Appalachian hillsides covered in tangles of thick rhododendrons. After two weeks in endless downpours of soaking rain, I was wet to the bone and as cold as an icy river. I was miserable and upset, and I let everyone in my group know it! One day, as I trudged through the wet undergrowth, I suddenly realized I was the one making myself miserable—it wasn't the cold or the rain, it was my attitude. Through Positive Reframing, I could tell myself a more empowering story. My heart started singing. It showed me that I could be soaked, cold, AND completely happy.

Use This Skill When…

- I want to remember there's goodness in the world.
- I am having a hard time and feel like it will always be like this.
- I focus on the mistakes made by me or others.

Meri—I woke up this morning very tense. I was juggling many balls and unsure how to get it all done. As I drove to my early morning walk with friends, I remembered a Positive Reframing thought practice: I could change all my "have tos" into "get tos." It was worth a try.

- I "get to" grocery shop—unlike those who don't have money, healthy food available, or time away from small children or elderly parents.
- I "get to" do the laundry—unlike those unhoused or without access to laundry facilities.
- I "get to" work—unlike those looking for a job, especially those with "different abilities" who many employers don't see as capable of contributing.

This Positive Reframing practice calmed me down. When I realized all I "get to" do, I felt fortunate rather than burdened by my list. Tasks that had been "chores" became experiences of privilege—more like a blessing than a curse.

I can Practice This by…

We can use the Resilient Mindset of Curiosity and ask ourselves, "How can I see this situation from a different perspective?" The story we tell ourselves matters. We can give ourselves more empowering stories by:

- **Reframing mistakes**. When I make a mistake, recognize that I have been given an opportunity to grow or to learn.

- **Reframing obstacles.** Practice changing how I see obstacles so they become opportunities to do something I had not thought of before. Where is the possibility?

- **Reframing negativity.** When people present me with negativity, try viewing their energy as their issue—that I don't have to absorb.

- **Rewind to reframe.** As soon as I notice I am getting off-center, "rewind" to the moment it happened and reframe with a new perspective as soon as possible. Catch it before it grows into something more significant.

Positive Reframing can also be helpful when we reflect on our past. Juana used Positive Reframing when she reflected on how the pandemic affected her. As a first-generation college student, she felt she finally hit her stride in her junior year. She was busy taking advantage of every opportunity that college offered. Then the COVID shutdown hit hard. She stayed at her university because it was the right decision for her family, but the isolation depressed her. This new time for herself led to soul-searching and eventually therapy. She spent more time sitting with her thoughts and feelings, learning to feel more deeply and process her experiences. With the few friends still in the area, Juana went on walks and enjoyed the beautiful nature in her surroundings. Now, when she looks back, she can see the gifts the pandemic gave her.

Modeling and Coaching This Skill for our Families

Jonah worked on this skill with his youngest son, Eddie, a college senior. Eddie had missed the deadline for student housing, and Jonah's former wife kept panicking every step of the way. That was not helpful for Eddie because each obstacle felt too big to handle. Instead, Jonah helped Eddie break down the problem into bite-size steps, seeing each step as an opportunity:

1. Need ideas for a room? Contact your brother for suggestions.
2. Is the room nice enough? Contact a friend to check it out.
3. Too expensive? Come up with a plan to earn some extra money to pay for it.
4. Need parents to sign a lease and get a security deposit? Ask us.
5. Does the college say it now has a room in the dorms? Negotiate to get out of the lease.

Once we learn how to break down our problems into manageable pieces, it is easier to see them as opportunities. With Positive Reframing, a "housing crisis" became "Eddie now sees that he can handle difficult issues"—an important life lesson he might not have learned without his obstacles.

Positive Reframing is tricky for principal Gideon, especially when he doesn't feel his most "resilient self" and his Protective Pattern of Attacking is emerging. Early in the pandemic, one of his three kids tested positive for COVID. Ugh! It was a false positive, but he didn't know that before picking up ALL his kids from school, worrying about the next steps, and becoming afraid and confused about what it all meant. During the inundation of emails, rapid testing, PCR testing, and concerns about missed homework, Gideon started Centering by Finding Gratitude for everyone's health. Then Positive Reframing helped him tell the kids, "Well, looks like you get a five-day weekend! Let's watch a family movie on a Wednesday night!" The surge in positive family energy reminded Gideon why it is important to model this skill for his kids. He demonstrated how to step back from being a victim of circumstances, unhook from a negative story that limited him, and invent a new lens to see through.

Practices to Model and Coach Positive Reframing:

- When things do not go as planned, I can share a different perspective with my family. Together, we can develop new plans: a Plan B, a Plan C, and maybe a Plan D.

- I can talk about what I am learning when I make a mistake.

- When things do not go the way my child wants, I can ask them if they are open to Positive Reframing. If they are, I can lead them through it. What new perspective can help them see a situation as more empowering?

When coaching others in the skill, we mustn't force others to have a positive reframe when it doesn't feel authentic to them. We can ask, "Would you like a Positive Reframe for that situation?" If they say no, we honor their feelings.

Activity: Conversations to Expand our Perspective

Exploring Positive Reframing with others is an incredible way to learn together:

- When something is throwing us off-balance, call a friend and have some straight talk together about what story we have in our mind and what would be a helpful reframe.

- When something has changed in our work or family, or an expectation has not been met, it can be a bonding experience to name what we are reacting to and what we might need to Let Go of. Then, we can look for a silver lining and collaborate on a more empowering story.

Group Activity: Finding Rainbows in our Storms

In a group, team, or family, we can ask everyone to think about who "helps us find rainbows" during stormy times, i.e., who are our allies when we are trying to overcome obstacles. Calling on those who can help us with Positive Reframing gives us Courage to use the skill.

Who are the rainbows in your clouds?

(word cloud: the birds outside, my best friend, kiddos i worked with, aunts, pups, my kids, po-po, my friends, uncles, my best friends, my therapist, colleagues, my dog, wife, inspirations, kids, cousin, dad, my husband, my daughter, mentors, mom, family, crickets, god son, my husband, friends, nephews, neighbors, my sisters, coyotes, nieces, grandmother, participants in training, my son, god daughter, birds, grandma, friday, my cat, jules, inspiring authors, my village, my puppies, my parents, strangers, maria, co-workers, my girlfriend)

Deeper Insights

"Words create worlds."
~ Abraham Joshua Heschel, Jewish theologian

Chuck—I was lying in a hospital bed the morning after my heart attack when the cardiologist stopped by to chat. He was a hoot, leaving me both laughing and crying by the end of his visit. I laughed because he was so hilarious—he said I needed a head like a coconut so stress wouldn't get to me. And crying at the relief I felt—he told me that the heart is the smartest organ in the body and can regenerate arterial connections to supply blood where needed.

The medical literature is filled with research on how a positive mindshift (Positive Reframing) can create changes in our body. Even thinking something will help us when it is actually benign—the placebo effect—can positively impact cellular health. What is less known is the "nocebo effect"—where negative expectations of a patient are linked to adverse outcomes. When we think negatively, it can literally harm our nerves and our immune system.

> **"Our thoughts and beliefs …
> have a profound impact on our physical health."**
> ~ Ellen Langer, renowned Harvard mind/body researcher

It may be that my cardiologist was invoking the placebo effect in me, but I'll take it. His Positive Reframing of my heart attack made me instantly believe in my ability to heal. I have kept his words at the forefront of my mind during and since my heart surgery, recovery, and healing.

Self-Discovery

- If I tend toward being a "glass half-empty" person, how might shifting to a "glass half- full" empower me?

- Ask myself if the story I am telling myself is working for me. Is it helpful?

- When things don't go as planned, how can I pivot my expectations?

- What expectations or judgments might I Let Go of to create a more empowering story?

- How might the Resilient Mindsets of Curiosity, Choice, and Courage be helpful in Positive Reframing?

Centering Skills

Chapter 25

Nurturing Myself

> "Nurturing yourself is not selfish—it's essential to your survival and your wellbeing."
>
> ~ Renee Peterson Trudeau, transformational coach

Meri—I first learned the Centering Skill of Nurturing Myself from my mother. She was a middle-school teacher in a tough neighborhood for students with learning disabilities. Some days, she had kids throwing chairs at her. On other days, she channeled their energy by coaching football. She kept her spirits up by swimming every day after school and then taking a nap. And then dealing with whatever crisis her four children threw at her. I learned a lot from my mother about how we should treat those who live on society's margins and how we need to involve parents to improve the lives of children. Yet, as a middle schooler myself at the time, I resented that she was unavailable as soon as she walked in the door. As an adult, I now realize she was teaching me something far more important: we need to Nurture Ourselves to nurture others. My mother modeled for me how challenges can be opportunities—if we have the physical, emotional, mental, and spiritual resources to deal with them. Nurturing Myself is our way of fueling up so that we are ready to go, so that We Are Resilient.

I didn't start my own exercise regime until my mid-thirties. Once I realized it was essential for my mental health, I became a convert. Swimming laps every day is where I Notice Myself and then Let Go of my anxieties and sorrows. I use Finding Gratitude, maybe some Positive Reframing, and even daydream a little. It is the fastest way for me to get Centered. Science confirms my experience—exercise can reduce anxiety and depression.

The critical thing to remember is that, ultimately, Nurturing Myself is not about adding one more thing to our "to-do" list or checking a box. It is about self-love. It is about knowing we are worthy of love and showing ourselves that love by giving ourselves what we need every day. Only by nurturing ourselves can we show up and be the best person we can be—for ourselves, those we care about, and the world.

> **"When you get to a place where you understand that love and belonging, your worthiness, is a birthright and not something you have to earn, anything is possible."**
>
> ~ Brené Brown, emotions researcher, TED interview

One day last winter, avid cook Beatrix found herself in a rut. She was grumpy, snippy, and NOT her most resilient self. She knew she was better when she cared for her body with exercise, healthy foods, and sleep. But on that day, something else was missing. So, she forced herself to check in to see what it was. Was she tending to ALL her needs or just her physical ones? When was the last time she:

- Connected with friends
- Blasted music and danced
- Played games
- Dressed up
- Took a break from social media

Through pausing and taking stock of how she was treating herself, Beatrix realized she was not playing enough. Being playful brings her joy. One of the core differences between Nurturing Myself and how most people think of "self-care" is the importance of doing something just for the enjoyment and pleasure of it.

Beatrix challenged herself to choose one joyful activity to engage in every day for the whole month of February (hey, it is doable, right? It is the shortest month!). To start, she blew out her hair, put on makeup, wore her favorite outfit, and took an extra-long walk while chatting with her best friend. The next day, it was time to blast some music. Choosing something new each day was perfect!

Nurturing Myself: What is it?

Nurturing Myself is loving ourselves by attending to our deepest needs—emotionally, physically, socially, and spiritually.

Our Centering Skills are strategies to bring us back into balance, helping us recover from a Protective Pattern or avoid using one completely. Nurturing Myself ensures we meet our needs and do tasks or only attend to others after filling our own bucket.

Nurturing ourselves is a skill fundamental to our wellbeing. Our needs are biologically hardwired into us, and ignoring them comes at a cost. We have emotional needs for paying attention to our feelings and creativity, physical needs for healthy food, adequate sleep, exercise, social needs for connection, and spiritual needs for nature, meaning, and purpose. When something difficult happens, we can nurture ourselves emotionally by giving ourselves empathy for all we have to deal with. We can acknowledge we are doing our best and forgive our mistakes.

Jonah, a 60-year-old tech professional, gives himself what his wife calls "Jonah time" several times a day. He loves the comfort of drinking a giant 28 oz cup of tea, which takes about 45 minutes. Jonah uses the time to reflect and perhaps read the newspaper. He usually drinks his first cup before his wife gets up, another at lunch, and the last one at the end of the day. While his wife says "Jonah time" is like clockwork, Jonah is unaware of the clock. When he has finished something, it's time for his break. He listens to his body and nurtures himself.

Nurturing Myself is different for each person. How can we care for ourselves with compassion? Like Jonah, we might need to build a micro practice into our day for slowing down and paying attention to our feelings.

Jaya never truly had time off as a primary care doctor because her pager was constantly buzzing. She was also a busy mother, having had three children within five years. Jaya never took downtime for herself or socializing with friends and had trouble asking for help. Now she looks back and sees she was a disaster waiting to happen.

When Jaya turned 40, immense work stress and career burnout—combined with severe stress-induced back problems—almost crushed her. Jaya's desperation forced her to learn to Nurture herself. She reduced her work hours and invested time in friendships, walks, and gardening. She also reinvented her medical practice through coaching courses. Rather than telling her patients what to do, Jaya learned to ask about their vision for health and wellness and then helped them meet those goals. She learned how to listen better and meet her patients where they are.

Her most significant transformation came through practicing Isha yoga and focusing on inner wellbeing. Practicing 45 minutes per day kept her centered and strengthened her resilience. As happens with many of us, she was disciplined for a while, but then the busyness of work and raising a family intervened, and she stopped her practice. One day, her teen daughter told her, "Mom, I liked you better when you were meditating." With this wake-up call, Jaya recommitted to her yoga and has been nurturing herself through it for the last eight years.

For many, attending to our bodies is the most challenging type of self-nurturing. Like Jaya, we have absorbed a Cultural Pattern that we can function like machines. While we would not expect our phones to work without recharging, we somehow expect our bodies to.

Caring for our bodies is proven to reduce the impact of stress. We function better with healthy eating, quality sleep, and moving our bodies regularly. If we are angry or frustrated, sometimes the best remedy can be nutritious food, a cup of coffee, a drink of water, sleep, or a walk. Moreover, we can take better care of those around us when we care for our needs.

For Arjun, a software engineer, after a challenging few months working hard on a gig on top of his full-time job, Nurturing himself meant connecting with others. He traveled to Los Angeles to visit close friends he hadn't seen in a long time and they played Dungeons and Dragons. He felt refreshed after the weekend and ready to return to work.

Nurturing ourselves may mean seeking others' support, compliments, and caring feedback. As it was for Arjun, a caring relationship—whether a family member, friend, or colleague—can be our best buffer when we are off-centered or lonely. Conversations, hugs, or sitting together quietly can work wonders for our spirits.

Finally, taking care of our spiritual needs—whether through practicing a faith tradition or ensuring we have meaning and purpose in our lives—is an essential part of Nurturing Myself. Jerome, a fitness industry COO, nurtures his spiritual life by waking at 5 a.m. every weekday (6 a.m. on weekends) to spend a quiet hour drinking coffee. As he sits reflecting in the dark, he tries to focus on God and prayer. His rules are no phone, other electronics, or reading. Some days are better than others. He reflects on his purpose and mission, which evolve over time. What are his responsibilities as an employee, a son, a husband, and a father? Jerome's regular practice of nurturing his spirituality gives him an uncommon groundedness and resilience.

Influence of Cultural Patterns

Jerome's father passed away when he was 11, and Jerome believed he had to rely on himself to figure out the world. His two older sisters were reeling from the incident, and his mom was trying to figure out how to raise the family on her own.

Fortunately, his parents had fostered the value of nurturing himself. They had cultivated his strong faith and supported his spiritual development. Jerome also played sports, which built confidence and helped him stay mentally and physically healthy. His mother reinforced how loved he was, always making him feel special. Jerome had learned to be comfortable being alone if needed, which helped when the neighborhood boys chose activities Jerome didn't want to follow. Almost 50 years later, Jerome is still committed to nurturing himself in ways he learned as a boy and spent his career helping others be active for optimal mental and physical health.

On the other hand, principal Gideon's parents did not model Nurturing Myself. When Gideon's mother was off-center, she moved into Hyper-Caretaking to the detriment of her own needs. Even when she contracted COVID, she refused to let others care for her. "Don't even consider me. I don't want to be a burden," she told Gideon and his wife. Though her health required it, she found it difficult to care for herself or to allow others to care for her.

Gideon's dad also used Hyper-Caretaking. Working and coaching in schools, his dad spent his life serving others. While Gideon was inspired by his dad's service to become a teacher and then principal, his dad veered too often into Hyper-Caretaking and martyrdom. Gideon's father would complain, "I was closing up at 10 p.m…" in a way that almost felt like bragging. His dad developed severe heart disease by age 50. Gideon felt deeply disheartened by his dad's refusal to nurture himself, which included not informing his children when he was hospitalized and thwarting any visits or attempts to connect and help. Gideon took his parents' "Don't Nurture Myself" messages into his adult life. When he first became a principal, he worked 6 a.m. to 6 p.m. until he burned out and had to find another job. Through that struggle, Gideon learned the importance of Nurturing Myself.

Ruby, a single mom and nonprofit professional, also had Cultural Patterns—and related Protective Patterns—that made it challenging to nurture herself. She was raised to believe that strong women don't waste time nurturing themselves because they have too much to do. Last winter, Ruby's three-year-old son, Leland, caught a cold and quickly passed it to Ruby and baby Shayla too. Two nights later, they all had a fever. Three days of constant caregiving with no respite exhausted Ruby. She felt like she was drowning, and her Protective Pattern of Distrusting emerged. She thought, "I can't do this! And I have no one to help me. I can't ask my mother or sibling for help because they all work. They can't afford to get sick either."

Just then, one of her friends texted her. Desperation helped Ruby use her Courage so she could *Speak Authentically*. She texted back, "I am not okay. I am stressed. I am a mess, with no shower, no food for me or the kids, and the house is a mess." It took so much Courage to let her friend know she needed help.

Her friend immediately responded. "I will wear a mask, but I'm coming right over. We will be okay." When her friend replied, offering help, Ruby bawled. She had so much gratitude for her friend's lifeline. Ruby's friend got food and medicine and cleaned up the house. Ruby's friend helped her nurture herself and meet her needs. Ruby now recognizes that she needs to modify her Cultural Patterns and nurture herself more regularly to avoid becoming so depleted in the future.

When Nurturing Myself is Difficult

Nurturing Myself is difficult for most people. Nurturing Myself is counter to American culture, which prioritizes hard work and individualism over caring and connection. Many companies have a business culture that doesn't recognize we cannot function well without meeting our own needs. Many of us also struggle with Nurturing Myself because of necessary caregiving burdens, our Protective Patterns, or a lack of boundaries.

When we are having difficulty using a Centering Skill, we can shift into our Curiosity Mindset and ask ourselves the following questions:

Am I using a Protective Pattern? Meredith's husband has a chronic condition, so she feels a need to be Hypervigilant to protect him. Even when he was healthy, Meredith, a corporate trainer, had difficulty nurturing herself. Giving herself compassion was not easy for her. She took a class with self-compassion experts Kristen Neff and Christopher Germer and started using the app *Unwinding Anxiety*. After learning how her brain sets up patterns that amplify stress, she meditates more to nurture herself.

Brenna worked to balance her high-level job with the needs of her aging mother and her children. As a daughter and mom, her desire to care for others sometimes veered into Hyper-Caretaking. Even when she damaged her knee and could barely walk, she flew down to care for her parents after her mother's surgery. One evening, she cooked dinner and cleaned up for her parents while balancing phone calls from her daughter, who had a hurt back, and trying to finish a work presentation. To reduce her Hyper-Caretaking and have time to nurture herself, Brenna is teaching her mom and children how to access other resources so they can support themselves better.

Am I drained by caring for family members or friends? Donna, a retired administrator, cared for her husband Chester after he had jaw surgery. For three months, she didn't have time for activities like water aerobics that nurtured her. After he recovered, she recognized how completely depleted she was. Donna knew she could better care for others when she cared for herself, so she recommitted herself to nurturing herself. She exercises regularly to keep strong, eats more mindfully, and takes courses with her husband to stimulate their minds. Together, they are deliberately expanding their social time for the support they both need. We cannot care for those we love when we are drained.

Do I have a more meaningful value that might help me Nurture Myself? *Chuck*—As a young father, my work came before family, which became a stress point in my relationship with my wife, Sandy. I did not yet understand how my Protective Pattern of Hypervigilance drove my perfectionism. When I was 12, my dad blew up at me for playing on our swing instead of mowing the lawn. I was so angry that I grabbed our lawn mower and pushed it, running up and down our vast, hilly yard until I finished. My injunction to myself was, "I can't play, or I'll get in trouble." I took this belief to heart, and my work came before anything else, including Nurturing Myself. Later in life,

Sandy and I did couples counseling, and I was shocked to learn that I was a workaholic. I realized I was either going to ruin my marriage or start taking time for myself, my wife, and our kids. I deeply loved my family, so I made hard changes to reorient my priorities.

Do I need to establish boundaries? When Audrey's boss asked her to take on extra duties, Audrey declined. Her boss was frustrated, and Audrey hated feeling she was disappointing her. Audrey likes to follow the rules, be a team player, and please people, which sometimes leads her to Hyper-Caretaking. The next day, Audrey explained to her boss that her son and daughter-in-law needed her to babysit because one was having surgery. She needed to support her family by protecting her health and declining extra duties. Her boss's attitude changed, and she became more empathetic. Establishing boundaries for ourselves and providing context for those boundaries to others can help us choose the skill of Nurturing Myself.

When NOT to Nurture Myself

Chuck—As an Outward Bound instructor, I took troubled teens into the wilderness on 21-day rites of passage courses. This grueling work often included long days of hiking off-trail through heavy rain in the rugged, steep mountains of North Carolina. I nurtured the sensitive feelings of these young people struggling with self-esteem, heavy backpacks, and harsh attitudes toward life. For one group, however, I had to move into emergency mode. A 16-year-old girl fell and punctured a lung. Because of this severe injury, our whole group had to focus on transporting her to a road to be picked up by ambulance.

There are many times, like in this experience, when being selfless is a valued priority. Putting off Nurturing Myself for brief periods can be necessary in work settings, to care for others, to meet deadlines, to support our communities, or in emergencies. In the long run, though, not nurturing ourselves has consequences that harm us, our families, colleagues, and communities.

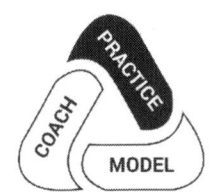

Practicing Nurturing Myself

Chuck—Since I didn't know the importance of Nurturing Myself for much of my life, too often I let my stress overwhelm me. Gradually, I learned that micro-practices make all the difference. While I learned to meditate in my twenties, I started with five minutes shortly after waking. One day, after wearing myself out shopping in a big mall, I stopped at a bench and meditated for five minutes. I was amazed by how it restored my sense of self and energy, and I realized this tool could help me throughout my day. I also learned about power napping in graduate school but didn't practice it regularly until I taught it to high-school teens in my wellness class as a school counselor. When I got tired, I put a small camping mattress under my desk and hung a "power napping" sign on my door. Often, five minutes of napping restored me fully. Finally, I began starting all meetings with a moment of silence. These short calming practices have become a game-changer for me and those around me.

Use This Skill When...

- I notice that I feel drained or overwhelmed.
- My inner critic and negative self-talk are bringing me down.
- I feel depleted, disconnected from others, or lost in my life.
- I need to care for others.

Knowing our needs and how best to meet them is essential. Design enthusiast Emilia's favorite way to Nurture Myself is to shower. When she feels stressed, and her brain is muddy, cleansing her body also cleanses her mind and relaxes her. As a freshman in college, she appreciates being separated from the stress of her phone and other digital distractions. She reflects on her thoughts in a long shower and gets more centered.

We can use the Resilient Mindset of Curiosity and ask ourselves: How can I nurture my body, emotions, mind, or spirit?

I can Practice Nurturing Myself by...

- Giving myself empathy, self-compassion, and kindness.
- Eating healthy foods that nourish me.
- Moving my body regularly and getting quality sleep.
- Choosing activities, play, and relationships that make me happy.
- Ensuring that I pursue activities that give me meaning and purpose.

Spend some time thinking about what might help with Nurturing Myself—to meet the needs of our bodies, minds, emotions, and spirits. Even five minutes can make a difference: feel the sun on our face as we walk into work, brew tea, Breathe Mindfully before transitions, dance to one song, or rub on scented lotion. Everyday activities, done with mindful love for ourselves, are great ways to practice the skill of Nurturing Myself. If we resist taking the time to do so, remember we are modeling the opposite of Nurturing Ourselves. It might be helpful to think about the advice we would give to a friend. Would we tell her to stay up to finish her work, or would we ask her to go to bed and give herself the rest she needs?

- **Nurturing my physical self.** Choosing nutritious food, moving my body, and getting enough regular sleep will nurture me at the most basic level. Notice when I feel healthy and strong and what has helped me feel this way.

- **Letting in compliments.** When someone gives me praise or appreciation, practice acknowledging and letting in the positive words.

- **Letting in my own genius.** Recognize and honor my gifts, talents, accomplishments, and personal genius. Each of us is uniquely gifted in an extraordinary way. Letting in my own goodness strengthens me.

- **Nurturing my creativity.** Take some time for creativity: Create a meal, garden, woodworking project, drawing, dance, song, or something playful that taps my imagination instead of chilling in front of the TV or social media.

- **Nurturing through connection.** Take some time for personal connection and conversation. Call a friend, write a letter, play a game, visit in person, or take a walk with someone to strengthen my relationships. Relationships can be a profound way of centering and Nurturing Myself.

- **Communicating my needs.** Let my family members or colleagues know when I need time or space to regroup, regain my energy, and Nurture Myself.

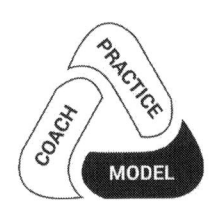

Modeling and Coaching This Skill for our Families

It took Jodi a long time to truly understand and embody how to love and care for herself. Though she had years of training and experience—as a school psychologist, a certified trauma-informed yoga and mindfulness teacher, and a facilitator of visual meditation—her priority was to be a successful professional rather than to listen to her body. All the people involved in her work—colleagues, children, parents, teachers—needed something from her, and she was happy to give it, but she wasn't attending to herself.

Jodi had several health crises in which her body cried out. When she was pregnant, she had some severe complications. At first, Jodi focused on learning more—as if books, courses, and more certifications would save her. That path led to a breakdown, bringing on panic issues and anxiety.

Later, her work at Headstart had a stressful federal review. She kept pushing through, but her eye swelled so much with pink eye-ish symptoms that she looked like a "zombie." When she saw her stress made her children afraid of her, she knew her emotions were out of control.

Finally, a self-care, meditation, and mindfulness podcast helped her listen to her body (Noticing Myself). This change in approach—listening inside to what her body was saying rather than expecting her body to do it all—forced her to slow down. She also learned to take moments to Breathe Mindfully and Find Gratitude for herself, stretching and exercising. Now, Jodi's favorite way to nurture herself is with a cup of tea, reminding herself to slow down and take in the present moment. She pays attention to what she sees and notices around her. She uses the Resilient Mindset of Choice—does she want to be positive or negative? Jodi now moves through the world differently, modeling for her children how to love themselves.

In her work, Jodi first guides people through self-love and play, especially school staff and administrators who don't feel they have time for it. She advises them to be more authentic and talk about feelings in meetings so they can model for colleagues, students, and families. Her most important message is that we don't have to wait for someone else to love and nurture us.

Chuck—When I was a young father and a workaholic, I unconsciously modeled unhealthy behavior I had learned from my family. I am grateful that my wife nudged me to be different so I could model for my children how to take care of their needs. We don't want our children to be so busy and stressed they can't see straight. We all want them to be healthy, happy, and connected as adults and to take care of their own needs.

Practices to Model and Coach Nurturing Myself

- When I need space to regroup and replenish my energy, I tell my family members what I need. I show my family that it's okay for me to Nurture Myself.

- I let my kids or spouse know when I am choosing Nurturing Myself.

- I ask my children what they do to feel nurtured.

Activity: Giving Myself Compassion

Sometimes, it is difficult to show ourselves kindness. Think of a challenging situation I am facing right now. If a friend told me about a similar situation, how would I kindly, with love, support, and advise them? Now, apply my kindness and support to myself.

Activity: Giving Myself TLC

1. Write on a sheet of paper a list of the actions that I am most likely to need when I am pulled off-center. Examples: Eat healthy foods, sleep, find alone time, express my feelings in a healthy way (e.g., talking, creating art, journaling), find reasons to laugh, recognize my strengths and achievements, and do something comforting.

2. Circle the activity I most commonly need when I am off-center.

Deeper Insights

"The more you value yourself, the healthier your boundaries are."
~ Lorraine Nilon, Australian author

Chuck—Nurturing Myself includes learning to hold healthy boundaries. Boundaries require loving ourselves enough to know what we need and communicating a firm line over which others may not pass. Understanding the importance of boundaries was difficult for me, as I grew up in an alcoholic family where few healthy boundaries were modeled.

My lack of healthy boundaries around work hurt my relationship with my wife. After the pandemic forced me to work from home, my lack of work boundaries became even more pronounced. My need to be Hypervigilant about work—constantly monitoring my phone messages, email, deadlines, etc.—meant my work spilled into our home life, into our kitchen, living room, and bedroom. Sandy sometimes felt like she needed to set up her own bedroom or leave the house to avoid being unseen, ignored, or trumped by my work. I didn't see how my early learned behavior hurt her.

When I finally saw how my lack of boundaries was damaging our relationship, I recognized the need for the agreements she had been requesting for a long time. Agreements about small things—like not using electronic devices at meals, in shared spaces, and in bed—gave us some significant gains in our relationship. I am learning to Nurture Myself by limiting how much work takes over my life. In turn, I am nurturing my relationship with my best friend, partner, and wife, who meets my most profound need for connection.

Self-Discovery

- Do I permit myself to Nurture Myself?

- What attitudes or beliefs have I learned that prevent me from Nurturing Myself?

- Which Protective Patterns get in my way of Nurturing Myself?

- Do I get my self-esteem predominantly from "getting stuff done?" How might this impact the time I take for Nurturing Myself?

- How strong am I at holding healthy boundaries around work, family, and play? Would a break from social media help me?

- How can I best model Nurturing Myself for my family?

Chapter 26

Living in the Heart of Resilience

---

*"Although the world is full of suffering,
it is full also of the overcoming of it."*

~ Helen Keller, American author and disability rights advocate

Chuck—Even in the midst of my heart attack, I KNEW I was going to be okay. I remember the intense pain, being hauled out of my bedroom by paramedics to the waiting ambulance, and the fearful look on my wife's face. I said to her, "Sandy, I've got this. Don't worry, babe." While this culminating experience from my childhood trauma brought me pain, anxiety, and emotional stress, part of me absolutely trusted that I would be okay. My heart attack opened me up to the profound richness of life. It revealed how I could live more deeply into my own heart of resilience.

My early trauma influenced unhealthy behaviors that took me decades to untangle. For much of my life, I thought I was a victim of this trauma, but exploring my resilience revealed an inner spirit of optimism and wonder at the miracle of living.

Like Chuck, we all experience difficulties, even daily. One of our *Protective Patterns* is triggered by a friend, colleague, spouse, or kids—or—we react to a world event, an illness, or the death of a family member. We might get angry, or sad, or frustrated. That same day, we may also experience incredible moments of joy and even ecstasy. Maybe we share a smile, laugh, or deep vulnerability with someone we love. We might enjoy a spectacular performance, the scent of a flower, or sitting on the porch on a hot summer day.

Living in the heart of resilience is holding both the difficulties and joys together—a both/and perspective. Many of us experience life in an either/or kind of way. We get caught up in darkness or dazzled by the light. When we are down, we can forget our family loves us, and when we are on a roll, we can forget that our ecosystem is in crisis. The We Are Resilient approach helps us develop the inner strength to hold both the difficulties and joy. Something throws us off-balance, and then we return to our center. When we live with more resilience, we can have a more joyful life.

Thriving in Uncertainty

> "Yet it really is possible to thrive amid uncertainty...
> it's about faith and self-trust— believing that
> whatever happens, you'll find a way through it."
> ~ Brené Brown, *Daring Greatly*

While the preceding chapters explored the various components of the We Are Resilient approach—each pattern, mindset, and skill—the full power to transform our lives comes when we use them all together.

Meri—We were informed last month that my husband Steve now has a rare lung disease, which is complicated to treat. While he is fortunate he can join a clinical trial, the various medication side effects are daunting, and the cure rate is only 50%. We are both weighed down by the uncertainty, which sometimes causes me to react badly. Last night, Steve asked a simple scheduling question, and my Protective Pattern of Attacking jumped out. Luckily, I noticed it after a couple of minutes. I Noticed Myself (what the heck happened?) and made a Choice to stop yelling. Nurturing Myself, I gave myself compassion for losing it. A few minutes later, I used my Courage and apologized.

Like Meri, we sometimes make choices that cause us shame. Identifying our Protective and Cultural Patterns helps us see ourselves more clearly. Then, we can move beyond our shame and see our similarities with people we consider "other" than us. Understanding our shared human condition ignites our compassion and empowers us to be more of the person we most want to be. And we realize that we have a choice in how we respond going forward. We can use our Protective Patterns—sometimes our best option—or choose Resilient Mindsets and Skills. After seeing and assessing the possibilities, we gain clarity to make better choices.

We all have times when we can be overwhelmed by uncertainty—whether it is a job change, evolving relationships, health issues, or stress in the lives of our loved ones. There is also an unending amount of uncertainty in our world, from climate change and political turmoil to the rise of Artificial Intelligence and new biotechnology. Practicing the mindsets, patterns, and skills helps us develop the inner strength and trust in ourselves to thrive. Despite all the physical, emotional, and financial stress that Meri and Steve face, their resilience helps them be generally upbeat and optimistic.

Resilience helps us know we are not at the end of any story. We can each create a new story—about ourselves, our lives, or the world—every day. Accessing our superpower of resilience strengthens us and helps us build a better life.

> "We must let go of the life we have planned, so as to accept the life that is waiting for us."
>
> ~ Joseph Campbell, American mythologist

Practice—Model—Coach

How can we each best share what we learn from the We Are Resilient approach? We do so most authentically and successfully when we practice it ourselves first. Though it is tempting to tell others what to do to improve their lives, we all learn best when others show us rather than tell us (called "modeling"). When we practice ourselves and model the approach, then we can more effectively coach others. We call this the Practice-Model-Coach method and encourage everyone to embrace this way of sharing. Whether we are a teacher, parent, health professional, or coach—it's all about practicing what we preach so we can share our learning effectively!

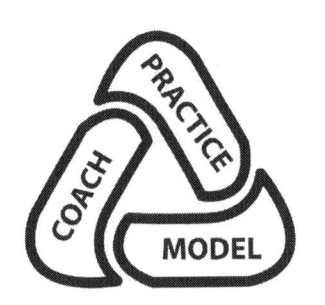

Practice using **Choice** to become better ourselves

Model using **Courage** so others can learn from us

Coach using **Curiosity**, compassion, and encouragement

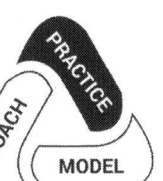

Practice Resilience Using Choice

Chuck—I walked into a team meeting, having just finished a busy morning of emails, deliverables, spreadsheets, and phone calls. My colleagues also came to the meeting with busy minds and their to-do lists. Sitting at the table, I noticed I felt overwhelmed and out of balance with everything on my plate. On top of that, my wife and I had been out of sorts with each other earlier that morning.

Rather than jumping into our agenda, I chose to pick up the Tibetan singing bowl on our table and said, "Can we bell in?" The group knew that "belling in" was code for pausing and using the Centering Skills of Breathing Mindfully and Noticing Myself. Everyone nodded with some relief as they anticipated stepping back from their stressful day. I picked up the bell, took a deep breath to begin Centering myself, and said, "Okay, let's bell in, breathe a little, and find our balance so we can do the good work we're here to do together." As we settled in, I offered some minimal suggestions. "As we begin, just notice that you're breathing ... drop into feeling the sensation you feel in your body ... the rise and fall of the breath ... the feeling of the air in your lungs ... and the movement of your belly." After a minute, I rang the bell softly three times, and the group's attention slowly and silently came back, focused and ready to work.

Practices and structures support our resilience and nurture our inner strength.

Spending a few moments feeling our feelings is powerful. As it did for Chuck, building it into our day and creating structures for practicing mindful awareness can help us tap into our resilience skills more effectively. Chuck and his team had created two structures to support them:

1. An agreement on how to begin meetings
2. Keeping a bell on the table—a physical reminder to use it

Agreements—whether just with ourselves or with others—spell out what we want to do and how we do it. Naming something makes it more likely to happen. A physical reminder is also helpful, as our lives are full of distractions that take us off course. Agreements and physical reminders make us more likely to choose our intended practices. They help us make choices that bring more joy into our lives.

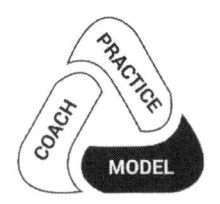

Model Resilience Using Courage

Meri—After my mother broke her leg and needed surgery, I spent long days in the hospital with her. Even more exhausting was negotiating four healthcare systems—the trauma hospital where she had her emergency surgery, the HMO system charged with her care, the skilled nursing facility where she was transferred, and the home health system I was trying to set up so we could move her home. My friends worried as my mother's health declined, and I juggled my job and family life. Surely, I had too much on my plate?

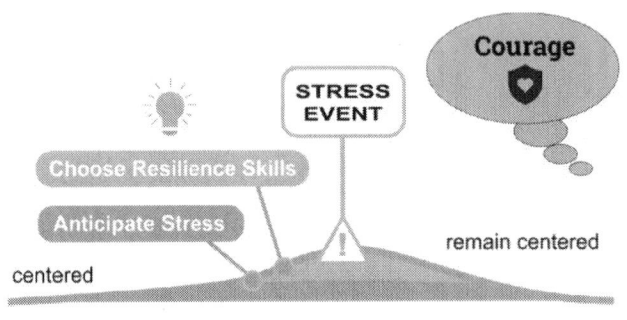

Anticipatory Resilience

Indeed, I had "too much on my plate," as most of us do. However, I could keep a pretty even keel through my ups and downs by relying on my mindset of Courage. When I received my brother-in-law's phone call about my mother's fall and ambulance trip to the emergency room, I was in a store, trying on new pants. As we frantically left the store, I used Breathing Mindfully to calm myself and Courage to listen to my heart. I loved my mom and, in my heart, I knew this day was coming. Courage helped me model resilience, so my whole family stayed a little calmer.

Living the We Are Resilient approach does not mean life is easy. Over the past several years, my resilience has been tested many, many times in small and big ways. COVID and the ups and downs of grant-seeking have buffeted our nonprofit. My stepfather and my mother have passed away, and we have had to dismantle their family home of almost 60 years. My husband has a rare disease and needs complicated treatment. Each time, I use the Resilient Mindset of Courage to lean into my values and stay the course of what I think I am meant to do. Choosing a path aligned with my values reduces stress because being authentic to myself eases the difficulty. Friends, family, colleagues, and those in our training classes learn how to strengthen their resilience when I use Courage to share my stories of dancing with the stress of life.

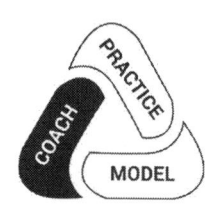

Coaching Resilience Using Curiosity

"My partner wants to start a family, but I want him to get a job first. He is angry about that. What should I do?" asked Nafuna in an email after a training session. Though I was very tempted to tell Nafuna what I thought, I took a deep breath. I have learned the hard way about the importance of Curiosity. Like most of us, when I tell people what to do, it is often ineffective.

Beginning with genuine Curiosity changes everything. So instead I asked, "What Protective Patterns came up in the conversation? What Resilient Mindsets could you have used? How might that have changed the conversation?" When Nafuna answered with a lengthy description of how the Protective Patterns cropped up and how using her Mindsets would have improved their conversation, I knew she had tapped into her own wisdom—the heart of her resilience.

Using Curiosity is especially powerful when working with those we supervise, educate, or parent. Asking a compassionate question can help others recognize what they already know. Curiosity helps others get to the heart of their emotional intelligence. Like Nafuna, people often have deep wells of insight and answers to their own questions and frequently answers to mine. Even small children can have amazing insight when we ask them compassionate questions. After some poor behavior when my daughter was young, I got curious about what was going on for her. "I feel sad because Daddy's not here," my daughter shared. This helped me to be curious about my own reactions and opened the way for us to discuss our mutual sad feelings about Daddy's frequent travel. We were strengthening our resilience together.

Living This Approach

We created the We Are Resilient approach to provide ourselves and others with the knowledge and skills to take small steps to transform from the inside out. We wanted this for the world, but we also needed it for ourselves. As we both have lived this approach, we have realized that it starts as a bucket of tools but gradually has become second nature and integral to who we are. The We Are Resilient approach is not a pill we take when things become difficult—rather, it has strengthened our mental, emotional, and physical immune systems.

We have now given it to you. Resilience is yours to use—both by birthright and as an Open Education Resource. Reading this book may have given you important insights. The real work begins now as you choose to practice living in your own heart of resilience.

As the stories in this book have demonstrated, small moments when we notice a pattern or use a mindset or skill—micro-practices—can significantly change our lives. Choose one or two practices and do them for a week, then add another practice. Create some structure so you have accountability for your practices. Over time, these practices and structures become like muscle memory, giving you more inner strength and joy.

As we gain awareness and repeat our practices in the same way or at the same time or place, we build habits that become part of who we are. We can be intentional about choosing both practices and structures. We invite you to consider:

- Which parts of this approach do you want to integrate into your life?
    - Which Protective Patterns do you use the most? When are they helpful, and when do they get in your way?

- Pause and reflect on which Cultural Patterns influence your judgments and expectations. When are they helpful, and when do they get in your way?
- Which Resilient Mindsets help you be your best self?
- Which Centering Skills will bring you the most joy?

• How can you practice what you have learned? Which micro-practices will you adopt?

• What structures will support your journey to becoming who you most want to be?

- Could you tape the Resilient Mindsets on the bathroom mirror? Post the We Are Resilient poster on the refrigerator?
- Do you have a friend you can walk with once a week and talk about resilience?
- Could you create a book group to read and discuss this book together?

• As you anticipate future challenges, which practices and structures will support you in those challenges?

"Strengthening your resilience is a journey of the heart: feel, love, and be transformed."
~ Chuck Fisher and Meri McCoy-Thompson

What's Coming

We live in a world of relationships, groups, and communities. We thrive most when our resilience helps us be attuned to ourselves and others. Resilience is coming back to balance and connecting with others. This book has focused on our Personal Resilience because self-knowledge is the first step to understanding and being sensitive to others.

Our next book will focus on how we can improve our Relational Resilience and Group Resilience. Connecting Skills strengthen our ability to adapt and respond to challenges in a relationship and increase our feelings of trust and safety with another person. Collaborating Skills effectively helps us solve problems together and exponentially improve our ability to innovate. Collaborating Skills also help maintain vision, purpose, and engagement when meeting challenges—in our families, social groups, work teams, and communities—which maximizes everyone's contributions.

We can't wait to share it with you!

We are Resilient

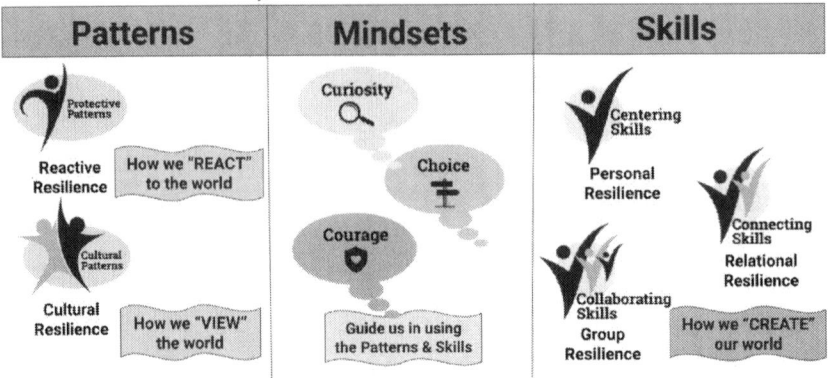

Patterns	Mindsets	Skills
Protective Patterns — Reactive Resilience — How we "REACT" to the world	**Curiosity**	**Centering Skills** — Personal Resilience
Cultural Patterns — Cultural Resilience — How we "VIEW" the world	**Choice**	**Connecting Skills** — Relational Resilience
	Courage — Guide us in using the Patterns & Skills	**Collaborating Skills** — Group Resilience — How we "CREATE" our world

Please visit www.dovetaillearning.org to be alerted about our next book and for more resources, courses, and training on the We Are Resilient approach. Our Open Educational Resources can be downloaded, adapted, and shared freely.

Printed in Great Britain
by Amazon